A lively, engaging history of The Great War written for a new generation of readers

In recent years, scholarship on World War I has turned from a fairly narrow focus on military tactics, weaponry, and diplomacy to incorporate considerations of empire, globalism, and social and cultural history. This concise history of the first modern, global war helps to further broaden the focus typically provided in World War I surveys by challenging popular myths and stereotypes to provide a new, engaging account of The Great War.

The conventional World War I narrative that has evolved over the past century is that of an inevitable but useless war, where men were needlessly slaughtered due to poor decisions by hidebound officers. This characterization developed out of a narrow focus on the Western Front promulgated mainly by British historians. In this book, Professor Proctor provides a broader, more multifaceted historical narrative including perspectives from other fronts and spheres of interest and a wider range of participants. She also draws on recent scholarship to consider the gendered aspect of war and the ways in which social class, religion, and cultural factors shaped experiences and memories of the war.

- Structured chronologically to help convey a sense of how the conflict evolved
- Each chapter considers a key interpretive question, encouraging readers to examine the extent to which the war was *total, modern*, and *global*
- Challenges outdated stereotypes created through a focus on the Western Front
- Considers the war in light of recent scholarship on empire, global history, gender, and culture
- Explores ways in which the war and the terms of peace shaped the course of the 20th century

World War I: A Short History is sure to become required reading in undergraduate survey courses on WWI, as well as courses in military history, the 20th century world, or the era of the World Wars.

Tammy M. Proctor, PhD is Department Head and Professor of History at Utah State University, Logan. She holds a doctoral degree in history from Rutgers University and has also taught at Wittenberg University. Previous books include *An English Governess in the Great War: The Secret Brussels Diary of Mary Thorp* (2017), *Civilians in a World at War, 1914–1918* (2010), and *Female Intelligence: Women and Espionage in the First World War* (2003).

T0341534

WILEY SHORT HISTORIES

General Editor: Catherine Epstein

This series provides concise, lively introductions to key topics in history. Designed to encourage critical thinking and an engagement in debate, the books demonstrate the dynamic process through which history is constructed, in both popular imagination and scholarship. The volumes are written in an accessible style, offering the ideal entry point to the field.

Published

A History of the Cuban Revolution, 2nd Edition
Aviva Chomsky

Vietnam: Explaining America's Lost War, 2nd Edition
Gary R. Hess

A History of Modern Europe: From 1815 to the Present
Albert S. Lindemann

Perspectives on Modern South Asia: A Reader in Culture, History, and Representation
Kamala Visweswaran

Nazi Germany: Confronting the Myths
Catherine Epstein

World War I: A Short History
Tammy M. Proctor

World War I

A Short History

Tammy M. Proctor

WILEY Blackwell

Registered Office
John Wiley & Sons, Inc., 111 River Street, Hoboken, NJ 07030, USA
John Wiley & Sons Ltd, The Atrium, Southern Gate, Chichester, West Sussex, PO19 8SQ, UK

Editorial Office
350 Main Street, Malden, MA 02148-5020, USA

For details of our global editorial offices, customer services, and more information about Wiley products visit us at www.wiley.com.

Wiley also publishes its books in a variety of electronic formats and by print-on-demand. Some content that appears in standard print versions of this book may not be available in other formats.

Library of Congress Cataloging-in-Publication Data

Names: Proctor, Tammy M., 1968– author.
Title: World War I : a short history / by Tammy M Proctor, Utah State University, Utah, USA.
Description: 1st edition. | Hoboken, NJ : John Wiley & Sons [2018] |
    Series: Wiley short histories ; 7713 | Includes bibliographical references and index. |
    Description based on print version record and CIP data provided by publisher;
    resource not viewed.
Identifiers: LCCN 2017015022 (print) | LCCN 2017016071 (ebook) |
    ISBN 9781118951910 (pdf) | ISBN 9781118951903 (epub) |
    ISBN 9781118951934 (cloth) | ISBN 9781118951927 (pbk.)
Subjects: LCSH: World War, 1914–1918.
Classification: LCC D521 (ebook) | LCC D521 .P77 2017 (print) | DDC 940.3–dc23
LC record available at https://lccn.loc.gov/2017015022

Cover image: Courtesy National Archives, photo no. 111-SC-32080

Set in 10/12.5pt Bembo by SPi Global, Pondicherry, India

10 9 8 7 6 5 4 3 2 1

Contents

List of Illustrations

Maps

Figures

Preface

The effects of World War I were far-reaching, from ruined landscapes to ruined lives.
This photo depicts part of the battlefield at Verdun, France, nearly a century after the war.
Source: Photo by author, 2004.

One hundred years after the battles that raged in northern France, it is still
possible to find copious evidence of World War I on the Western Front. Pieces
of munitions, sometimes even unexploded shells, sit on the side of the road
awaiting pickup by the army's disposal squad. One can glimpse the scarred shell

holes and remains of trench networks in wooded copses just off the highways and byways of the region, and small tourist signs point to memorials, cemeteries, and places of importance. While the Western Front is perhaps the best-known area of fighting between 1914 and 1918, it is not the only landscape disrupted by war. Stone trenches line the mountains between Italy and Austria, and remains from the war appear in remote areas of eastern Europe and western Asia. Monuments and markers point to places around the world where refugees fled, where enemy aliens were interned, and where wartime disasters unsettled communities. World War I had an impact—not just on physical landscapes and families—but on the social, religious, economic, political, and cultural frameworks of the twentieth-century world. This impact was uneven, and some areas experienced only a whisper of war's reshaping potential, but large numbers of people across the globe saw their worlds turned upside-down.

This short history of World War I cannot tell the whole story of this conflict, which was waged from 1914 to 1918 (officially) and which straddled more than a decade of serious global violence. Instead, my aim is to suggest for students interested in the history of the war a broad framework or way of seeing that will help them make sense of all the other materials they read and watch and hear. Each chapter answers a central question about the war and its aftermath, and at the conclusion of every section there is a timeline and select reading list for context. Ideally, when they finish the book, readers will want to go looking for more information about all the ideas that have only been suggested here.

The central aim of *World War I: A Short History* is to provide an accessible and concise overview of the first modern, global war. Many people have a cursory knowledge of the events of World War I, and most understand the stereotypical narrative that has developed, namely that of an inevitable but useless war, where men were slaughtered as a consequence of the poor decisions of out-of-touch senior officers. This trope, widely used in both scholarly and popular works, developed out of a narrow focus on the Western Front and particularly through the writing of a British version of the war. Many films and novels feature this story of the war, using the narrative of senseless war to frame the tales of individuals caught up in a futile machinery of violence. A good example is the film *Gallipoli* (released 1981), in which poor communication and a leader who is far from the front and immune from the realities of battle sends young men to their deaths. More recently, the film *Joyeux Noel [Merry Christmas]* (released 2006) humanizes the experience of fighting and loss through the stories of individual men and officers, but demonizes the military command as without pity or understanding. It is this sense of a disconnect between the bloodshed of ordinary people and what seems to be a heartless attitude on the part of the military leaders that has captured the attention of a generation.

The ubiquity of this image of World War I makes it a fascinating topic. However, it also demands the production of a new volume for classrooms that challenges this narrative. What is needed is a corrective to this vision of the war, one that digs deeper into the mechanisms by which battle was waged for more than four years. Here, each chapter re-establishes the broader context of the war by including the rest of the fronts: Italy, Russia, East Africa, and Mesopotamia, to name some of the more important war zones. The war encompassed and affected a broad swath of humanity, and this book brings some of those voices back into the story of the conflict. By doing so, the Western Front story gains a back-story and a necessary complexity. Many leaders acted in concert with their allies, and often an offensive in one sector was coordinated to help another sector advance. With poor communication and uncertain transport/supply trains, officers and civilian officials struggled to understand the many moving parts that made up the war effort around the globe. Here, students will get a sense of some of those challenges.

Each chapter of this book is arranged in a loose chronological fashion with a featured year of the war framing the discussion. In addition, each chapter contains a wide-ranging geographical coverage of the topic with short, specific examples to help support this view of war. Because the common narrative is so strong, the book provides an equally strong counter-narrative to help displace current myths about the war. The story of this book is focused around the linked questions—to what extent was this war *total*, *modern*, and *global*? Readers are encouraged to answer these questions for themselves as they progress, using the tools in each chapter. Perhaps at this point, readers might be thinking—who really cares? Is World War I all that significant anyway in the scheme of things? This book argues that the war was a pivotal point in world history in the twentieth century for three main reasons.

First, it gave concrete reality to the possible. By this, I mean that ideas that had emerged in laboratories and factories, in diplomatic offices and imperial outposts, now could be tested in the social experiment that was war. World War I featured the development of new weapons, which were tested and perfected in the field, with deadly results. Well-known examples include tanks, aerial bombs, and poison gas delivered in shells. The war also witnessed the birth of a broad coalition of charitable and humanitarian organizations with the express aim of alleviating the suffering of victims of war. Some of these organizations survived the war as international and permanent agencies devoted to the lives of war victims or children displaced by violence. Certainly, ideas about what could or should be done for the victims of war were transformed by this conflict. Governments also expanded to meet the needs of a modern wartime economy and society; many nations created whole sections to handle pension claims from widows and veterans, for instance. States also codified international agreements and rules for passports. Tax structures that had been reformed during the war became permanent fixtures of life. In short, World War I wrote the rules for what war meant in the modern world, while simultaneously reforming governments, societies, and economies.

Second, the experience of World War I fundamentally reshaped geopolitical lines, not only reframing power blocs but also redrawing political boundaries. Four well-established empires in Eurasia disappeared as a result of the war (German Empire, Austro-Hungarian or Habsburg Empire, Russian Empire, Ottoman Empire), and many other states emerged as new entities. Examples include Poland, Czechoslovakia, and Yugoslavia, to name only a few. Imperial lines outside of Europe also changed, with the creation of a category of states known as mandates. Many of these mandate states, such as Syria and Iraq, faced tutelage from European nations (France and Britain, respectively), and while they looked forward to eventual independence, this timeline was uncertain and highly managed by their imperial masters. It is also important to remember that the war displaced vast numbers of people, many of whom lost their citizenship along with their homes. The population exchanges between Turkey and Greece fundamentally restructured religious, political, and cultural life in those two nations and upended the lives of nearly two million people. Russian refugees from a variety of regions including modern Georgia, Azerbaijan, Ukraine, and Belarus streamed into cities seeking work, many of them classified as "stateless." To summarize this point, the modern political landscape was born out of World War I.

Finally, World War I set the stage for the extremist politics of the interwar period and ultimately served as a major factor in the outbreak of World War II. It was a precursor. The unprecedented numbers of people involved in the war meant upheaval in the postwar period as soldiers sought to reintegrate into society. Families faced personal challenges with the return of their loved ones, but at every level—household, neighborhood, town, nation—people sought to make sense of the war and return to something that could be perceived as "normal" life. For many, this proved impossible, and the growth of paramilitary units, many of which contained disaffected ex-soldiers, threatened social harmony. Revolutions, civil disorder, and economic instability also plagued postwar nations. Framed by the perceived problems of the peace treaties in many parts of the world, grievances and disorder gave way to extremist political solutions. Fascism, along with Stalin's version of communism, gained traction by the late 1920s. In this climate of political experimentation, military *coups d'état* and authoritarian regimes marked interwar politics around the world. Even nations with democratic traditions experienced unprecedented concentration of power. For instance, the only US president to win an election four times was an interwar leader, Franklin D. Roosevelt.

These three themes are important reasons for studying World War I, but they are not the only reasons that the war's legacy is still important more than

100 years later. Unlike World War II, the 1914–1918 war remains a contentious event. The British Parliament squabbled in 2014 about how to commemorate the war in their nation, and journalists often raise the specter of the war in explaining political divisions in the Middle East or the rise of nationalism in the last 100 years. *World War I: A Short History* details the multitude of ways that the war functioned as a rupture between the wars of the past and the wars still to come. As British poet and novelist Thomas Hardy wrote in his 1918 poem, "And There Was a Great Calm": "There was peace on earth, and silence in the sky;/ Some could and some could not, shake off misery:/ The Sinister Spirit sneered 'It had to be!'/ And again the Spirit of Pity whispered, 'Why?'" Hardy posed the ultimate question asked by the survivors as they contemplated the armistice: Why? This book will explore that question.

Citations

Page *Source*

x *Gallipoli*. 1999. DVD. Directed by Peter Weir. Paramount Pictures.

x *Joyeux Noel [Merry Christmas]*. 2006. DVD. Directed by Christian Carion. Sony Pictures Home Entertainment.

xiii Hardy, Thomas. "And There was a Great Calm." 1918. Accessed December 18, 2015. http://www.poetryfoundation.org/poem/248470

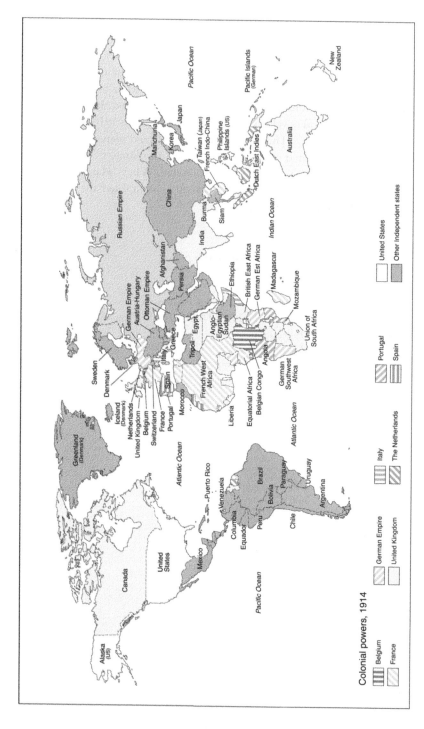

Map 1 The world in 1914.

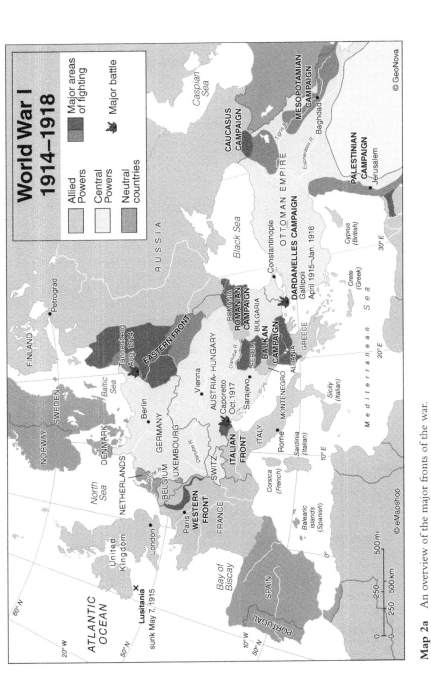

Map 2a An overview of the major fronts of the war.

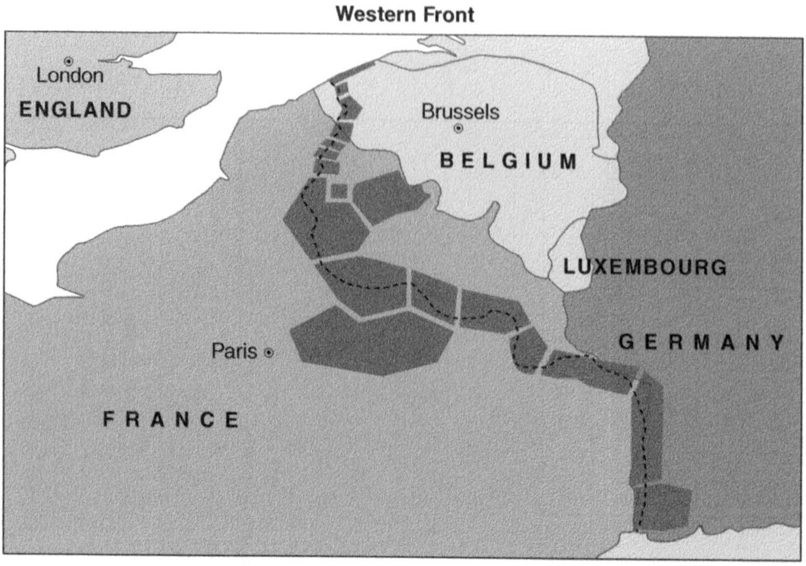

Western Front

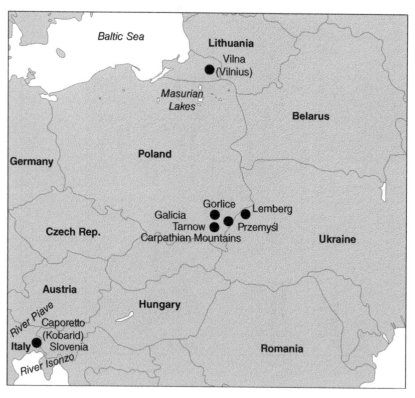

Map 2b The Western Front in 1915.

Map 2c Important sites on the Eastern Front.

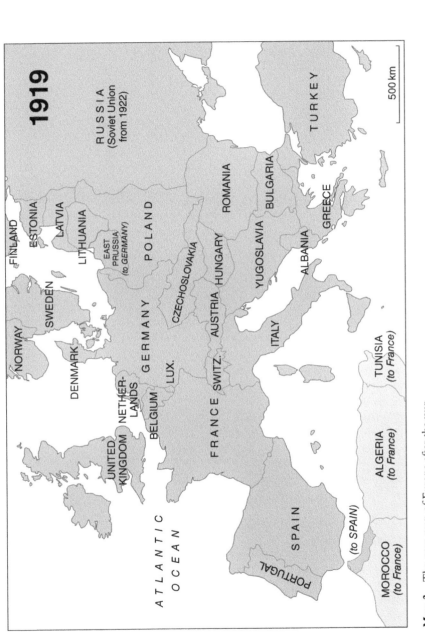

Map 3 The new map of Europe after the war.

Acknowledgments

Writing a textbook, especially a short history about a complicated global topic, has been an adventure for me. I would never have attempted such a book without 20 years of teaching this material. The students I have taught always questioned and challenged me, provided new insights on the war, and, in the case of my Fall 2015 World War I class at Utah State University, read the manuscript of this book and provided a critique. To all the undergraduate students with whom I have worked at Utah State, Wittenberg University, Lakeland College, Princeton University, and Rutgers University: you have my sincere gratitude. I would also like to offer my thanks to Dr. John McGowan and his honors course in Fall 2015 at the University of North Carolina–Chapel Hill for reading part of the manuscript and offering suggestions. While all mistakes are, of course, still my own, these additional student eyes provided excellent feedback for the book. My colleagues at Wittenberg and Utah State and elsewhere have engaged in countless conversations about teaching, scholarship, and the meaning of life, and I thank them all for helping me maintain a balanced view of what is important. Special thanks to to all my colleagues and friends, but especially to Christian Raffensperger, Nancy McHugh, Molly Wood, Joe O'Connor, John Flora, Leslie Keeney, Carmen Hernandez, Dar Brooks Hedstrom, Amy Livingstone, Susan Grayzel, Sophie de Schaepdrijver, Jeannie Banks Thomas, and Laura Gelfand for their good counsel and friendship.

I want to thank Dr. Catherine Epstein, editor of this short history series, for sharing her own manuscript and book on Nazi Germany. She has provided advice, speedy feedback, and encouragement throughout this process. Editors and other staff at Wiley-Blackwell have also provided excellent advice as they have shepherded this book through the editorial process.

Acknowledgments

My thanks go to Peter Coveney, Jayne Fargnoli, Haze Humbert, and Denisha Sahadevan for their help. In addition, I appreciate the constructive suggestions I received from anonymous reviewers of the initial proposal and of the draft manuscript.

As always, I would like to recognize the support of my families—both the Proctors and the Shirleys. Finally, my thanks go to my husband, Todd Shirley, for his patience and good humor as I worked on this project.

1

Why and How Did War Break Out in Summer 1914?

Figure 1.1 The war began with an assassination in Sarajevo, but the first fighting of the war occurred in Belgrade, Serbia. In this photo Serb children "play soldier" in their wartime nation. *Source*: Imperial War Museum.

World War I: A Short History, First Edition. Tammy M. Proctor.
© 2018 John Wiley & Sons Ltd. Published 2018 by John Wiley & Sons Ltd.

Who Started the War?

This question is at the heart of one of the biggest debates in modern history, one which has been raging almost since World War I began more than 100 years ago. The question of war blame sparks emotion, nationalism, and shame, but it is not the most important way to understand the war. Instead, scholars and students of history should focus on a different question about the war's origins, namely: How and why was a global, total, modern war possible in 1914? Rather than considering who is responsible for the war's outbreak, students must think about *how* a local assassination turned into a global conflict, and they must imagine "the journeys travelled by the key decision-makers."

Perhaps the single most important thing to remember about the world in 1914 is that it was full of nation-states and nations seeking to become states. The Enlightenment and the French Revolution gave rise to understandings of a "nation" as an entity composed of people who belonged together and who shared a sense of identity. In turn, these ideas helped create radical notions that power belonged to the people and that political decision-making should reflect the common good. Of course this raised a central question, namely what makes a group of people belong to each other? In response to that question, men and women sought to understand their lives in relationship to the markers of their identities: language, culture, religion, ethnicity. People differentiated between the *state* where they were official subjects and the *nation* to which they truly belonged. For instance, a Czech speaker might live in the Habsburg Empire but secretly dream of a Czech nation-state. In other words, nationalism arose to challenge the authorities of states and empires, and by 1914, nationalism was undermining many of the traditional powers in Europe and around the world.

This new understanding of a nation defined citizens as people with responsibilities to those who shared their "nation," which meant that the privileges of political participation came with the need for defense of those principles. By 1914, true nation-states had citizen armies to fight wars, and most early twentieth-century states conscripted or drafted these citizens to fight when the need arose. Multinational empires understood the simmering tensions of nationalism within their midst, and sometimes these states only called up citizens they thought might be loyal. Other states relied on voluntary enlistment but still framed their call to arms as a national duty and stigmatized those men who refused to fight.

Nationalism was not the only defining factor for the political powers of 1914, most of whom were empires of either land or sea. Identities transformed through such imperial conquest as well. A nationalist leader such as Mohandis Gandhi (1869–1948) built his ideology through contact not only with his place of birth in India, but through his imperial education in Britain and his early work experience in South Africa. In other imperial settings, people faced the creation of new national or ethnic identities based on the classification and boundaries designed by imperialist officials. In South Africa, for instance, officials created legislation that marginalized leaders, expropriated land, and renamed societies such as the Zulu or the Basotho, lumping them together despite historic enmity. Even those states that were not directly under imperial control, such as China or Mexico, often saw their choices regarding trade and foreign policy severely limited by the intrusions of great powers.

From the British Empire's control of a quarter of the globe by 1914 to the Russian Empire's massive contiguous land empire, a few states controlled the destinies of many of the world's people. Imperialism created unequal relationships that helped shape not only the Great War but especially its aftermath. Map 1.1 shows a snapshot of the world in 1914 as a guide. When colonies and dependencies form part of the figures, small European states such as Britain counted massive populations and land areas in their total numbers. Appendix 1.1 at the end of this chapter provides a brief comparison of the main empires of 1914 and sets the stage for discussion of the war.

As a way of understanding the powerful states, their allies, their enemies, and those marginalized by these imperial politics, let's embark on a grand tour of the world in 1914.

A Grand Tour of 1914

A traveler wanting to circumnavigate the world in spring 1914 would probably use many of the same conveyances that the fictional character Phileas Fogg utilized forty years earlier in Jules Verne's popular novel, *Around the World in Eighty Days* (1873). Horse-drawn vehicles, steamships, coal-fueled steam railways, and small boats still featured prominently in the lives of travelers in the early twentieth century. However, newer contraptions had also made an appearance on the scene—streetcars, subways, and automobiles, as well as airplanes and zeppelins. To traverse the empires of the world, a traveler moved between the conveyances of the past and the machines of the future, from hiking in rugged terrain with animal pack trains to whizzing through urban streets in an automobile. A traveler had to be prepared for extremes of heat and cold and for long delays. This global journey might begin with a boat ride down the Thames River.

United Kingdom

London in 1914 was a metropole that served as a shipping, insurance, and banking capital for the largest overseas empire in the world. From a dock at Westminster pier near the Houses of Parliament, political hub and legislature of one of the world's most successful constitutional monarchies, our traveler (imagine that it is Phileas Fogg repeating his journey) would float past teeming wharves full of imperial commerce toward the maritime center of Greenwich, a sleepy suburb just east of the City of London. The British metropolis marked time for the globe in 1914. Since 1884 Greenwich had served as the divider between east and west, the home of the Prime Meridian, the standard for Greenwich Mean Time, and the location of 0° longitude. Shipping charts, international time standards, rail timetables, and astronomical calculations revolved around this suburb of London and its Royal Observatory perched on a hill above the river. The observant traveler might also spend a little time walking under the River Thames in the state-of-the-art foot tunnel that opened in 1902, little imagining that this space would serve as a bomb shelter for civilians during the war to come.

Embarking again downriver, passengers might glimpse the Royal Arsenal at Woolwich, which would employ nearly 40 000 munitions works by 1917. As the riverboat headed toward the English coast, Fogg might take note of volunteers training in military maneuvers in a nearby field, as part of their service in the Territorial Force. With no widespread system of conscription, Britain's small professional army relied upon the idea that if a war came, lightly trained volunteers would step up to contribute. The last major town the passengers might notice before heading into the marshy expanse leading to the English Channel would be Tilbury on the north shore, a fort town that became a gathering place for horses destined for war service in Europe. Fogg and his companions could have still traveled further down the river in the spring of 1914, but during the war a bridge of boats blocked access at Tilbury and allowed for passage of troops across the river.

Travelers had a decision to make at this point about their next destination. For those people wanting to cross the Channel to Europe in 1914, boats left from several smaller ports on Britain's east coast. Britain was a nation of ports, with a rich naval and shipbuilding history. If Fogg had instead sought passage across the Atlantic, he might have traveled by train to the larger ports such as Liverpool, Glasgow, Hull, Bristol, Plymouth, Southampton, or Newcastle to board a large liner, such as the RMS *Lusitania*, one of the Cunard line's most luxurious and speedy passenger ships that had been sailing the Atlantic for seven years. Ireland's ports, which not only served as conduits for passengers and goods arriving from around the world, were also a possible point of embarkation. In fact some of the newest and best liners were assembled in shipbuilding centers such as Belfast. With a successful test of Marconi's wireless in 1898 on the northern Irish coast, ship-to-shore and ship-to-ship communication became a reality as well. The ships docking in Belfast and Liverpool came from ports all over the globe, carrying beef from Argentina, gold from South Africa, grain from the United States, coffee from Brazil, tea from Ceylon, and more. These ports truly demonstrated

4

the global nature of commerce by 1914 and the emphasis the United Kingdom put on overseas commerce, the Royal Navy, and maritime matters.

French Republic

However, in 1914, our traveler's intent is to cross the Channel to France because as an adventurer and innovator, he plans to travel to Calais using a new-fangled device, the airplane. Several pilots are training for an upcoming cross-Channel race in July 1914, so Fogg convinces one to take him along on a flight from Dover to Calais. Manned flight in flimsy planes with sputtering small engines was just over a decade old, and few could have predicted the need that war would produce for pilots. The Channel looked calm to Fogg from his perch above the water, and there was as yet no sign of the bombers (both airplanes and zeppelins) that soon would be crossing the Channel. Once on solid ground again, Fogg considers a trip to Bruges, Belgium, to buy some of its famous lace or to Ypres, which housed a beautiful medieval Cloth Hall. Both cities soon will figure prominently in the war, Bruges as a German seaport and Ypres, as one of the bloodiest and most active sectors on the Western Front. Fogg, however, decides to forego the pleasures of Flanders (such as beer and waffles) in the interest of time.

Fogg opts to take a train to Paris, the capital of the French Empire. France, the only republic in Europe at the time, prospered from its imperial trade and its industrial expansion. In the French capital, Fogg rides the Paris Métro, a sparkling and efficient new subway system with ten lines and the capacity to carry millions of travelers each month. Fogg's destination, Paris's Gare de l'Est rail station, served as the entry point for his next journey—on the Orient Express, a long-distance train. Reading newspapers and journals while he waits, Fogg observed that modernism had taken over the French capital. From the scandalous and exotic dance routines by Mata Hari to Igor Stravinsky's *Rites of Spring* ballet, which seemed to break all the rules of classical music, Parisians lived in the midst of cultural regeneration and change. Artists Pablo Picasso and Georges Braque's collaboration had created a whole new form of painting and sculpture known as Cubism, which had solidified into a cultural movement by 1914. The streets of Paris thronged with workers and students from all over France and from its imperial holdings in Algeria, Indochina, and West Africa. Artists, radicals, and entrepreneurs from around the world sought success in the French capital.

While waiting for the train, Fogg also witnessed a labor demonstration outside the station in Paris. France's labor unions actively sought improved conditions for workers, and many French people felt an affinity for the socialist politicians clamoring for a more equal society. One of these socialists, Jean Jaurès, was internationally renowned as an orator, a member of the Chamber of Deputies, and a reasonable voice for socialism's demands for workplace protections, unemployment insurance, and an equitable nation. One of his most ardent causes was pacifism. Jaurès was adamantly opposed to war and militarism in French society, and he had spent much of 1913 and 1914 protesting the mandatory draft of French young men. Like other socialists, he worried that war would derail the international movement of workers' rights and create a storm of nationalism. Although Fogg did not know it, this demonstration foreshadowed the tragic murder of Jaurès in August 1914 by a pro-war assassin.

German Empire

As he boarded the Orient Express for Strassburg (today Strasbourg), Fogg heard a mix of languages on the train. Strassburg itself, formally a French city in Alsace, had been under Germany's control since France's humiliating defeat by Prussia in the Franco-Prussian war of 1871. The town contained pro-German and pro-French families, and both nations viewed Alsatian loyalty as questionable. The region had featured prominently in one of France's most important political divides in recent history, the Dreyfus Affair, when a Jewish French army officer from Alsace was accused of espionage. The decade-long dispute and legal proceedings exposed a nation struggling with antisemitism and the separation of state from religion. While Dreyfus was eventually pardoned, the "Affair" activated ultra-nationalism and xenophobia while also motivating both the political Right and Left. Ultimately the Dreyfus Affair led to international pressure on France from its friends and allies alike.

With the few hours he had in Strasbourg, Fogg stopped for a nice meal and some famous wine from the region. In the distance he could see both the Vosges Mountains, a rugged expanse that became a significant part of the Franco-German battles of 1914 and 1915, and in the opposite direction, the Rhine River, a major artery for commerce. After his brief stay, he reboarded the train toward Munich, the southernmost city in Germany and capital of Bavaria, once independent state but now a state in the German Empire reigned over by the Kaiser, Wilhelm II.

Of all the countries in western Europe, Germany had transformed itself the most in the 40 or 50 years before 1914. As a new nation in 1871, the German Empire turned its attention to building colonies outside of Europe while also expanding its industrial capacity, especially in the chemical and steel industries. Fogg's view from the train would have reflected much of this change—the new consumer goods and prosperity from German economic and overseas development, the factory complexes, and the new infrastructure in transport and communications. This industrial might was soon put to the test by an unprecedented war. Germany also maintained an agricultural heartland, but the boundaries of these two worlds of agriculture and industry had created tensions in the social and political fabric. With the largest mainstream socialist political party in Europe, the SPD, Germany had a politically astute working-class that was organized and active. Fogg no doubt would have observed the urbanization of the Rhineland areas amid the fairytale castles of Germany's past, but his trip took him nowhere near the real heart of the new German state, Berlin, which was capital of both Prussia and the German Empire.

Habsburg Empire

Munich's location near the Austrian border meant that Fogg was soon able to reach Vienna, the Austrian imperial capital of the Habsburg (Austro-Hungarian) Empire, and then to its counterpart, Budapest, in the Hungarian part of the dual monarchy. The splendor of these towns struck Fogg immediately, especially the Baroque beauty of Vienna and the commercial bustle of Buda and Pest, twin cities separated only by the Danube River. Unlike Germany, Austria–Hungary had not sought overseas expansion in the late nineteenth century. Instead, it fought to hold its empire together in the face of burgeoning nationalist challenges from its multiple ethnic, religious, and linguistic minorities. The peculiar political system that governed the empire included an aging emperor who was fearfully ill in spring 1914, Franz Josef, and an unusual power-sharing arrangement, with two prime ministers, one for Austria and one for Hungary. Despite political tensions and conflict in its Balkan border regions, the empire flourished, and Vienna served as a cultural capital for Europe. Home of Sigmund Freud, whose exciting breakthroughs had revitalized the field of psychology, and Gustav Klimt, who was part of a different modernist art impulse than the one that Fogg saw in Paris, Vienna buzzed with activity.

Fogg had a decision to make in Hungary about whether to continue toward the Ottoman capital of Constantinople or take one of the spurs to another destination. Serbia was an enticing prospect because of its relatively new status as a kingdom and its rugged natural beauty. Serbia and its neighbors had just emerged from two wars over territory in the region, and there was an optimism and vitality to its public life, especially in the capital city of Belgrade. Another reason Fogg was drawn to Serbia was his curiosity about the place to which he had contributed through a war relief fund to help victims of the recently concluded Balkan Wars. He wanted to see the people behind the charitable appeals. But, despite his interest, Fogg decided to continue on his regular journey with a stop in Romania's capital, Bucharest, on his way to the Ottoman center of Constantinople (Istanbul). He was grateful that the train went directly to the city; thirty years earlier passengers had had to go to the Black Sea port of Varna and take a steamer to reach Constantinople.

Ottoman Empire

Stepping off the train in Ottoman territory, Fogg was struck first by the beauty of the great mosque and former church, the Hagia Sophia, which dominated the skyline. The year 1914 was a pivotal one in Ottoman history because it initially marked a year of peace after a revolt and two Balkan wars, and it also was a time when the Young Turk faction had consolidated power under a constitutional monarchy and begun efforts to modernize the city and its empire. From railway construction to naval purchases, the Ottoman authorities hoped to compete with western empires in industrial and geopolitical strength. The Ottoman capital city was a diverse multiethnic, multireligious metropolis that served as a crossroads for goods moving from the Black Sea to the Mediterranean Sea. The city, and indeed the empire, housed significant minority communities including Jews, Armenian Christians, and Kurdish nomads. These groups had been clamoring for more autonomy and had been challenging imperial authority. Had Fogg taken a cruise of the Bosphorus and Dardanelles straits, he might have noticed how the Ottomans had fortified and improved their maritime defenses, with such changes as antisubmarine nets and enlarged gun emplacements. A military observer would certainly have noted that Ottoman preparedness had improved substantially as a result of the Balkan Wars in 1912 and 1913.

Other Empires

At this point in his journey, Fogg left the train that had been his home for the last few days. He prepared to set off to India, on a steamship—one of a number of British merchant ships headed through the Suez Canal for points east. The Suez Canal, which opened in 1869, had become a key strategic and commercial site by 1914, and it had proved profitable in the early twentieth century because of the thriving imperial trade flowing through its 120-mile length. Also, given its location near major oil reserves and its importance for shortening the journey between European and Asian ports (especially in India), Britain took responsibility for protecting the canal and its neutrality by guarding the canal with troops stationed in Egypt. Britain's commercial interests also played a role, since in May 1914, the British government bought a controlling share (51%) of the wealthy Anglo-Persian Oil Company, thereby strengthening its ties to the area. In 1914 alone, "oil output ... reached 273,000 tons." From a British point of view, the canal had to remain in its hands, especially in time of war.

As the ship exited the canal zone, Fogg reflected on the changed political boundaries of the African continent as they steamed past Sudan and Eritrea. While the British had maintained a longer presence in the region, especially in their control of the port of Aden (in modern Yemen), the Italians were newcomers in colonization of northeast Africa, taking control of Libya, part of Somalia, and Eritrea in the late 1880s. Like Germany, Italy sought to join the quest for overseas colonies and hoped to build a reputation as a major European power in the twentieth century. Unlike Germany, by 1914 Italy had not industrialized to the extent that its neighboring European countries had, and it remained a highly divided country in terms of wealth, language, literacy, and political loyalties. Even the building of an empire could not erase its north–south divide nor its serious population drain as workers left for opportunities in other nations.

Fogg's ship did not dock in the Christian kingdom of Ethiopia, one of only two African states that remained independent of European rule in 1914. (The other, Liberia, had been established in the 1820s by the United States as a home for freed slaves, so it had a unique status and protection.) Throughout the rest of the continent, European control was the norm, and the rest of the territories had formal or informal colonial status. European officials drew new boundaries, built railways, and established settlements, but they also brought missionaries, teachers, and soldiers, disrupting established norms of family life, agriculture, and politics. Empires also empowered certain local elites, rewarding individuals for collaboration with the new foreign regimes. When war did come, these leaders gained in importance as they led their peoples into foreign conflicts.

Following the route of centuries of merchants, Fogg's ship traversed the Indian Ocean and had a choice of one of three main urban port centers in British India—Madras, Bombay, or Calcutta. Fogg's ship stopped in Calcutta, on the east coast, which in many ways was the heart of British India. The area had hosted British traders from the East India Company for nearly 300 years, and the resulting Anglo-Indian community there was unlike much of the rest of the subcontinent. Fogg recognized the importance of India's commercial ports, and its vast markets for imperial goods, to Britain's sense of itself as a world power. The Indian army, numbering nearly 150,000 men, played an important role in Britain's imperial defense. Certainly, the outbreak of war a few months later would plunge India into the global conflict.

From India, Fogg chose to visit another industrializing and modernizing nation-state, Japan. Of all the powers in the world, Japan was in some ways the most surprising, having defeated both China (1894–1895) and Russia (1904–1905) in short wars. East Asian power had focused for most of world history around China and its dynasties, but Japan's rapid modernization in the 1870s had led it to challenge European powers in industrial and imperial might. As a small island nation, Japan needed raw materials, and its search for those resources had led to annexation of Taiwan and Korea. China, Japan's near neighbor, had little ability to intervene in Japanese imperialism as it had been carved up into a series of spheres of influence by Europe and the United States. At the port of Nagasaki, Fogg remembered that this had been the single gateway for trade between Europe and Japan for more than 200 years; today it hosted ships from around the world.

In 1914, Fogg now had the option of leaving Japan's west coast port of Tsuruga, traveling by fast boat to Vladivostok, and then taking the Trans-Siberian railway back to London, a trip that took only two weeks under the best conditions.

Russian Empire

While a trip across the vast expanse of the Russian Empire appealed to Fogg, he chose merely to stop in Vladivostok and see the fortress under construction there near the bustling commercial port. Russia's defeat in the Russo-Japanese war and its subsequent revolution in 1905 had led to limited political reforms and to a new focus by Russian officials on securing its borders and improving its army and navy. Still, social and political unrest persisted. Russia's leader, Tsar Nicholas II, latest representative of the Romanov ruling dynasty, knew that his empire had an advantage in terms of population, and that Russia had experienced more than half a century of economic and industrial growth. However, despite impressive growth and change, it was also apparent in 1914 that Russia still lagged behind modernized and modernizing states in industrial might, income per capita, and literacy. Russia was primarily a rural, agricultural empire. It was also the largest contiguous multiethnic empire in the world, and it was capable of raising an enormous army. As such, it was a force in world politics. Fogg knew that a long train journey through Russia would demonstrate the vast land and resources of the Romanov Empire, and that he could observe the variety of peoples now under Russian imperial control. However, he wanted to circumnavigate the entire world, so he turned east, to the Pacific.

United States and Canada

Fogg departed from Vladivostok on a sea route to San Francisco in order to spend some time in the United States, the leading industrial nation by 1914. Having survived a bloody civil war in the 1860s and built its own empire by 1898, the United States was booming. Migrants from around the world came seeking work, and a westward migration had created new states. The United States in 1914 was in the midst of an era of regulation and progressive social causes, making cities and workers the objects of intense reform efforts. US officials, meanwhile, sought to continue economic growth in the western hemisphere and to replace European predominance in important parts of South America's export trade. The United States was also warily watching the revolution raging in Mexico on its southern border, and stepping up its naval program to better connect the mainland with colonies in Hawaii and the Philippines. The United States was a nation on the move, with working-class immigrants seeking new lives in the industrial centers on the coasts and in the Great Lakes region, agricultural laborers looking to California and the Midwest, and Americans of all backgrounds relocating to the land-rich western reaches of the nation. Fogg's stop in San Francisco was so brief that he only got a glimpse of this dynamism before traveling up the coast to Vancouver Island, Canada, where he boarded a train headed to Halifax, Nova Scotia.

As he crossed Canada, Fogg witnessed many similar trends to those in the United States and unbeknownst to him, traveled the route that hundreds of thousands of Chinese civilian contract workers would take on their way to the Western Front in just a few years. In the years before the war, European immigrants, enticed by generous incentive programs, flocked to Canada for work in industry and agriculture. Many of these guest workers would soon face imprisonment as enemy aliens because they hailed from empires at war with Britain and its dominions. In fact, despite a sizable and vocal French-speaking population, signs of Canada's loyalty to the British Empire abounded, making it clear what role Canada would play in a British war.

From Halifax, Fogg completed his last leg of his world tour with a transatlantic voyage over much of the ocean recently crossed by the ill-fated *Titanic*, which had sunk just two years earlier. Little could he know how dangerous Atlantic waters were about to become. With the outbreak of war, German U-boat submarines began patrolling Atlantic shipping lanes, seeking to damage the British blockade that was slowly strangling German supplies.

As he made his way home from Southampton to London, Fogg reflected on this brief survey of the world, marveling at the signs of global interconnectedness that had not been present in the same way just a few decades earlier. The world he saw in 1914 was one of massive inequities—in wealth, political power, social mobility—but it was also a world that seemed to have created balances to control conflict. All that changed in the summer of 1914.

Tensions in 1914

What Fogg's tour of the world failed to uncover were the simmering tensions that lurked between and within the nations he visited. War in summer 1914 was not merely the result of a single poor decision, nor was it an inevitable reaction to a political assassination. Instead it was a culmination of specific political actions in 1914 and a whole string of decisions in the years leading up to the war. As most historians will agree, World War I is an excellent example of the concept of historical *contingency*. This concept means that war might occur, but it might not; it was not foreordained in any way. War happened in 1914 because real people assessed their choices, made calculations about consequences and possible outcomes, and then acted on those decisions. This contingency is what makes studying World War I so fascinating because the questions of "What if" and "Why?" abound. The rest of this chapter will list some of the probable underlying causes for war and the certain actions and decisions that led to the outbreak of a local war that transformed into a world war in 1914.

Nationalism

One of the most significant underlying factors in the outbreak of war was the growth of nationalism in the late nineteenth and early twentieth centuries. The concept of nationalism arose as a result of the revolutions of the eighteenth century in the United States, France, and Haiti. By overthrowing monarchies and establishing new institutions, revolutionaries proposed an idea of citizenship that relied on people to participate in the politics and defense of the nation. Benedict Anderson famously explained this concept as an "imagined community" in which human societies define belonging by concepts such as language, ethnicity, religion, and shared history, rather than mere personal acquaintance. This notion of nationalism had gained strength by the early twentieth century and had become a vital feature of modern life.

Nationalism contributed to the war in a number of ways. First, cultural nationalism exploded as a force in the nineteenth century. Common people found identities in the traditions of the past—folklore, language, music, art, dance, poetry, and other cultural forms. In Scotland, folklorists collected songs and ballads for a new generation, while in Bohemia, political leaders began to talk of a Czech identity based on language and history. Languages that had been nearly lost to time were revived to help link people to their heritage, and schools began to encourage children to learn "folk" languages such as Irish, Welsh, and Flemish. Cultural nationalism created a strong bond and sense of group identity, but it also served to divide groups and to emphasize differences. Second, by 1914, many men and women had achieved a certain level of literacy through religious or state-sponsored educational initiatives. In elementary schools, children learned a national or imperial history that shaped their understandings of citizenship, duty, and rights. Curricula utilized historical events and "national" literature to teach the basics of reading, writing, math, and civics. Even in imperial contexts, mission schools taught a version of the European national story as an explanation for the growth of empire and for the place of its citizens. Nationalism became an important tool for governments seeking to motivate or mobilize populations. In 1914 men who were called to war largely answered that call, many out of a sense of obligation and duty to the nation-state. The lines between Germans and French and Turks and Britons hardened through the hatred and bloodshed of war, but these divisions had already been established well before hostilities commenced.

12

Eastern Question

Another significant factor in the war was a long-term and lingering conflict that historians know as the "Eastern Question." Certain areas of the world were diplomatic hot-spots because of their histories or their strategic importance to multiple nations. One such hot-spot in the nineteenth and twentieth centuries was the Ottoman Empire, whose territories and the surrounding borderlands faced upheaval. From an empire that had once reigned supreme in the eastern Mediterranean, the Ottomans had suffered loss of territory, financial bankruptcy, and internal revolt, making it vulnerable to interference from other powers. The problem was that these outside powers had competing interests in the region, which created conflict. The British had clear economic and strategic goals to protect their empire in India, to create markets for their goods and investments (such as railways), and to maintain open international waterways for their shipping. The Russians also knew what they wanted, which included protected access through the Dardanelles for their grain shipments from the Black Sea. The French, who invested heavily in infrastructure and business in the region, also sought markets, access, and political support. In similar ways to what was happening in China with the slow crumbling of Qing dynasty power and the escalation of outside interference, the Ottomans contended with an onslaught of advice, funds, and threats from other world powers. One of the areas where this battle for survival occurred was in the Balkans, which had long been the location for contending Austro-Hungarian and Ottoman control and which was now experiencing a nationalist revival. In short, the Eastern Question led to instability in southeastern Europe, the Middle East, and the Persian Gulf, and increased vulnerability of minority populations. The presence of significant oil reserves in the area only complicated the picture.

Industrialization

Industrialization and the competition for resources and markets that accompanied it also played a role in the war. As nations experienced industrial growth, they underwent urbanization, population increases, and labor militancy in addition to changes in families and workplaces. Regions that achieved only sluggish industrial growth saw themselves falling behind other nations in infrastructure, national wealth, and social indicators such as literacy. Throughout Europe, grinding poverty, high rates of infant mortality, and poor wages still plagued vast numbers of people. In other parts of the world, the impact of globalizing and industrializing European and North American states led to disappearance of local industries, exploitative labor systems, and disruption of the social fabric of lives. European urban workers, in particular, organized to meet the challenges of industrialization, creating effective trade unions to lobby for better wages and conditions and eventually founding major political parties to make the case for laws protecting workers. By 1914 organized labor made a compelling case for peace across national borders, but when war came, few were able to withstand the claims of nationalism and patriotic duty that silenced much of the protest. Additionally, the insatiable industrial needs of the wartime state would push up wages and create jobs for those who were not fighting, opening the doors of factories to increasing numbers of women, youth, and immigrants.

Militarization

Many historians speak of the long nineteenth century as a time of peace between the Congress of Vienna in 1815 and the outbreak of the world war in 1914. Yet, this century was built on warfare. From national wars of liberation in Greece and Serbia to revolutions in France to the Crimean War to the American Civil War to imperial wars around the globe to the Russo-Japanese War to the Balkan Wars, this was far from a century of peace. Europeans, however, did get used to a version of war that could be celebrated in heroic fashion. The Franco-Prussian War of 1870–1871, for instance, was short and had clear goals, and it led to the creation of a modern French Republic and a new German Empire. Individual stories of heroism circulated in the new popular press to bolster national understandings of the war. Likewise, the Anglo-Boer War of 1899–1902 served as a wake-up call to the British nation about its lack of preparedness, but it, too, was short and distant, making it the stuff of heroic tales. Robert Baden-Powell, the hero of the siege of Mafeking, used his fame from the war to launch a new organization in 1907, the Boy Scouts, which institutionalized militarism for the masses. War was present, but it did not touch the majority of European populations in a personal and immediate way until World War I.

War had lodged itself in the imaginations of many people by 1914, however. The creation of mandatory periods of military service for young men in every major European country (except Britain, which had a robust voluntary training system) meant that whole generations of young men had some stake and experience in the waging of war. In addition, many amateur societies trained men for war or warlike activities (e.g., shooting), and irregular militias of volunteers emerged in areas where nationalist unrest was prevalent (e.g., Ireland). Women, men, and children across generations learned about a romanticized version of war through popular novels, stories, and songs. Espionage stories, tales of imperial adventures, and shock stories about future invasions all sold briskly at the turn of the century. The shadowy enemies of these tales invariably changed, but the notion that defense of nation in time of war was an important duty of all who lived in that nation became a truism. War and its accompanying values of sacrifice, duty, heroism, and glory took on a transcendent form in political treatises, poetry, and art. Laurence Binyon was only able to publish a poem such as his "For the Fallen" in the London *Times* on September 21, 1914, because of a half-century of cultural messages that glorified war as a pure sacrifice for patriotism and nation:

> They went with songs to the battle, they were young,
> Straight of limb, true of eye, steady and aglow.
> They were staunch to the end against odds uncounted;
> They fell with their faces to the foe.
>
> They shall grow not old, as we that are left grow old:
> Age shall not weary them, nor the years contemn.
> At the going down of the sun and in the morning
> We will remember them.

This sentiment that dying for one's country was an honor accompanied a whole generation of people to war in 1914.

Technology

Finally, it is important to remember that technological innovation had led by 1914 to a revolution in the means of waging war. Not only did nations amass weapons that were designed to be used in air, on land, and at sea, but they also now had the capacity to feed, clothe, transport, and communicate with armies that would have been unimaginable even 50 years earlier. Therefore, when considering the technology of war, it is also important to remember the invention of refrigeration, canning, radio, telephones, electricity, vulcanized rubber, and other processes that made war on the scale of World War I even possible. In terms of the actual weaponry of war, military expenditure soared. Among the six so-called "great" powers (Germany, Britain, France, Austria-Hungary, Russia, and Italy), money spent on defense more than quadrupled between 1870 and 1914. Germany's spending on defense and armament saw a particularly massive increase in the early twentieth century, from a per capita expenditure of $1.28 in 1870 to $8.19 in 1914.

Some of this spending focused on research and development of war materials. Although all major countries spent money on building navies prior to the war, both Germany and Britain invested considerable amounts on naval innovation, with the creation of massive modern battleships with big guns, quicker high-speed destroyers, and torpedo-laden submarines. Russia and Austria-Hungary built railroads in the lead-up to the war, understanding that rail lines would be crucial for mobilization in the event of a European war. Other innovations that became important in 1914 included breech-loading rifles, machine guns, high explosive shells, field guns and mortars, poison gas shells, and airplanes, just to name a few. The most destructive, expensive and frightening weapon of the war in 1914 was artillery. In fact, the majority of wounds in the war were inflicted by shell or mortar, making artillery the most feared machine for front-line soldiers. These new weapons required a transformation in treatment of the wounded, but the medical profession only slowly adjusted to the devastating injuries that modern weaponry inflicted on bodies. As they did innovate, new surgical strategies, drugs, wound regimens, and triage procedures appeared at the fronts.

Alliances

Many histories of World War I emphasize a system of alliances as the driving mechanism that, once activated, drew Europe inevitably into war. Although it is true that the great powers of Europe organized themselves into two camps in the late nineteenth and early twentieth centuries through a series of treaties, mutual assistance pacts, and alliances, these agreements had an informality that left them less binding than many states had hoped. Germany, Austria-Hungary, and Italy joined together in the Triple Alliance in 1882, but the weaknesses of that agreement became clear when Italy not only declined to join the war with its allies in 1914, but actually fought against them after 1915. Russia, France, and Britain's Triple Entente of 1904 was not a mutual defense alliance—rather, it was a loose agreement; without the German violation of Belgian neutrality, Britain's ability to appease popular opinion in order to aid its allies by joining the war would have been in doubt.

In fact, it was not the strength of alliances that led countries to fall like dominoes into war, but instead it was the fear that promises might be broken and the uncertainties of support that made government officials willing to act. The alliances and agreements allowed for small states to play on the fears of great powers. The powerful states, in turn, imagined complex scenarios that sometimes led to reckless or poor decisions. In other words, the alliance system was important but not necessarily for the reasons that many think it was. Alliances were weak and uncertain, or merely imagined, leading decision makers to take calculated chances after guessing what other nations might do. This created an unstable and volatile diplomatic environment in 1914.

Prior Conflicts

The world in 1914 was certainly a complicated place, but it was not a place where a global war seemed probable or even that possible. In the decade leading up to 1914, several major conflicts and wars had been successfully contained to local regions or had been solved with diplomatic negotiation. The two Balkan wars, while terribly destructive and painful for those involved, each lasted less than a year and seemed to have concrete goals. The Italian campaign to annex

Libya in 1911 was likewise a quick expedition. Showdowns between major powers in Bosnia, in Morocco, in China, in Sudan, and in Rhodesia all ended with treaties or negotiated settlements. There was no reason to think that war might break out between even a few powers, let alone all the major world empires. War occurred because in the summer of 1914 leaders made decisions based on three concepts: past knowledge of conflict, questions of national security, and assumptions about their futures. The catalyst and later the justification for these decisions was a terrorist act on June 28, 1914.

The Journey to War in 1914

Students with little knowledge of World War I often have heard of the assassination of June 28, 1914, and today visitors to Sarajevo can stand in the (bronzed) footsteps of the assassin and imagine the events of that day. In reality, the assassination of the heir to the Austrian throne, Franz Ferdinand, and his wife, Sophie, in the streets of Sarajevo barely registered in the world news reports except as a terrible tragedy. Other political leaders had been assassinated by terrorist groups or individuals seeking vengeance, so while it was a tragedy, it need not have sparked a world war. For example, Tsar Alexander II of Russia died from an assassin's bomb in 1881, and US President William McKinley was assassinated by an anarchist in 1901. Reports, then, of Franz Ferdinand's death initially described it as a terrible act of violence and a blow to the Habsburg monarchy. What turned an act of violence into a catalyst for war were the reactions by diplomats and political leaders in the month that followed. Each used the event for purposes beyond the scope of the actual assassination. This series of actions and decisions is usually called the "July Crisis," which in turn activated the "Guns of August." How did it happen?

The background context of the Eastern Question is significant here. As Ottoman control of the Balkan peninsula continued to crumble in the nineteenth century in the face of popular revolutions and resistance, Serbia, Montenegro, and Romania all gained independence from the Ottomans, followed by recognition from the great powers. Bulgaria sought a similar independence in 1908, sparking Austria-Hungary to annex Bosnia-Herzegovina at the same time. Crisis was averted only because of intervention from the major powers, who recognized this annexation as a legitimate one under rules established years earlier at the Treaty of Berlin (1878). Bosnia and Herzegovina became part of the Habsburg Empire, but many Serb nationalists lived and worked in Bosnia and saw Bosnia's natural and national future as part of a greater Serbia. Therefore, when the heir to the Habsburg throne visited the capital of Bosnia on the most important Serbian national holiday of the year, it was not entirely surprising that he was the target of violence.

The shooter, Gavrilo Princip, was 19 years old and one of seven conspirators who set out to murder the heir. The first assassination attempt of the day wounded members of Franz Ferdinand's party, but the Archduke chose to continue with his itinerary at least through a planned speech at City Hall. After this speech, the archduke wanted to visit the wounded from the first assassination attempt, but the change in itinerary confused the drivers who went down the wrong street. When told to reverse, the drivers had to push the car back because cars did not yet have a reverse gear. At this moment, Princip was in the right place at the right time to make his move. He stepped up on the running board of the car and, with two shots at point-blank range, he hit both Franz Ferdinand and his wife. By lunchtime that day, both were dead, and Princip, "who was trying to shoot himself," was in custody.

What was unknown at the time, though suspected, was that Serbian government officials had aided and armed these conspirators, who were part of a secret organization known as the Black Hand. It was this suspicion of Serbian culpability along with a deep sense of insecurity that led Austria-Hungary to move toward punishing Serbia for this crime. Another way to perceive this event is as a spark for another Balkan war, fought locally over the boundaries that had been at stake since the Bosnian annexation crisis and the creation of Bulgaria in 1908. Each Balkan conflict, in 1912, 1913, and 1914, sought to deal with the tensions over boundaries and political power in the region. What is important to understand is how this Third Balkan War turned into World War I. The answer to that is complicated and has been the subject of heated debate among historians for a century. This is where the issue of contingency reappears and becomes important to the analysis. The move from local conflict to global war occurred because of choices made by political leaders in a number of states and because of a "shared political culture." By examining each of these states separately, it is easier to see the pattern that emerges by late July 1914 and to construct a timeline that expanded war in the Balkans to war around the world (see Timeline in Appendix 1.2, at the end of this chapter).

First, Austria–Hungary, reeling from the shock of the assassination and angry at what appeared to be Serb complicity, appealed to its allies for support and aid should it challenge Serbia. Austria–Hungarian officials wanted reassurance because they feared retaliation from the Russian Empire, which had appointed itself protector of Slavic peoples and friend to Serbia in a grand gesture years earlier. Russia was also wary of any attempt by Austria–Hungary to expand its boundaries into former Ottoman territory. The Habsburg foreign minister, Leopold Count Berchtold, was an experienced diplomat who had served in Britain, France, and Russia prior to the war. The assassination had been a personal tragedy for him because he and his spouse had been close friends with the archduke and his wife. Berchtold and other Austro-Hungarian leaders agreed that some action had to be taken to respond to this provocation, but without solid proof of Serb involvement, and without the backing of allies, they were reluctant to act too rashly. Berchtold, therefore, sought German assurances of support should the Habsburgs challenge Serbia. He sent a messenger to Germany on July 5.

Meanwhile in Germany, many political leaders felt sympathy for the Habsburgs and quite quickly saw the need for some response. By the time the Austrian messenger left Berlin on July 7, Kaiser Wilhelm II, Chancellor Theobald von Bethmann Hollweg, and Under-Secretary of State Arthur Zimmermann had agreed upon support for their ally. Basically, the Emperor and his officials saw Austrian action against Serbia as justified, and German leaders had faith that the war would be localized, as the earlier Balkan Wars had been. Some historians have argued as well that Germany might have had a preventive war in mind. Certainly German leaders looked uneasily at growing Russian military and industrial expansion, and they spoke among themselves in bellicose terms. Some saw war coming to Europe in the near future and perhaps viewed this as an opportunity to fight while Germany was still relatively strong. In any case, the Germans did promise support in vague terms to the Habsburgs in what has become known in the historical literature as the "blank check," implying support in any eventuality. In hindsight, it looks like both Austria-Hungary and Germany were engaging in very risky behavior, especially given the possible Russian reaction. The Central Powers gambled on the idea that Russia would not intervene.

The Russian Empire watched events in early July 1914 very carefully while also hastily making contact with its own allies, particularly France. Raymond Poincaré, president, and René Viviani, prime minister, who had already been scheduled to make a state visit to St. Petersburg, arrived on July 20 in the Russian capital city. Given events in the Balkans, the meeting turned into a much more pointed conversation between the French leaders and the Russian foreign minister, Sergei Sazonov, and his sovereign, Tsar Nicholas II. Both Russia and France agreed on two main concepts, namely that Serbia could not be held responsible for the terrorism of individuals and that the two must stand firm as allies in the face of possible aggression by the Central Powers. As the French leaders sailed home, Austria-Hungary delivered an ultimatum to Serbia.

Serbia, the small state at the center of this crisis, proclaimed its innocence in the assassination plot. In fact, major officials in the Serb government had secretly directed, funded, armed, trained, and supported the assassins of the Black Hand, which other nations suspected but could not prove at the time. In early July, Serb leaders appealed to Russia for support in case of Austrian retaliation. When the ultimatum arrived at 6 p.m. on July 23, it was immediately clear to Serb officials that it was designed to fail. Serbia would have to agree to a violation of its sovereign status and allow Habsburg investigators to work in Serbia itself. Anyone in Serbia who had thought the Germans would restrain their ally now faced an imminent war with the Habsburgs. However, the Serbs also had received assurance from Russia on July 25 that assistance was guaranteed, and the Russians had begun a partial mobilization. The Serbs delivered their answer that same night, accepting all but two of the Habsburg terms unconditionally. They balked at demands that would allow Austria-Hungary to participate in police inquiries and prosecutions within Serbia, calling these a violation of sovereignty and the Serb constitution. By midnight, the Austro–Hungarian army had received orders to mobilize.

In Britain, Foreign Secretary Sir Edward Grey had tried to stay out of the growing crisis in Europe in the early days of July. July 24 was one of the first documented Cabinet discussions of the problem, and even at this time, the discussion focused on a proposed mediation by Britain, Italy, France, and Germany. Britain had guaranteed Belgian neutrality and promised to safeguard it by treaty in 1839, but popular opinion showed little support for British intervention on the continent in 1914. Kaiser Wilhelm II saw British action as improbable, especially because he had heard a rumor from his brother that their cousin, George V (monarch of Britain), had promised to stay clear of a continental war. These mixed messages and lack of clear direction from London meant that not only did Germany calculate on Britain's neutrality, but France and Russia looked nervously at their ally.

Once leaders realized what was happening, it became harder to stop the logic of their own decisions from dictating actions. Kaiser Wilhelm II even sought a last-ditch escape from war by telegramming his other royal cousin, Tsar Nicholas II. These notes between kings on July 29, known subsequently as the Willy–Nicky telegrams, failed to avert crisis and served as evidence of how far the statesmanship of an earlier era between elites had changed by 1914. Things escalated quickly between July 28 and August 5, by which time all the major players were involved in the war. It is important to remember that during this week the conflict might have been contained had any of the main powers backed down or developed serious mediation strategies, but none did. Each remained steeped in its own political calculations, its fear of the others, and a sense of invulnerability that is hard to fathom by the modern student of history.

Historians have argued about what tipped the balance in July 1914, and several candidates have emerged—Germany's blank check, Austria-Hungary's ultimatum, Serbia's answer, Russia's mobilization, Britain's ambiguity, France's fatalistic approach to war. All of these contributed to the crisis, but the main trigger was fear. Britain feared Russia's expansion in the eastern Mediterranean and Afghanistan, Germany feared Russian invasion, France feared German invasion, Austria-Hungary feared internal revolt and loss of territory, Belgium feared violation of its neutrality, Serbia feared Austria-Hungary, and the Ottoman Empire feared all the great powers. This was a situation in which small actions were magnified by the atmosphere of fear.

Conclusion

By the time the first shots were fired by Austria-Hungary in Serbia's capital city of Belgrade in late July 1914, war preparations had begun in a number of countries. Ultimately, the Austrian attack on Serbia on July 28 made a German decision necessary. Additionally, the Russian general mobilization of July 30 also pressured Germany to act. Germany issued ultimatums to Russia and France on July 31, and then declared war on Russia on August 1 and France on August 3. As soon as news broke of the German invasion of Belgium on August 4, Britain declared war as well. What seems peculiar in all this is the fact that Austria-Hungary and Russia, who in many ways had precipitated the crisis over Serbia, did not go to war with each other formally until August 6. For the remaining global powers, 1914 became an opportunity to advance foreign policy objectives or a chance to remain outside the fray. Japan, for instance, saw an opportunity in the war to expand its power in the Pacific vis-à-vis China and Russia, while the United States declared its official neutrality. Fence-sitters such as the Ottoman Empire and Italy eventually chose a side, the Ottomans joining the war in November 1914 on the side of the Central Powers, and Italy rejecting its alliance with the Habsburgs and the Germans in order to join the British and French in May 1915.

Amidst all this diplomatic maneuvering and posturing, the people of the states involved got drawn into the fray, whether they wanted to be or not. Some historians have claimed that an almost universal popular enthusiasm reigned in the streets of the nations declaring war, but recent scholarship has demonstrated a much more varied response. While some did welcome war as an exciting event that would transform societies, many others dreaded leaving livelihoods and families.

To return to the question of the chapter—How and why did this war happen? The answer is not that common people demanded it, but instead, high-stakes decision-making among a small group of political and military elites led to war. It is true that these elites depend upon the loyalty of their populations, and every decision made in July 1914 was predicated on the idea that the people of their nations would answer a call to arms. Those citizens did answer the call, with the result that millions around the world found themselves caught up in a global, modern, total war that would reshape their nations' futures.

Citations

Page   Source

2   "the journeys travelled ...." quoted in Christopher Clark, *The Sleepwalkers: How Europe Went to War in 1914* (New York: HarperCollins, 2013), xxviii.

4   Figures drawn from Angela Woollacott, *On Her Their Lives Depend: Munitions Workers in the Great War* (Berkeley: University of California Press, 1994), 29.

8   "Oil output," quoted in Hew Strachan, *The First World War. Volume I: To Arms* (Oxford: Oxford University Press, 2001), 774.

12   "imagined community," concept drawn from Benedict Anderson, *Imagined Communities: Reflections on the Origin and Spread of Nationalism* (London: Verso, 1991).

15   "they went with songs ...." Laurence Binyon, "For the Fallen," *The Times*, September 21, 1914.

15   Figures drawn from Joachim Remak, *The Origins of World War I, 1871–1914*, 2nd Edition (Orlando, FL: Harcourt Brace, 1995), 86.

18   "who was trying to shoot himself," quoted in Margaret MacMillan, *The War That Ended Peace: The Road to 1914* (New York: Random House, 2013), 552.

18   "shared political culture," quoted in Clark, *The Sleepwalkers*, 561.

Select Bibliography

Afflerbach, Holger, and David Stevenson, eds. *An Improbable War? The Outbreak of World War I and European Political Culture before 1914*. Oxford: Berghahn Books, 2007.

Carter, Miranda. *George, Nicholas and Wilhelm. Three Royal Cousins and the Road to World War I*. New York: Vintage, 2011.

Clark, Christopher. *The Sleepwalkers: How Europe Went to War in 1914*. New York: HarperCollins, 2013.

Fromkin, David. *Europe's Last Summer: Who Started the Great War in 1914?* New York: Alfred A. Knopf, 2004.

MacMillan, Margaret. *The War That Ended Peace: The Road to 1914*. New York: Random House, 2013.

McMeekin, Sean. *The Russian Origins of the First World War*. Cambridge, MA: Harvard University Press, 2011.

Mombauer, Annika. *The Origins of the First World War: Controversies and Consensus*. Harlow, Essex: Pearson Education, 2002.

Neiberg, Michael S. *Dance of the Furies: Europe and the Outbreak of World War I*. Cambridge, MA: Harvard University Press, 2011.

Otte, T. G. *July Crisis: The World's Descent into War, Summer 1914*. Cambridge: Cambridge University Press, 2014.

Remak, Joachim. *The Origins of World War I, 1871–1914*, 2nd Edition. Orlando, FL: Harcourt Brace, 1995.

Strachan, Hew. *The First World War. Volume I: To Arms*. Oxford: Oxford University Press, 2001.

Appendix 1.1: Important States in 1914

State	Political Picture in 1914	Land area	Population
Austria-Hungary	Habsburg Empire (1556–1918) Franz Josef	0.6 million km²	50.6 million
Belgium (+ colonies)	Monarchy (1831–present) King Albert I	2.4 million km²	23.0 million
France (+ colonies)	Republic (1870–1940) President Raymond Poincaré	11.2 million km²	88.1 million
Germany (+ colonies)	Wilhelmine Empire (1871–1918) Kaiser Wilhelm II	3.5 million km²	77.7 million
Italy (+ colonies)	Constitutional Monarchy (1861–1946) King Victor Emmanuel III	2.3 million km²	37.6 million
Japan (+ colonies)	Empire (1868–1947) Emperor Taishō	0.7 million km²	74.2 million
Ottoman Empire	Sultanate (1453–1918) Sultan Mehmed V	1.8 million km²	23.0 million
Russian Empire	Romanov Empire (1613–1917) Tsar Nicholas II	22.1 million km²	176.4 million
Serbia	Kingdom (1882–1918) King Peter I	48 500 km²	2.9 million
United Kingdom (+ colonies/ dominions)	Kingdom (1801–present) King George V	33.3 million km²	446.1 million
United States (+ colonies/ dependencies)	Republic (1783–present) President Woodrow Wilson	9.6 million km²	106.3 milllion

Sources

Broadberry, Stephen, and Mark Harrison. "The Economics of World War I: An Overview." In *The Economics of World War I*, edited by Broadberry and Harrison, 3–40. Cambridge: Cambridge University Press, 2005.

Baταković, Dušan. "Storm over Serbia: The Rivalry between Civilian and Military Authorities, 1911–1914." *Balcanica* XLIV (2013), 307–356.

Schremmer, D. E. "Taxation and Public Finance: Britain, France, and Germany." In *The Cambridge Economic History of Europe* vol. 8, edited by Peter Matthias and Sidney Pollard, 494. Cambridge: Cambridge University Press, 1989.

Appendix 1.2: Timeline from June to August 1914

June 28, 1914	Assassination in Sarajevo of Franz Ferdinand, heir to Habsburg throne
July 5, 1914	Austria-Hungary sends a messenger to Germany to seek support
July 7, 1914	Messenger conveys German "blank check" of support for its ally
July 20, 1914	French President Poincaré arrives in St. Petersburg for a state visit
July 23, 1914	Austria-Hungary presents Serbia with a 10-point ultimatum
July 25, 1914	Serbia replies to ultimatum, accepting all but two provisions
	Russia assures Serbia of its support
	Austria-Hungary orders a targeted mobilization against Serbia
July 26, 1914	Russia begins a partial mobilization
July 28, 1914	Austria-Hungary declares war on Serbia and invades
July 29, 1914	Willy–Nicky telegram exchange begins
	Russia declares a general mobilization
July 31, 1914	Austria-Hungary expands to a general mobilization
	Germany declares a "state preparatory to war"
	Germany issues ultimatums to Russia and France
	Britain asks Germany and France for assurances about Belgian neutrality
August 1, 1914	France orders a general mobilization
	Germany orders a general mobilization
	German troops invade Luxembourg
	Germany declares war on Russia
August 2, 1914	Germany issues ultimatum to Belgium asking for free passage
August 3, 1914	Germany declares war on France
August 4, 1914	Germany declares war on Belgium and invades
	Britain declares war on Germany
August 6, 1914	Austria-Hungary declares war on Russia
August 12, 1914	Britain and France declare war on Austria-Hungary
August 17, 1914	Russia invades Germany
August 23, 1914	Japan declares war on Germany

2

1914. Was This War a Total War?

Figure 2.1 Ordinary people found themselves in extraordinary circumstances during the war. Here an Ottoman prisoner of war cuts his Australian captor's hair at Gallipoli in 1915. *Source*: Imperial War Museum.

World War I: A Short History, First Edition. Tammy M. Proctor.
© 2018 John Wiley & Sons Ltd. Published 2018 by John Wiley & Sons Ltd.

On July 30, 1914, shells rained down on Belgrade, Serbia, from Austro-Hungarian artillery. Days later, German troops entered the tiny state of Luxembourg and began a brutal invasion of Belgium that featured executions of civilians, destruction of property, and hostage-taking. During the invasion, German soldiers looked nervously over their shoulders, seeing themselves as vulnerable targets for civilian snipers. German troops had been raised on stories of the dangers of sharpshooters in France and Belgium from literature of the Franco-Prussian War. Later that same week in Britain, the counterespionage office arrested suspected spies and began the process of registering all known "aliens" (people of foreign birth or nationality) in the country in preparation for the internment of many of them. In Russia, manufacturers of all kinds of goods began mobilizing in order to dress, feed, and equip a massive army, bigger than anything the empire had seen up to this point. French refugees in border zones took to the roads, hoping to escape the violence they knew was coming. This impressionistic list frames the big question of Chapter 2, namely *What is "total war," and was this a total war?* In the popular media during the beginning of the war's centennial in 2014, much was made of the fact that World War I was a transformative conflict, an unprecedented conflagration. This chapter will focus on the first few months of fighting in 1914 and then examine the concept of total war in order to understand how this war was different from those that preceded it. By studying the definition and meaning of total war early in the book, we will have the opportunity to test the concept's usefulness and limitations for describing World War I.

The War in 1914

A month after the assassination of Franz Ferdinand in Sarajevo, Austria-Hungary launched a war with Serbia on July 28, 1914. When it became apparent that war had indeed arrived, outbursts of popular enthusiasm erupted in many major cities in Europe. In a now famous photo taken in front of the *Feldherrnhalle* in Munich an excited young Adolf Hitler is part of a boisterous crowd cheering the war. Photos of other European cities also capture crowds of young men smiling at the approaching war. Yet, despite these outbursts of war fervor and jingoism, many dreaded the coming of the war rather than welcoming it. For farmers, it was hard to contemplate leaving their harvests in the field to report for military service, for instance. Working-class socialist and communist leaders also opposed war on principle and faced a difficult choice between class ideology and calls to nationalism. In fact, given the cares and concerns of most ordinary people, why did so many men report when they got the call?

What spurred men to report for duty or to enlist in 1914 in most cases was a sense of responsibility as citizens to support their nations and to defend them against threats. Since each government explained its aims in 1914 as defensive and protective, populations accepted this duty in the first months of the war. In every country, ordinary people "went to war believing that their government had no choice but to fight a war of self-defense." Yet, as many authors have pointed out, most people who went to war in 1914 had little conception of what was to come. There was a widespread feeling that the war would be short, and for a generation raised on heroic literature and adventure tales, war seemed to have a glorious and almost regenerative cast. Poetry of the prewar period supported this notion, with young men being told that war was a game with rules to be followed and glory to be won. In Sir Henry Newbolt's poem, *Vitaï Lampada* (1897), a cricket game turns into a blood-soaked imperial battle with a schoolboy/soldier heroically proclaiming "Play up! play up! and play the game!" In Germany, Isolde Kurz's poem, *Vaterland* (1914) makes a similar point: "At the close of the iron game, pure hands of saviors will award the lot you won: the crown of fame." The war in 1914 that citizens of the combatant empires joined was not the war that they thought it was, and the early battles of 1914 on every front made this clear. As German soldier Paul Hub wrote to his wife in October 1914, "All around me the most gruesome devastation … I didn't think war would be like this." By October, and certainly as 1914 drew to a close, a new sense of war consciousness had emerged among ordinary people. Although the first shots of the war were fired by Austria-Hungary in its invasion of Serbia, fighting had broken out on a number of fronts by early August (see Map 2a).

Western Front

The Western Front in 1914 constituted a bloody war of movement as Germany and France sought to execute their prewar military plans and deliver a knock-out, war-ending blow. The Germans set into motion their Schlieffen Plan, sending troops into Luxembourg and Belgium and beginning a sweeping movement toward the English Channel and toward Paris. Quickly, the German offensive was bogged down by unexpected Belgian resistance, first at Liège, then in other towns in Belgium, and the German troops found it difficult to keep their armies supplied as they moved. In August the Germans faced British and French troops along the French–Belgian border near Mons, but these early clashes were not decisive and led to a retooling by both sides. France's initial war plan called for an attack along the boundaries of Alsace and Lorraine and in the northeast corner of the country near Metz. The mountainous terrain there led to terrible fighting conditions. The Germans gained ground in the region, then promptly built trenches and defensive works while the French retreated to safe positions. It was a devastating blow for French morale, with casualties reaching more than "200,000, of which over 75,000 were dead in just a few days of desperate fighting." (See Map 2b.)

It is hard to imagine the sight of these early moments of combat, where a clash of eras was on display. The bright reds and blues of nineteenth-century uniforms had been designed to allow for identification of enemy from foe on a battlefield filled with musket smoke. In the evolution to industrial warfare, most armies had not yet shed these ill-suited brilliantly colored clothes, although Britain and Germany had already modernized. The French army, as Sir Edward Spears noted in his memoir of 1914, showed bravery, yet he was struck by the waste of life: "The sense of tragic futility of it will never quite fade from the minds of those who saw these brave men, dashing across the open to the sound of bugles and drums, clad in the old red caps and trousers which a parsimonious democracy dictated they should wear, although they turned each man into a target."

Like the French, the Germans and the British also advanced into machine gun and artillery fire in head-on assaults that resulted in enormous loss of life. Most armies had not yet adopted hard-shelled helmets, so the soldiers had only soft caps to protect themselves from artillery. All the nation's infantry soldiers carried enormous amounts of heavy equipment including rifles, ammunition, tools, and clothing, all of which made it difficult for them to move quickly or defensively. During this early period in the war when soldiers were expected to march miles in a day fully loaded with supplies, exhaustion ruled the day. When the fighting did occur, tired soldiers who had sometimes left their supply lines behind fought in bitter battles for territory. Even the small, professional British regular army, which had had recent experience in its imperial wars, still was decimated in 1914 by fierce fighting over large distances in the defense of French territory. In each battle, casualties mounted, and military planners sought to adjust their plans to finish off their opponents and thus end the war. All of these armed confrontations between early August and early September became known as the "Battle of the Frontiers" and featured four national armies: German, French, Belgian, and British.

For these four armies, who had been battered by the first month of fighting and who were frustrated by the lack of clear victories, the decisive clash of 1914 became the series of battles known collectively as the "Battle of the Marne." In early September, the Germans moved troops and sought to outflank or maneuver around the allied forces in order to encircle Paris and force a quick surrender. The combined French, British, and Belgian forces, in turn, hoped to stop this German advance and perhaps outflank and surround German troops. The two sides fought viciously for a week, with reinforcements being moved into position as holes opened up in the fronts. Famously, Paris taxicabs brought some French soldiers to the front because of shortages of rail transport. When the dust settled in mid-September, the Germans' plan to take Paris and end the war in the west in six weeks was destroyed. More to the point, by mid-September, it was becoming clear that "neither army on the western front … was adequately prepared to fight a modern war."

After the Battle of the Marne ended in both sides falling back to safe areas and digging trenches to protect their positions, the fighting moved west as each side continued to try to break through the enemy lines, surround them, and end the war. The autumn battles continued in September and October in the Aisne, Marne, and Meuse river regions and near Ypres, Belgium, with the opposing forces racing to get ahead of each other. All attempts to outflank the enemy failed. Historians call these maneuvers the "Race to the Sea." By November 1914, the effect of the Western Front battles on the Frontiers, the Marne, the Aisne, and in Flanders (Ypres) was to create a long, thin front almost 600 miles long from the Swiss border with France to the English Channel.

Along this front, soldiers began to dig deep trenches for protection against artillery and the winter that was approaching. Germany occupied all of Belgium except for a small strip of Flanders along the Channel coast. In the northern zone of this coast, which was in a low-lying flood zone, Belgian troops had opened the dikes and flooded the land, making it impossible for the Germans to continue towards the coast. South of the flooded area, the British occupied a small area of Belgium and northern France. For the rest of the front, the French army stretched its forces along the length of the emerging trench network to Alsace and Lorraine. In that eastern frontier region and especially in the Vosges Mountains, Germany held the high ground and dug fortress-style trenches that were reinforced with concrete. Casualties were awful on all sides: combined fatalities in the four armies exceeded 600 000 men. Those who remained in December 1914 sat exhausted in trenches and contemplated a much longer war than most had anticipated.

This shift, from a war of movement to a fixed front, is one of the most enduring images of World War I in the popular imagination. It also marks the moment when the myth of a short heroic war was destroyed, which is perhaps why so many people are fascinated by the highly romanticized story of the Christmas Truce of 1914. The truce was a short interlude of fraternization on Christmas Eve and Christmas Day in isolated sectors of the Western Front and Eastern Front, although the truce between Russians and Austrians is virtually never mentioned. Letters and oral histories recount the exchange of gifts of chocolate and cigarettes, random games of football, Christmas trees in No Man's Land, and singing of hymns or carols, providing a much-needed break from the war. Because of these informal holiday ceasefires that in some areas ruled the day, popular accounts today depict these events as an act of defiance against war. Yet it is important to remember that this truce was an isolated series of events; in many areas of the front, the war continued as usual on Christmas Day, and people continued to die. For those who were involved, the truce was significant "even if its contemporaneous meaning was not the defiant moral that was imposed on it long afterward."

Perhaps what gives the Christmas truce its symbolic meaning and what captures attention is the idea of what might have happened if the soldiers in 1914 had just refused to fight. Or maybe the idea that sticks with readers today is the notion of a spontaneous truce marking a moment in the war where innocence was lost. While there were later informal truces throughout the war, especially in order to bury the dead, no other truce had the tragic pathos of this first Christmas in popular memory of the war today.

Eastern Front

While the Western Front in 1914 was a tale of quick movement and bloody clashes leading to a stalemate, the Eastern Front told a slightly different tale in 1914. The 1000-mile Eastern "Front" was actually three separate sectors during the war, which included: a) East Prussia, Poland, and the Baltic (Estonia, Latvia, Lithuania); b) the region known at the time as Galicia (today parts of Poland and Ukraine); and c) the southern front in the Balkans (Serbia and its neighbors). Initially it looked as if some of the battles in all three of these zones might be decisive. Serbian forces, under Radomir Putnik, invaded parts of Hungary while the Habsburg forces, under the overall command of Franz Conrad von Hötzendorf, moved into Serbia. Fighting was vicious on this front with much of the combat occurring in the mountains and around the capital city of Belgrade, which changed hands twice. None of these battles were decisive for either side, and when the winter weather descended in December 1914, the Serbs and the Austrians had entrenched, having gained virtually no territory. Worse for the Austrians, their war with Russia had decimated their ranks, and Conrad had to pull men and resources away from this sector of the war.

Russia was a fearful opponent not just for the Habsburgs but also for the Germans, given its sheer size. The Russian army lumbered into action by mid-August, and its first forays against the Austro-Hungarian army in Galicia brought success. Warfare in this zone in 1914 looked like wars of the past: "complete with cavalry skirmishing in the gaps between the armies and dramatic maneuvering as both sides sought the flanks of their opponents while desperately fending off threats to their own." During these early battles of movement, the Russians took control of major rail hubs and cities, occupied almost all of the area by December 1914, and besieged the large fortress city of Przemyśl. On the Habsburg–Russian front, it was apparent that the Habsburg army would need support from their German allies against the Russians.

Meanwhile on the East Prussian front, the Russians also experienced early success with a defeat of the Germans at Gumbinnen on August 20, mostly through strength in numbers. German military commander, Helmuth von Moltke, replaced generals on the Eastern Front days later with the competent team of Paul von Hindenburg and Erich Ludendorff. This proved a crucial step for the Germans when their armies next met Russian forces. The Germans crushed the Russians at back-to-back confrontations in the Battle of Tannenberg and the Battle of Masurian Lakes, which were fought in late August and early September 1914. At Tannenberg, perhaps the best known and most important battle of 1914 on the Eastern Front, German forces attacked the Russian Second Army, which suffered from poor communication, difficult terrain, and uneven leadership. The battle was a disaster for the Russian Empire. Germany took more than 90 000 Russian prisoners and celebrated the victory at home, where the place had historical resonance as the site of an important medieval battle for the Teutonic Knights. The victory in 1914 was proclaimed in Germany as a vindication of the Knights' defeat 500 years earlier, and it became one of the most important battles in the history of the war. It established "Hindenburg and Ludendorff as popular heroes." For the Russians, on the other hand, the loss was a national blow because of the high casualty rate. Alexander Samsonov, the Russian general at the battle, committed suicide as a result of the devastating loss. (See Map 2c.)

In the third sector of the front, in Poland, the Germans had less success. Rain and poor conditions as well as a spirited Russian defense stopped the German advance toward Warsaw. The Germans gained some territory (most notably the town of Łódź) but had to retreat and dig trenches to prepare for winter. The Austro-Hungarian forces who also participated in this push into Poland also failed to meet their objectives and suffered serious damage. Therefore, like the Western Front in 1914, by December the massive Eastern Front (double the length of the Western Front and with more problematic terrain) had also turned into a stalemate as each army faced winter in trenches. Combined losses on the Eastern Front in 1914 neared 2.5 million casualties (dead, wounded, and missing). While waiting for the spring thaw, most military planners set to work on a new set of priorities and plans.

African Fronts

Germany had thrown most of its military resources into the fronts of Europe, but it also faced the problem of protecting its overseas colonies. Throughout the world, Entente troops invaded German colonies immediately upon the declaration of war. One of the most contested zones for colonial conflict was East Africa (today's Tanzania and Kenya). In 1914, residents of East Africa knew war had come when the British navy blockaded German colonial ports at Dar es Salaam and Tanga. Both German and British colonial governments had small armies already in place in East Africa composed of European officers and African soldiers, so these formed the nucleus of units that would expand to fight for the whole period of World War I. In East Africa, the war immediately became one that relied on transport and supply. Perhaps most importantly, both armies needed human porters to carry all weapons and goods because animals were useless in a region where tsetse fly was deadly to them. Beginning in autumn 1914, the European-led forces of African colonial subjects fought a mobile war where the only military objectives were limited—armies fought to destroy each other's railways, communications systems, and ports. Despite being outnumbered, the German force, under the command of Paul von Lettow-Vorbeck, won an important early battle against British and Indian forces near Tanga. For the rest of the war, small isolated groups fought over vast territories in East Africa with a terrible loss of life, especially among the human porters.

In other African colonies, such as Togo, Cameroon, and Southwest Africa, combined British, Belgian, and French forces attacked German colonial possessions. Again outnumbered, German colonial armies lost a series of skirmishes and eventually surrendered. For Africans, the war brought occupation by the enemy as well as hardship. Wartime requisitions of goods, animals, and people took a serious toll on local populations. One of the advantages that the Allies possessed in the fight over African territory included the proximity of their own colonial populations. Particularly useful for Britain was the participation of South Africa, which was part of the British Empire. Its participation was at first threatened by an internal rebellion from its Boer residents in 1914, who still remembered their war just a decade earlier with Britain and who had little interest in fighting for the British Empire. It was not until the rebels had been defeated in December 1914 that South Africa was able to contemplate sending large numbers of officers, soldiers, and laborers to other fronts for imperial combat.

Pacific and Australasia

While the Pacific theatre of war was quite small, it had meaning for twentieth-century history as a precursor for World War II. Japan entered the war on August 23, creating an ally for France and Britain in the Pacific that could police German colonial holdings there. Almost immediately the Japanese and British navies blockaded the main German port of Qingdao in China in order to force the small garrison there to surrender. The city held out for two months under siege before capitulating in November 1914; German men of military age were sent to Japanese internment camps and Japan occupied the city. Other Pacific colonies such as Samoa, New Guinea, and Micronesia provided goods and human labor for the war effort, especially as the war dragged on into its third and fourth years. Although a relatively quiet sector in World War I, the Pacific established a broader Asian and Pacific presence for Japan and fueled its prewar imperialist aspirations.

32

Ottoman Fronts

One of the most important developments in the war in 1914 was the entry into the conflict of the Ottoman Empire in November. This was particularly important for the Russian Empire as it opened up another front for it to defend, this time in the Caucasus Mountains. Russian and Ottoman forces met in battle in the region days after war was declared near Erzurum, but it was the Ottoman attack of December 1914 near Sarikamiş that was most memorable. Turkish leader, Enver Pasha, seriously miscalculated the winter conditions and the equipment his soldiers needed: "Without tents, fuel or firewood, thousands of men died of exposure. Fully one-third of the corps died in the snows of the mountains." The continued fighting decimated Ottoman troops, and left only about a quarter of the original invasion force still standing by January 1915. Out of an original group of 100 000 soldiers, only 18 000 survived. This disaster early in the war shaped Ottoman policy in 1915 and probably helped justify deportations of so-called internal enemies a few months later.

Ottoman forces also fought in the eastern Mediterranean. Britain landed a force of British and Indian troops in Mesopotamia (modern Iraq) upon the outbreak of war and took control of Basra by the end of 1914. However, the entry of the Ottomans increased the stakes and expanded the front in the whole region today known as the Middle East. Oil was an important resource in the area, so most of the combatants had an interest there. Additionally, the Ottoman Empire was technically still the center of the Islamic World as the site of the caliphate. This was potentially disastrous for Britain and France because of fears that Muslims within their empires might embrace their religious identities instead of their national or imperial obligations. These fears proved unfounded when Ottoman religious leaders issued a *fatwa* (Islamic religious ruling) calling for all of Islam to unite. Muslims living in the British and French Empires demonstrated a stronger tie to empire and nation than to religious solidarity, and the notion of a united Muslim front remained merely a fantasy. As the war progressed, France and Britain diverted more and more troops to Mesopotamia, Palestine, and Egypt, creating the need to bring imperial soldiers to these areas. Millions of men from India, Australia, New Zealand, and African colonies saw service on this front, especially with the invasion of the Gallipoli peninsula in 1915.

A quick overview of the war situation on December 31, 1914, shows a bleak picture for military planners, soldiers, and civil populations. On virtually every front, fighting had stalled, and in each case, soldiers had fallen back to defensive positions and dug trenches to wait for spring. Nations raced to increase production of munitions and other supplies as it became apparent that this would neither be a short nor an easy war. Commentators also began to notice that this war had new characteristics that set it apart from anything that had been seen in the past. While the phrase "total war" had not yet been coined, people began to discuss what kind of conflict this 1914 war might become.

Defining Total War and Its Debates

In the long history of conflict, many military planners, theorists, and politicians have sought the perfect formula for a successful war. Questions of strategy, logistics, justice, morality, and politics have served as the subjects in the study of war. Jurists, politicians, philosophers, and generals throughout written history have struggled to understand why war occurred, what a moral or "just" war might look like, and how success in war might be insured. However, with the advent of the modern age and the development of nation-states in the wake of the French Revolution, understandings of war in nineteenth-century Europe crystallized around the ideas of Prussian soldier and theorist Carl von Clausewitz (1780–1831). His posthumous writings, which were published by his wife in the 1830s, became foundational reading for students of military strategy and for political leaders. His most famous work, *On War*, lays out a vision of conflict based primarily on his observations of the Napoleonic wars. Clausewitz's ideas rested on the concept that a modern state required a regular standing army, and he theorized that a decisive battle between two regular armies could determine the victor of the war itself. In this formulation, generals had to possess a level of strategic genius because they needed to set up the conditions that enabled such a big, decisive battle. Soldiers had to be well-trained, well-armed, and well-cared-for so that they could perform when the time came.

Despite the fact that Clausewitz lived and died nearly a century before World War I, he recognized and identified many elements that became important in the fighting of this twentieth-century conflict. First, he wrote at length about the fact that a victory meant nothing unless an enemy could break the will of the people. For Clausewitz, the rise of nationalism had redefined the role of the citizen and engaged more people in war. Clausewitz knew that irregular forces could continue to fight, that internal divisions could disrupt a military campaign, and that people were unpredictable. Second, he made it clear that war could never exist in isolation from other forces, particularly political forces. Clausewitz explicitly understood war as a political act with political consequences. Sometimes this idea is translated into a pithy quote—"war is politics by other means." Thirdly, for Clausewitz, leadership mattered. Leaders with courage and vision—he uses the term genius more than once—had power to win or lose battles. This is perhaps why his work became standard reading in military academies around the world in the nineteenth century. Clausewitz thought that military leaders, working in conjunction with political leaders, could mold the course of a conflict.

While Clausewitz's theories of war were important, nuanced, and significant, he wrote in a period before significant industrialization. Clausewitz never saw a machine gun, an airplane, a submarine, a gas shell, or a tank. Perhaps even more significantly, he had never seen an army transported by rail or fed from a depot filled with tinned goods. His wars were smaller wars with different weaponry, fewer soldiers in a battle, and much more limited firepower. Therefore, while generations of military leaders in Europe were trained in Clausewitz's theories about the power of a decisive, well-planned battle, the nature of wars changed in the nineteenth century.

Two harbingers of the transformations accompanying modern, industrial war were the Crimean War (1854–1855) and the American Civil War (1861–1865). Both wars demonstrated the destructive capacity of artillery and rapid-fire. The Crimean War pitted professional armies from Britain, France, and the Ottoman Empire against Russian forces and demonstrated the need for military reform. The war led to army reorganization and medical reform in both Britain and France. The Crimean War also foreshadowed the wars to come in terms of the destructive capabilities of newly emerging technologies of war. The American Civil War resembled World War I even more closely. This conflict featured citizen armies on both sides, deliberate military targeting of civilians for strategic goals, trench warfare, and unprecedented injuries from shrapnel and other projectiles. As such, this conflict's brutality and violence served as a warning of what might come when multiple nations possessed such powerful weaponry and mass citizen armies. One important lesson from the American Civil War was the significance of industrial capacity; the North produced more guns, clothing, and food, creating a major advantage over the more rural South over the course of four years of war. Another lesson was the importance of the Northern blockade of Southern ports, which crippled the Confederacy's economy. In short, for those paying attention, the Civil War signaled a new kind of warfare.

One observer who took a keen interest in the changing nature of war and who wrote presciently about the future of war was Jan (or Ivan) Bloch (1836–1901), a Polish banker. In his 1899 book, which was translated for American audiences as *The Future of War*, he described the devastation that he expected to accompany a modern war. As someone who spent much of his career developing railway networks, he understood the role technological and industrial change might play in the fighting of a war. For Bloch, the big change from the Napoleonic period to the late nineteenth century was the possibility of war on a massive scale. Bloch theorized that armies that could be fed for months or years on end from railways with industrially-produced clothing and food could also find themselves in an impossible stalemate. Massive battles with dreadful casualties, famine in the cities, and environmental destruction were all features of Bloch's analysis. In a famous line, Bloch predicted the trenches of World War I, telling journalist W. T. Stead that "The spade will be as indispensable to the soldier as his rifle." For Bloch, making clear the terrible scope and destruction of war might help avert such a catastrophe, and he became a tireless campaigner for peace.

Others like Bloch sought to create institutions of peace in the nineteenth and early twentieth centuries that would either end war or at least mitigate its damage. Swiss businessman Henri Dunant (1828–1910) convened the first Geneva convention (1864) and created the International Committee of the Red Cross. Both endeavors aimed to protect medical personnel and the wounded during times of war through treaties and a neutral, international organization. Some other proponents of pacifism and protection in war were quite unlikely candidates for this sort of interest. Alfred Nobel (1833–1896), the Swedish inventor of dynamite, used his earnings from armaments manufacturing to create a Peace Prize in his will. American steel entrepreneur Andrew Carnegie (1835–1919) funded an Endowment for International Peace (1910) a decade later.

It was not only tycoons and manufacturers who took an interest in questions of peace. Socialists and communists met in a series of congresses in the years before the war and articulated their opposition to war between nations. Quakers and other pacifists held meetings aimed at the promotion of peace. This burgeoning peace movement tapped into growing internationalist sentiments in the late nineteenth and early twentieth centuries and led to a series of conventions and initiatives that addressed the nature of war. Delegates from multiple countries met in The Hague (Netherlands) in 1899 and 1907 and in Geneva (Switzerland) in 1906. The agreements provided loose "laws" for warfare that included treatment of enemy populations, prisoners of war, and allowable methods of war. More than 40 nations signed The Hague convention in 1907, signaling a growing interest in multinational agreements. Yet there was no solid mechanism for making sure states followed these rules and guidelines. It is also important to note that many of the real issues raised by World War I in 1914 were new, which meant they were not covered by these earlier conventions. Even Bloch, who had a vision of future war and who was invited to The Hague meeting in 1899, did not predict the ethical issues raised by World War I.

Clausewitz and Bloch may have set the stage for the expectations that political and military leaders brought to war in 1914, but it was the war itself that shaped a new conception of war theory. The first to coin the concept of "total war" in print was German World War I General Erich von Ludendorff in his work, *The Total War* (1935). Ludendorff, of Tannenberg fame, described World War I in hindsight, but it is important to remember that the concept of total war he explained was designed for future use. Looking back, after almost two decades, on Germany's defeat in World War I, Ludendorff argued that Clausewitz's ideas about war were outdated and obsolete. Instead, World War I had started a process that would culminate in a successful war of the future, namely one in which a nation's military would wage war on the total society of its opponent. Total war relied on annihilation and extermination of the enemy population for total victory to be achieved. Every citizen of the enemy nation was a target in this conception of war, and every resource that could be mobilized for the war effort should be activated. Therefore, in Ludendorff's description, total war meant turning all the nation's peoples, industries, political mechanisms, armed forces, and land into a huge military camp. Only when that process had been completed would the mass national effort be launched against every man, woman, and child in the enemy nation.

Ludendorff's term "total war" became the focus of scholarly debate in the period after World War II, a conflict that seemed to fit Ludendorff's discussion. Historians in this debate defined total war in a variety of ways as they worked with the concept. First, total war could mean state control of society for the purpose of waging war, and often total mobilization of humans and resources becomes a stated goal. Second, total war could describe a state's war aims, which might range from unconditional surrender to total destruction of an enemy. Finally, total war sometimes is used to outline a state's principles of war, typically violations of shared conventions of what is considered a "just" or "moral" war. Taken together, these features of total war suggest a conflict that breaks the boundaries of past behavior and that encompasses the majority of people in a state. In other words, total war refers to a "radicalization of warfare" and a "complete mobilization" of resources.

Was World War I such a war? Did the nation-states of 1914 to 1918 effectively mobilize all their people and resources then pursue policies and strategies that ruthlessly targeted enemy populations? The answer is a qualified one. States employed strategies of total war throughout the period from 1914 to 1918 and indeed in the conflicts that followed, but a truly total war remained an impossibility for most of the nations. To truly mobilize all people and resources required a measure of organization and funding that was difficult to attain. The rest of the chapter will look at the ways in which war assumed the trappings of a total mobilization of people and resources, a "total war" mentality, while also outlining the obstacles and limitations of this concept.

Total War: Mobilization of Men and Resources

As the warring states saw their military preparations turn into actual declarations of war by early August 1914, officials began to consider what a mobilization might look like in the context of a general war between European industrial nations and their empires. States closed their borders, diplomats scrambled to leave enemy territory, and local leaders sought to calm worried citizens. Many countries restricted movement of citizens and visitors, initiating passes or setting up no-go zones near military installations and munitions centers. Banks limited hours, restricted withdrawals, and tried to control possible bank panics. Very early in the war some states closed theatres, banned alcohol sales, and managed other aspects of everyday life. In other words, there was no ignoring war in 1914 for most of the states affected.

Military leaders immediately knew that they needed to focus upon logistical matters, which included transport of troops, animals, munitions, and supplies. Rail networks buzzed with activity, and frontier towns saw their populations balloon with the influx of soldiers being mobilized. States moved to secure ports as well, and naval personnel scrambled to remove themselves from enemy waters. In the combat zones, it was possible to use rivers or canals for transport, but unlike wars of the past, water transport had mostly given way to motorized vehicles, rail, and draft animals. By 1914, road surfaces had improved considerably from the nineteenth century, but they remained vulnerable to destruction or obstruction during poor weather. Also, they were initially difficult to navigate during invasions because of large numbers of refugees using the roads to flee. In order to cope with the vast numbers of humans and supplies, a logistical revolution took place in the years preceding 1914. Military planners created bases of operations from which they could supply and feed their armies, which were a feature of modern war that set World War I apart from earlier conflicts. Virtually every battle in the early part of the war stalled at some point because of logistical issues with movement of munitions, men, or other supplies.

Control of rail lines, waterways, and roads was crucial at the start of the war. For instance, one of the problems that the Germans faced in their invasion of Belgium in August 1914 was that the Belgian army destroyed rail lines as they retreated. The German army needed to move men and supplies by train, so it scrambled to repair quickly the destroyed rails. Ultimately, this slowed the German advance considerably, especially given the fact that only about 15% of the length of track had been repaired by the beginning of the Battle of the Marne. Dependence on trains also made rail lines vulnerable to espionage and resistance networks, who employed train watchers to count troops and arms and who sabotaged trains, when possible. On the Eastern Front, limited rail networks made a big difference in the ability to move troops. For example, "Russia could direct 260 trains a day against Austria-Hungary, whereas the Austrians could only manage 153 in reply…"

Economies mobilized immediately in 1914. Economic planners also moved into high gear in order to secure the funds to pay for the war through loans and reserves. The first few days of the war led to a survey of industrial capacity in each nation at war, and eventually many manufacturers turned their factories toward war production. Automobile firms such as Renault and Citroën in France took on war work, sometimes even building new factories, while other manufacturers such as I. G. Farben chemicals (Germany) and Bata shoes (in the Czech Republic today) saw an expansion in their business because of wartime demands. Wartime officials also secured natural resources such as oil, coal, wood, metals, wool, and cotton as best they could, although the initial stage of the war led to the loss of some vital commodities for the combatants. For example, the coalfields of northern France near Lille fell under German control in 1914 and remained firmly in German hands until near the end of the war.

These fledgling moves to steer economies toward war production only accelerated as the war progressed and eventually vast bureaucracies formed to manage trade, production, rationing, transport, and communications in most of the combatant states. By 1915, Britain and Germany were engaged in fierce economic warfare. The British blockaded the continent and the German state committed itself to unrestricted submarine warfare against Allied shipping. These two countries also battled for control of foreign exports, such as beef and coffee in South America. Britain pursued this economic war by creating a blacklist of German companies in neutral areas, putting pressure on other states to curtail German trade. Nations used their own purchasing power as bargaining chips in any dispute over import/export and access to ports. Once the United States entered the war, it also used the wartime economic sanctions to its advantage, displacing both British and German firms from many established markets in the western Hemisphere while they were tied up in wartime matters.

Finally, even domestic economies felt the war's impact. States controlled agriculture and food production in a variety of ways from the first days of the conflict. Farmers very quickly found out that their crops were subject to government census and seizure in times of shortage, and, with rationing, everything from the size of a loaf of bread to the amount of sugar a household might possess fell under official scrutiny. Governments regulated animals as well, requisitioning animals that could be of use to the war effort. Horses and mules played a particularly important role, but dogs, camels, and pigeons also "served." At home, civilian animals could be seized for war use as well. Germany even slaughtered millions of pigs in 1915 in order to reduce the numbers of animals that needed fodder. If any single feature of World War I signaled a striving toward total war, the ruthless economics of the wartime states may be that feature.

Total War: War Aims

Another way of understanding the concept of total war is to consider the combatants' reasons for fighting. One of the stereotypes associated with World War I is that it was futile and that the states involved had no war aims. In fact, all the major combatants had specific aims in 1914, but as the war developed, each combatant's aims changed considerably, especially as the fighting intensified. This chapter will explain the initial aims, ambitions, and plans during the formative period of 1914 (and for some states, 1915), then later chapters will focus on the ways in which these aims and plans shifted.

Each state at war began with military plans and specific goals for their armies and navies. Many of these plans were conceived in the late nineteenth and early twentieth century in the event of a wider European conflict, so they reflected planners with nineteenth-century outlooks. The most famous of these plans is the Schlieffen Plan, which articulated an ideology developed in the 1890s and then recorded in a document drawn up in 1905 by Alfred von Schlieffen, Chief of the German General Staff at the time. Schlieffen's idea was to avert a two-front war by focusing on a quick knock-out blow to France by encircling Paris, while then turning attention to the Russian front. The plan, developed nearly a decade before the actual war, underwent change as subsequent members of the General Staff tested it in war games and tweaked it in their discussions. Helmuth von Moltke, faced with a real war in 1914, used the Schlieffen Plan as a tactical outline, knowing that he risked a broader war with the violation of Belgian neutrality and also understanding that both France and Russia had improved their manpower and mobilization since the German plan was initially drafted. In 1914, then, Germany's main military aim was to avoid a protracted two-front conflict by targeting the Western Front for a quick offensive. However, one big flaw in the plan was the speed with which the soldiers would move, creating a situation where they left their supply lines behind them. Another miscalculation was in not considering a Belgian armed response to the invasion. Despite these problems, the plan was a bold outline for dealing with an intractable problem by employing a decisive offensive.

France, on the other hand, had begun developing more defensive war plans after their disastrous defeat in the Franco–Prussian War of 1870–1871. Their major strategy was to build a series of forts to defend French borders and to bolster railway construction in order to more quickly move troops. Over the course of the next 40 years, a series of plans were developed in the French military, but the one in force in 1914 was Plan XVII, developed by Joseph Joffre, Chief of the French General Staff. This plan focused French mobilization of forces on the eastern border with Germany, along the boundaries of the former French provinces of Alsace and Lorraine. With Italy's declaration of neutrality, the French did not need to guard the Alps, which helped the army in concentrating their forces. The good thing about the plan was that it provided a quick and efficient mobilization, which was crucial for France in 1914.

In the cases of both Germany and France, military planners assumed that decisive battles and good strategy would create a situation where the political aims of each state could take over on the Western Front. The Russian Empire also had a war strategy on paper in 1914, called Plan 19, which was initially developed in 1910. Like Germany, Russia needed to plan for multiple enemies, and Russian military planners needed to coordinate manpower both on the border with Germany and on the border with Austria-Hungary. Because of worries about whether the French could withstand a German attack, the

Russian leaders adjusted their plan to include a quick attack on East Prussia even if all the manpower was not yet in place. They also hedged their bets a bit by spreading out forces on the frontier with Austria-Hungary and in the space between these two areas of operation, possibly diluting Russian strength in any one area. Like the German and French plans, the Russian strategy included long-held ideas about grand strategy and calculated guesses that reflected real anxieties about mobilization times and effectiveness of allies.

Other belligerents also developed plans in the years before the war. Austria-Hungary relied on an offensive strategy, but like Russia, Habsburg planners contended with multiple fronts and a mathematics of probability. For instance, officers debated just how many soldiers should go to Galicia versus to the Serbian front. In 1914, Austria-Hungary split its forces and hoped for the best. Ultimately, Austria-Hungary's fate and its planning were tied closely to the fortunes of Germany. Similarly, Britain relied heavily on French war plans in order to deploy its forces and coordinate an attack. Of all the original combatants in the autumn of 1914, Britain had the least developed war plan, and it was the only one of the five states at war without a military conscription program (draft). Instead, the British invested heavily in its navy, which functioned alongside a tiny professional standing army, half of which was stationed around the world to protect the Empire. Because their priorities were different, Britain's leaders encouraged voluntary military training at schools as a way of maintaining some level of readiness without investing in a full-scale official military training program. Therefore, whereas the other states counted their soldiers in the millions in 1914, Britain sent a small force to the continent of only about 100 000 men in the first wave of August 1914. Their job was to prevent the encirclement of Paris by bolstering the French line in Flanders. Likewise, the small Belgian army worked to stop the Germans from gaining further territory in autumn 1914. They drew a line to stop the German advance by opening the dikes and levees in the Yser region in late October 1914, creating a flooded wasteland over which the Germans could not travel.

While the general staffs tinkered with their war plans, the politicians of each country had other goals and aims in mind. Nationalism had increased the pressure from minority groups to grant additional rights or recognitions, but it had also exposed problem areas where national claims did not necessarily align with imperial or state borders. Therefore, political leaders aimed through the war to resolve some of these niggling issues. Italy, although it did not join the conflict until May 1915, made it clear to possible allies that the reclamation of lands in the northeast and along the Adriatic were key goals. France also had territorial acquisition in mind, namely winning back the two provinces of Alsace and Lorraine from Germany. In fact, many of the political goals of the states at war focused around acquisition or reacquisition of territory or resources. Like Italy and France, territorial claims dominated their political war aims. These calls for "reclaiming" land that they considered stolen or lost is known by the term *irredentism*, which became a major feature of twentieth-century politics and propaganda in these two countries and others.

Germany and Britain had other concerns. Both saw themselves as world leaders and wanted to consolidate those positions at home and abroad. Britain had led nineteenth-century industrialization and built a massive global empire, but by 1914, its economic position and its empire faced the dual threats of internal agitation for change and external challenges from new world powers such as Germany and the United States. Germany, a new nation in 1871, saw its role as one of "catching up" to nations such as Britain, so in 1914, there was a sense that war would provide a demonstration of German progress and might. One historian has encapsulated this competitive spirit between Germany and Britain, noting: "For the Germans this was a war to change the world; for the British this was a war to preserve a world. The Germans were propelled by a vision, the British by a legacy." This quote implies that not only was there a political or economic component, but that these nations also had a cultural sense that war might determine their destinies. In 1914, Germany and Britain both proclaimed their aims in going to war as honorable ones—for Germany, it meant supporting an ally, Austria-Hungary, and for Britain, it meant honoring past obligations, namely insuring Belgium's neutrality.

While the British and Germans looked suspiciously at each other, the Habsburgs, the Romanovs, and the Ottomans had long tenures as the imperial overlords of their vast multiethnic, multi-religious, and multilingual empires, but each had suffered from serious challenges to imperial authority in the years before the war. For Russia, the loss to Japan in 1905 and the Revolution that followed that defeat had shaken the confidence of the ruling elite and foreshadowed challenges to come. Austria-Hungary's industrial backwardness had led to internal weakness politically, and its outdated dual power system slowed decision-making. The ongoing crises in the Balkans and the assassination of the heir to the throne all exposed its problems. Finally, the Ottoman Empire had already restructured after a 1911 revolt from a young group of western-influenced modernizers, the Young Turks. Additionally, the Balkan Wars and the minority movements within the empire increased a sense of threat for political leaders. Thus, each of these historic empires conceived of this war as a war to bolster imperial authority, to deal with border and minority disputes, and to expand their political and economic power.

On the surface, each state made the claim that its declaration of war was based on self-preservation and defense, while in reality, each state had long-held goals and fears that shaped decision-making in the summer of 1914. None of the states seemed to have planned for a long war; it was only gradually that their conceptions of warfare were radicalized. Certainly, none of the leaders in 1914 called for total destruction of the enemy, despite increasingly harsh propaganda campaigns that painted the enemy as almost sub-human. Instead, the states at war fell into the practices of total war and revised their aims to fit a changed situation over the course of five years of fighting. The war itself and the methods that evolved between 1914 and 1918 required totalizing mechanisms for production and management of the war, which in turn necessitated new methods for fighting the war.

Total War: Methods of War

One feature of war that was not new was the targeting of civilian lives and property during the violence of invasion. Imperial wars of expansion in the nineteenth century took a devastating toll on civilian lives and property, and European wars such as the Thirty Years' War (1618–1648) and the Napoleonic Wars (1803–1815) had led to looting and destruction of whole villages in the path of war. So, it was not necessarily a surprise when the brutal Russian invasion of Galicia in 1914, the Austrian treatment of Serbs, and the German attacks on Belgians all demonstrated the initial violence that accompanies the first weeks of battle. Outside of Europe, civilians also faced the realities of wartime invasion and occupation. Allied forces made immediate plans to occupy German colonies in German-controlled areas such as Micronesia, Samoa, and Papua New Guinea as well as areas of East and West Africa. In Samoa, occupying forces from New Zealand arrested German officials and interned them, established curfews for all inhabitants, and controlled all communications. Japan invaded Micronesia in the autumn of 1914 and remained there into the 1920s. Both Britain and Germany recruited massive numbers of soldiers and carriers for their campaign in East Africa where humans replaced pack animals as beasts of burden. The inhumane conditions of their service led to exceedingly high rates of disease and death.

Civilian populations in Europe also got a taste of what a total war might look like as early as August 1914 when zeppelins bombed the Belgian city of Antwerp and the French capital, Paris. The war brought further innovations from the air, including bombing from airplanes, air raid shelters, blackout orders, warning sirens, and aerial battles. Civilians understood from the heavy casualties of fall 1914 that this war had the ability to devastate their neighborhoods and families. On the Western Front, the British casualty rate was more than 60% between August and December. Germany and France lost a combined 1.7 million soldiers to casualties in this same period. The Eastern Front was no better. The Habsburg (Austro-Hungarian) army had lost 300 000 men by the end of the first three weeks of the war, and Russia suffered more than half a million casualties by the end of the year. As this news traveled home, communities began to absorb the reality of what this war might mean.

Most people knew that war brought casualties and deaths, but World War I, as it continued for years, almost certainly transformed the meaning of war for populations around the world. It is this transformation that leads to a sense that 1914–1918 constituted an historical watershed—a break with the past. What changed? This war was different in four main ways, all of which contribute to debates about the nature of total war. First, World War I witnessed the mobilization of more men for military service than had ever been seen in world history up to this point. In other words, the *scope* of the war made it different. Second, this conflict reached every corner of the globe in some way, from actual battles in places such as Qingdao in China to economic warfare in Chile. World War I was a truly *global* affair with postwar repercussions that upset geopolitical balances around the world. Third, World War I employed methods of war that skirted the lines of what many people considered to be "fair" in battle—chemical warfare, submarine warfare, deliberate starvation, forced labor, hostage-taking. What military leaders deemed *modern methods* called into question all the high-minded aims that nations claimed had drawn them into conflict. Finally, the war eroded and eventually *destroyed many of the political certainties* of the past. By 1918, four empires had dissolved, revolutions had emerged in multiple cities, and the victorious nations faced the task of putting the pieces back together. It is important to note that this happened without a clear victory on the battlefield in 1917 or 1918. Instead the nations at war just agreed to stop fighting. These features emerged over time and were not immediately apparent when the armies began clashing in 1914. However, glimpses of the carnage to come and increasing scope of the war had emerged as early as December 1914.

Conclusion

By the end of 1914, most of the war's fronts had been established, and the populations involved now knew that this would be neither a short nor a heroic war in the ways that they had imagined. As conceptions of the war shifted, so too did justifications and methods. One example of these shifting attitudes may help make the transformation of 1914 clear. In October 1914, a group of well-known German academics published a manifesto defending German actions to the civilized world, often called the Manifesto of 93. In their public letter, these 93 intellectuals denied German responsibility for the war, saying that no one in Germany wanted war. Next these intellectuals expressed their support for German military might as an important and self-preserving feature of the German nation and culture, asserting that their Kaiser's aim was "universal peace." Almost immediately universities and academics around the world responded with their own open letters, in many cases outlining German crimes against culture such as the burning of the university library at Louvain in Belgium in August 1914. Thus, the manifesto initiated a global debate about the notion of "civilized" warfare, the question of war guilt, and the reasons for the war itself that continued through the war and into the postwar period. This manifesto is important because it demonstrated the need as early as October 1914 for a defense of the war aims that had been laid out just two months earlier. This letter also shows the firestorm of recrimination and blame that would ultimately fall on those who lost this war.

As this chapter demonstrates, World War I certainly contained features of "total" war, but as a later generation who survived World War II understood, most historians agree that only hints of a truly totalizing war experience accompanied World War I. Some see the war as a precursor or a harbinger of forces still to come, and certainly the seeds of the regimes of Stalin and Hitler were planted during World War I. One thing that is very clear is that economics mattered in 1914–1918, just as Bloch had predicted. The breakdown of mechanisms for feeding soldiers and civilians played a major role in civil unrest. In turn, the collapse of German and Austro-Hungarian economies, rather than a military victory in the field, led to the armistice of 1918. Another important factor to remember is that states mobilized vast sections of their economies and societies for war, and they intended to fight as total a war as possible. For people living through the war, it felt like a momentous time in world history, and many commented on the multiple ways that it transformed their lives and their outlooks. Much of the rest of this book will explore in detail these transformative changes while also examining the things that stayed the same.

Citations

Page	Source

Page *Source*

27 "went to war believing…" quoted in Michael S. Neiberg, *Dance of the Furies: Europe and the Outbreak of World War I* (London: Harvard University Press, 2011), 119.

27 "Play up!…" Henry Newbolt, *Vitaï Lampada* (1897) available from http:// exhibits.lib.byu.edu/wwi/influences/vitai.html

27 "At the close of the iron game…" quoted in Margaret R. Higonnet, ed., *Lines of Fire: Women Writers of World War I* (New York: Penguin, 1999), 454.

27 "All around me…" quoted in Svetlana Palmer and Sarah Wallis, eds., *Intimate Voices from the First World War* (New York: William Morrow, 2003), 34.

27 "200 000 …" quoted in Peter Hart, *The Great War: A Combat History of the First World War* (Oxford: Oxford University Press, 2013), 50.

28 "The sense of tragic futility…" Edward Spears, *Liaison 1914: A Narrative of the Great Retreat* (Garden City, NY: Doubleday, 1931), 37.

28 "Neither army on the western front…" quoted in Eric Dorn Brose, *A History of the Great War: World War One and the International Crisis of the Early Twentieth Century* (Oxford: Oxford University Press, 2010), 66.

29   600 000 figure drawn from John Keegan, *The First World War* (New York: Vintage, 2000), 135–136.

29   "even if its contemporaneous …" quoted in Terri Blom Crocker, *The Christmas Truce: Myth, Memory and the First World War* (Lexington: University Press of Kentucky, 2015), 18.

30   "complete with cavalry …" quoted in Hart, 87.

31   "Hindenburg and Ludendorff as popular heroes" quoted in Ian F. W. Beckett, *The Great War*, 2nd Edition (Harlow, UK: Pearson Longman, 2007), 76.

31   2.5 million casualties figure drawn from Brose, 75, 79.

33   "Without tents, fuel or firewood …" quoted in Rob Johnson, *The Great War & the Middle East: A Strategic Study* (Oxford: Oxford University Press, 2016), 160.

33   18 000 figure drawn from Johnson, 163.

34   Carl von Clausewitz, *On War*, Translated by J. J. Graham (London: Routledge, 1966).

35–6   "The spade will be …" quoted in Stead introduction to I. S. Bloch, *The Future of War*, Translated by R. C. Long (New York: Doubleday & McClure, 1899), xxvii.

36   "total war" concept drawn from Erich von Ludendorff, *Der Totale Krieg* (München: Ludendorffs Verlag, 1935).

37   "radicalization of warfare" quoted in Daniel Marc Segesser, "Controversy: Total War," in *1914–1918-online. International Encyclopedia of the First World War*, doi: https://doi.org/10.15463/ie1418.10315

38   "15%" figure drawn from Martin Van Crefeld, *Supplying War: Logistics from Wallenstein to Patton*, 2nd Edition (Cambridge: Cambridge University Press, 2004), 129.

38   "Russia could direct …" quoted in Hew Strachan, *The First World War. Volume I: To Arms* (Oxford: Oxford University Press, 2001), 292.

41   100 000 men figure taken from Michael S. Neiberg, *Fighting the Great War: A Global History* (Cambridge, MA: Harvard University Press, 2005), 17.

42   "For the Germans …" quoted in Modris Eksteins, *Rites of Spring: The Great War and the Birth of the Modern Age* (New York: Doubleday, 1989), 119.

43   "On the Western Front …" all figures drawn from Beckett, 75–77.

44   "universal peace" quoted in Martha Hanna, *The Mobilization of Intellect: French Scholars and Writers During the Great War* (Cambridge, MA: Harvard University Press, 1996), 80.

Select Bibliography

Beckett, Ian F. W. *The Great War*, 2nd Edition. Harlow, UK: Pearson Longman, 2007.

Bloch, I. S. *The Future of War*. Translated by R. C. Long. New York: Doubleday & McClure, 1899. Preface by W. T. Stead.

Brose, Eric Dorn. *A History of the Great War: World War One and the International Crisis of the Early Twentieth Century*. Oxford: Oxford University Press, 2010.

Chickering, Roger, and Stig Förster, eds. *Great War, Total War: Combat and Mobilization on the Western Front, 1914–1918*. Cambridge: Cambridge University Press, 2000.

Clausewitz, Carl von. *On War.* Translated by J. J. Graham. London: Routledge, 1966.

Crocker, Terri Blom. *The Christmas Truce: Myth, Memory and the First World War.* Lexington: University Press of Kentucky, 2015.

Eksteins, Modris. *Rites of Spring: The Great War and the Birth of the Modern Age.* New York: Doubleday, 1989.

Hanna, Martha. *The Mobilization of Intellect: French Scholars and Writers During the Great War.* Cambridge, MA: Harvard University Press, 1996.

Hart, Peter. *The Great War: A Combat History of the First World War.* Oxford: Oxford University Press, 2013.

Hastings, Max. *Catastrophe 1914: Europe Goes to War.* New York: Knopf, 2013.

Hiery, Hermann Joseph. *The Neglected War: The German South Pacific and the Influence of World War I.* Honolulu: University of Hawaii Press, 1995.

Higonnet, Margaret R., ed. *Lines of Fire: Women Writers of World War I.* New York: Penguin, 1999.

Horne, John, and Alan Kramer. *German Atrocities 1914: A History of Denial.* New Haven, CT: Yale University Press, 2001.

Johnson, Rob. *The Great War & the Middle East: A Strategic Study.* Oxford: Oxford University Press, 2016.

Keegan, John. *The First World War.* New York: Vintage, 2000.

Ludendorff, Erich von. *Der Totale Krieg.* München: Ludendorffs Verlag, 1935.

Morrow Jr., John H. *The Great War: An Imperial History.* London: Routledge, 2005.

Neiberg, Michael S. *Dance of the Furies: Europe and the Outbreak of World War I.* London: Harvard University Press, 2011.

Neiberg, Michael S. *Fighting the Great War: A Global History.* Cambridge, MA: Harvard University Press, 2005.

Newbolt, Henry. *Vitaï Lampada* (1897). http://exhibits.lib.byu.edu/wwi/influences/vitai.html

Palmer, Svetlana, and Sarah Wallis, eds. *Intimate Voices from the First World War.* New York: William Morrow, 2003.

Segesser, Daniel Marc. "Controversy: Total War." In *1914–1918-online. International Encyclopedia of the First World War,* ed. by Ute Daniel et al. (Berlin: Freie Universität Berlin). doi: 10.15463/ie1418.10315

Strachan, Hew. *The First World War. Volume I: To Arms.* Oxford: Oxford University Press, 2001.

Van Crefeld, Martin. *Supplying War: Logistics from Wallenstein to Patton.* 2nd Edition. Cambridge: Cambridge University Press, 2004.

Appendix 2.1: Timeline from July to December 1914

1914	*IMPORTANT EVENTS*	*BATTLE*
July 30	Austria-Hungary shells the Serb capital of Belgrade	
August 3	German invasion of Belgium	
August 7	British Expeditionary Force begins landings in France (to 16th)	
	France begins invasion of Alsace/ Lorraine/Ardennes (to 23rd)	Battle of the Frontiers
August 17	Russia begins invasion of East Prussia (to 20th)	Battle of Gumbinnen
August 24	German armies enter France (to Nov. 11th)	
August 26	British capture Togoland (West Africa)	
	Russian and German forces clash in East Prussia (to 30th)	Battle of Tannenberg
September 5	German and French armies (to 10th)	First Battle of the Marne
September 9	Russian and German armies clash	Battle of Masurian Lakes
September 14	Beginning of "Race to the Sea"	Battle of the Aisne
October 14	German, French, Belgian and British armies (through November)	First Battle of Ypres
October 27	Belgians open the Yser sluices, flooding a portion of the land	
November 5	British forces capture Basra (Mesopotamia)	
November 6	Surrender of Qingdao (China) to Japanese and British	
December 22	Ottoman offensive begins at Sarikamiş	Battle of Sarikamiş
December 24–25	Christmas Truces	

3

1915. How and Where Was the War Fought?

Figure 3.1   The Western Front evokes images of endless trenches and destroyed environments. One strategy employed to stop the German Army's advance in Belgium was the flooding of the battlefield by the Yser River. Here a sentry guards the flooded zone.
Source: Photo of scrapbook page by author: Brand Whitlock Papers, Library of Congress.

World War I: A Short History, First Edition. Tammy M. Proctor.
© 2018 John Wiley & Sons Ltd. Published 2018 by John Wiley & Sons Ltd.

One of the most enduring features of World War I was the way in which it transformed landscapes. In the Julian Alps between Italy and Slovenia, one can still see the trenches carved into the mountainsides, while the rippled fields of the Western Front in Flanders continue to disgorge shrapnel, weapons, and other detritus of war. Not only were such physical landscapes reshaped but political, familial, psychological, and societal terrain altered during and after this conflict. New borders meant changing notions of personal and national identities, while the barrage of injury and death transformed households and villages. Therefore, for students wanting to dig into the war's history it is important to understand the vast variety of these wartime landscapes. The next two chapters will explain these transformations by examining the spatial aspects as well as the human side of the geographical reshaping. By 1915 several zones of conflict had emerged as a result of the war, and in these zones the major transformations of the twentieth century emerged.

For anyone taking a survey of the battlefronts in early 1915, the war looked static (see Map 3.1). Most of the offensives had stalled, winter had set in, and serious trench networks had emerged on both the Eastern and Western Fronts. Military and civil leaders alike began to consider the problem of "stalemate," which was a term borrowed from the game of chess. In its original meaning, a player cannot move any pieces without going into check. This seemed a perfect description of the situation of the war by early 1915—no one could move without catastrophic losses, and normal strategies appeared illogical. Not only was stalemate a conundrum in terms of accomplishing any strategic goals, but it cost a lot of money to keep millions of soldiers in the field waiting for something to happen. Governments who were draining their treasuries began borrowing and taxing to finance the war. Action was needed, but the question of what action seemed an open one. Generals knew that outflanking maneuvers were impossible in most of the entrenched battlefronts of the war, so they faced either frontal assaults with great casualties or some other creative approach. Planners had several ideas for how to address the stalemate, and each in turn made an appearance in 1915. Every plan depended on the idea of a big breakthrough that would knock the enemy out of contention, and this concept remained a constant throughout the rest of the war. This led to experimentation in terms of military tactics and technologies.

1915 and the Problem of Stalemate

A popular notion about how to deal with stalemate was to develop technology that would enable the big breakthrough that would crush enemy forces. Armies experimented with handheld weapons such as flamethrowers and brass knuckles, but they also sought to create defensive equipment such as body armor that would provide an advantage. When battlefield advances did not provide a breakthrough capacity, planners turned to a broader field of vision in their search for new technologies. One such advance was the widening of the air war to include aerial bombing of civilian and military targets by zeppelins and planes in order to break morale and destroy resources. Another was an expansion of unrestricted submarine warfare by the Germans, especially in the Atlantic, which culminated in the sinking of the passenger liner, RMS *Lusitania*, in May 1915. Eventually, other advances addressed these changes, nullifying their effectiveness. For example, the creation of air raid shelters and warnings limited damage from bombers, and the development of camouflage paint and protective convoys for ships neutralized some submarine activity. For each technological breakthrough, it seemed that a counter-technology quickly emerged.

Perhaps the best known technological shift in the waging of war came on land with the German use of chemical warfare (gas) beginning in April 1915 at the Second Battle of Ypres. The use of gas, delivered first in canisters and then in artillery shells, changed the battlefield but never broke the stalemate. While the Germans had piloted the use of gas on the Eastern Front in January, the attack was only partly successful because much of the gas froze in the wintery environment. The April attack was part of the Second Battle of Ypres, and Germans deployed chlorine gas in a quiet sector populated with Belgian, French, and Algerian troops near the Belgian town of Boezinge. The German use of gas led to panic among the troops who first faced the cloud of chlorine, but the attack did not have the desired effect and the attacking forces did not capitalize on the confusion nor gain much territory. In fact, the Second Battle of Ypres was technically an Allied victory, but at a high cost in lives for both sides.

The April battle did set a precedent for use of chemical weapons, and once the door was opened to chemical agents, all the armies began using gas, thereby negating any advantage. Soon all sides possessed versions of the major poisons used in gas warfare, most importantly chlorine, phosgene, and mustard gases (the latter in 1917). Almost immediately, each state went to work fabricating protective gas gear, especially masks, for humans and animals at the fronts and behind the lines. The gas masks that evolved over the course of the war became increasingly sophisticated with rubberized seals and fine air filters to catch particle contaminants. While gas was used and in fact its usage increased by all combatants as the war progressed, it never did more than create anxiety, fear, and grievous injury in those exposed. The disruptions that gas caused could not deliver the big breakthrough in the overall war that the belligerents sought.

Another idea for breaking the stalemate in 1915 came with massive coordinated counter-offensives that utilized artillery barrages to prepare the attack. The Germans and Austrians launched such an offensive at Gorlice-Tarnow where they had a numerical advantage over Russian troops in May 1915. This maneuver was hugely successful and eventually moved the entire front with Russia to the east, and "in a week, the Russians had lost 210,000 men, including 140,000 prisoners of war." The Central Powers drove the Russian forces hundreds of miles back and occupied the Baltic States; German and Habsburg forces continued their push, retaking much of Galicia and taking control of Poland before bogging down in autumn rains. Despite this great victory and major territorial gains, no end to the conflict was in sight, and German and Habsburg armies faced another winter with all the problems of supply that entailed. The Russian forces absorbed the blow, regrouped, and created a new line of defense in Russian territory. Soldiers on all sides awaited spring.

The British also launched a March 1915 coordinated offensive on the Western Front that aimed to cut off Germans from their railway supply lines. The Battle of Neuve Chapelle began with a short, intense artillery barrage in which the "British fired more artillery shells in those thirty-five minutes than they had fired in the entirety of the Boer War." While the Germans initially retreated in the face of this surprise attack, they soon regrouped and the lines returned nearly to their original position prior to the battle. Part of the problem for the British is that their communication and command systems broke down with the quick movement in the initial hours of the battle. Yet Neuve Chapelle had provided hope that a properly run offensive might succeed in ending the war. The French and British tried a coordinated series of attacks in May 1915 at Vimy Ridge (French) and Aubers Ridge (British) but both were dismal failures with high casualty rates.

On the Western Front, while the Germans were busy with their Eastern Front offensives, the British and French tried one more series of offensives in autumn 1915, mostly in the areas of Champagne, Artois, Loos, and the Vosges Mountains. These battles led to massive casualties but no decisive change in the fortunes of either side. Despite the fact that none of these offensives led to lasting victory or "breakthrough," they provided a direction for military planners who imagined that offensives could work, if only the artillery barrage and the numbers of men were bigger. What planners had not yet figured out was how superior the defensive measures had become by 1915; deep trenches, new tactics, and better reconnaissance had created an even larger advantage for defenders during a massive offensive.

Still, leaders sought the elusive surprise that might end the war. Another way that nations thought they might break the stalemate and end the conflict was by changing leaders. Helmuth von Moltke, who had begun the war in charge of the German Imperial Army, was replaced before the end of 1914 by Erich von Falkenhayn, who was in turn replaced by Paul von Hindenburg after the failure of the Battle of Verdun in late 1916. On the Allied side, the British replaced Sir John French as Commander-in-Chief in December 1915 with the First Army Commander, Sir Douglas Haig, in order to effect some change in the state of affairs on the Western Front. Perhaps the most famous, or infamous, situation where a nation's military leadership changed during the war was in August 1915 when Tsar Nicholas II decided to assume the role of Commander-in-Chief of the Russian army himself, demoting his cousin Grand-Duke Nicholas. The Tsar had little military training or talent, but more importantly, his presence in the field left Moscow and its civil government without a leader. In each case, personal characteristics in these men helped change the flavor of the conflict, but none of these leadership changes really disrupted the problem of the war's stalemate.

The last of the ways in which governments sought to erase the stalemate was through the involvement of new battlefronts and new allies. Both sides hoped to involve Italy in the war, but in 1915, it was the Entente that made Italy the best offer for postwar compensation in the form of territorial acquisition. In May, the Italian government declared war against Austria-Hungary and mobilized its forces for a conflict primarily to be fought against the Habsburgs in the mountains of northern and northeastern Italy. By June of that same year, Italians under the leadership of Luigi Cadorna launched an offensive on the Isonzo front against Austrian troops. It was the first of more than a dozen such clashes between 1915 and 1917, and what quickly became apparent was that the Italian fronts were not going to provide a break in the stalemate of the war. Instead, a new area of stalemate developed in the mountain passes of the Julian Alps and the *Alto Aldige* (the Alpine border between Italy and Austria). More than 230 000 Italian soldiers were wounded or died in 1915 alone.

Another nation joined the conflict in the Balkans in autumn 1915, Bulgaria. Like Italy, Bulgaria sought assurances of postwar territorial gain from its participation, but unlike Italy, the Bulgarians chose to join the war on the side of the Central Powers. As with its Balkan neighbors, Bulgaria had been engaged in a series of wars beginning in 1912 that aimed to expand Bulgarian territory and power in the region. With the outbreak of war in 1914, Bulgaria hoped to gain more land from a defeat of Serbia. In fall 1915 after a multipronged attack on Serbia by Bulgaria and its allies, especially Germany, that pushed Serbian troops to the historic site of the medieval battle of Kosovo (the Field of Blackbirds), Serb commander Radomir Putnik ordered a massive retreat to the coast over mountainous terrain. Conditions for the soldiers, civilian refugees, and Habsburg prisoners of war were terrible: "few had shoes, many wore rags as 'uniforms'. Typhus and dysentery ravaged the men." British and French navies evacuated the remains of the Serbian army to the Greek island of Corfu and eventually to the city of Salonika, creating yet another area of stalemate where men sat and waited for the war to return to them.

Earlier in 1915, while Italy was still hovering on the fence about whether to join the conflict, Britain decided to mount an attack in spring that would open up another front for action. One of the main proponents of an amphibious landing on the Ottoman shores was Winston Churchill, First Lord of the Admiralty (British Royal Navy). Churchill thought that the Dardanelles provided an opportunity to protect British strategic interests in the area, draw attention and manpower from other fronts, and provide a breakthrough for Britain and its allies. As it was conceived, the attack at the Gallipoli peninsula was a combined naval and land maneuver that required coordinated landings of men from naval ships onto narrow beaches below steep headlands and ridges. The landing force that tried to scrabble onto beaches at six different landing sites under machine gun fire in April 1915 was a multinational one, composed of French and British forces, many of whom were imperial citizens. These troops were outnumbered by Ottoman forces, who held the high ground, and Entente forces were further hindered by lack of intelligence about the region where they were headed. Within a few weeks of the landing, stalemate reigned in this sector as well.

Gallipoli became a flashpoint in the history of the war for New Zealanders and Australians especially, but it has become an important part of postwar Turkish national identity. For the British imperial troops, known as ANZACs (Australian and New Zealand Army Corps), who landed and held for nine fruitless months a small bay known as ANZAC Cove, Gallipoli was remembered as the first major test of their soldiers. Later in the campaign they participated in a disastrous second landing at Suvla Bay in August. Above the scattered beaches and behind barbed wire and scrubby steep terrain, the enemy Ottoman forces commanded high ground that created an advantage. In Gallipoli, as in most of the other battle zones of 1915, a stalemate seemed inevitable as weapons and terrain made a "breakthrough" impossible. By the time the Allied forces fully withdrew, in January 1916, no land had changed hands, but the combined casualties hovered around half a million.

The notion that stalemate was an unsustainable state of affairs had lodged deeply in the war planning rooms of each of the belligerents by the close of 1915. The murderous casualties should have served as a lesson about the nature of modern war and the problem of offensives, but the idea of the "attack" was deeply ingrained in the military planning of the period. Everyone took stock of the lessons they thought they had learned in the first year and a half of war, and each sought a "breakthrough." One historian has called 1915 "a formative experience, one in which the lines of development which would be followed through into the battles of 1918 were put in place."

War "Fronts" or Zones of Conflict

Combat Zones

Perhaps the most well-known "Fronts" of World War I are its combat zones. These included the major fighting arenas in western, eastern, and southern Europe, but by 1915 these zones also encompassed the Mediterranean coastlines, North Africa, the Middle East, East and West Africa, and China. If one considers the war at sea, the world's large bodies of water also became combat zones.

Popular understandings of combat zones often focus on the soldiers in these zones, but it is important to remember that service personnel, civilians, officials, animals, and medical staff also populated these areas. Those living in combat zones witnessed periods of intense inaction, boredom even, punctuated by sustained fighting and movement of the fronts. These were inherently unstable landscapes with an ever-changing human and animal presence.

Combat conditions varied substantially across time and space. The early confusion and movement of the war in northern France, for instance, gave way by 1915 to massive trench networks, many of which were constructed with timber, stone, and other building materials stripped from nearby lands. The combined toll of such building and of increasing artillery bombardments left a desolate landscape captured brilliantly in photographs and paintings of the period. The living creatures inhabiting the Western Front fought daily battles with the terrain and climate, enduring endless mud and standing water. In the winter, freezing temperatures, snow and ice all made living underground a trial. Enduring both cold and stifling air, diggers worked in dark and silence to tunnel under the opposing trenches in France and Belgium in order to cache explosives. For soldiers living in those trenches, good boots, wool socks, and other comforts could mean the difference between trench foot or frostbite and a tolerable existence. Nothing could really erase the stench of trench life, however, with nearby dead bodies, large numbers of unwashed men, and numerous animals enlisted for war service (mules, horses, dogs). Of course, such numbers of animals and men also meant the presence of rats and mice, lice, and other insects.

Countless letters, diaries, and novels spoke of the troglodyte world of dirt and vermin that men endured. In his 1929 novel, *The Middle Parts of Fortune*, Australian veteran Frederic Manning describes in graphic terms life on the Western Front. Manning's description of a trip to a latrine points to the nastiness of life and the coping mechanisms of soldiers: "on this insecure perch they sat, and while they sat there, they hunted and killed the lice on their bodies ... they had been through it, and having been through it, they had lapsed a little lower than savages, into the mere brute." Their multitasking here echoes the darkly humorous accounts in frontline soldiers' newspapers, which often spent an inordinate amount of time on descriptions of hunting rats and lice, making a joke that only insiders to the trench experience really understood.

While those in western Europe sat in wet trenches, soldiers in the mountain ranges along the imperial frontiers of Europe faced the harrowing challenge of fighting a war at altitude. In the Alps (Italy/Austria), the Caucasus Mountains (Russia/Turkey), and the Vosges Mountains (France/Germany), soldiers and laborers hauled all their ammunition, weaponry, and supplies up steep paths and rock faces in order to maintain entrenched areas high above river valleys. Sanitation and supply were constant battles, and poised as they were on mountaintops, soldiers fought against driving snow, lightning strikes, and exposure to all the elements.

Photographs from the period show women hauling food on their backs, men hacking out ice caves for storage of supplies, and priests conducting religious ceremonies on rock outcrops hundreds of meters above the ground.

Many of the alpine troops relied on skis and dogsleds to move through the terrain. Others marched in full gear on narrow mountain paths. Italian soldier Virgilio Bonamore described his mid-summer 1915 climb to trenches in the mountains above the Isonzo River: "I can't recall a more tiring march; many men pass out ... there is something epic about our cautious approach in the dark, in total silence. Now and then, in the more difficult passes, someone falls off the edge. They fall without making a sound, as we have been ordered. All we hear is this pitiful sound of a body with a rifle hitting the ground." Once he reached his position, Bonamore put down his knapsack, which rolled off his ledge into a deep ravine. Such descriptions are common to the experiences of mountain-bound soldiers, and to make matters worse, access to the amenities of daily civilian life, which were relatively close in zones such as France and Belgium, were mostly off-limits for Italian and Austro-Hungarian soldiers living in the mountains.

In Mesopotamia, Gallipoli, and Palestine, a different battle with the landscape and the elements was waged. Scoured by sandstorms that hurt their eyes and their skin, soldiers tried to keep their guns, food, and other supplies free of sand. They fought sunstroke in temperatures that could top 120 degrees Fahrenheit and savored their tenuous water supply. On the Gallipoli peninsula (in modern Turkey), Entente troops relied on ships to bring in water and food. These vital supplies were then transported by mule train to the sandy dugouts that soldiers had built for protection. Soldiers in Mesopotamia (modern Iraq) also complained bitterly about the heat, the sand, and the difficulty of fighting in desert terrain. While alpine soldiers hauled munitions on dogsleds, the Mesopotamian troops relied heavily on camels for moving supplies. The armies faced basic problems such as finding clean drinking water and transporting men and goods in an inhospitable terrain. Morale suffered not only because of these logistical difficulties, but also because most of those overseas troops stationed in the Middle East never got home leave during their four years of war.

Perhaps one of the most difficult experiences of war was faced by soldiers on the Serbian front (later expanded to include Romania and Bulgaria), where poor sanitation arrangements and shortages of food, water, and supplies exacerbated epidemic levels of disease. In brutal fighting leading up to December 1914, both the Serb and the Habsburg armies suffered dreadfully high casualties in a battle over the city of Belgrade. Habsburg units, fearing civilian resistance, attacked and executed nearly 5000 civilians in the early weeks of the war. The Serb army survived this first series of battles, but later in 1915, Austria and its allies occupied Serbia. Even though the bulk of the Serb army, many medical units, and a number of civilians retreated to the promised safe haven in Greece by 1916, their numbers were still decimated by exposure, malnutrition, and diseases such as cholera and typhus. Once in Salonika, where Allied forces awaited them, the Serbs found conditions little better in an area that German writers dubbed the "war's largest internment camp" because of the inactivity of the zone.

Another combat zone that took a major toll on human life was the East African theatre in the war. Through four years of cat-and-mouse fighting in what is today modern Kenya, Tanzania, and Uganda, the German and British armies utilized millions of African men and women as soldiers and "carriers" of supplies for their war. Tsetse fly populations were so large in this zone that pack animals died and could not be used, and the terrain was by turns marshy, forested, and mountainous, making mechanized vehicles impractical. Therefore, human porters were enlisted to carry the army's munitions and supplies over hundreds of miles, and many of these carriers were forcibly impressed into service and then retained through force. While it is unclear how many died in service to these European nations, this was a deadly combat zone with casualties in the millions. East Africa was one of the few regions that featured almost continuous movement during the war, with German General Paul von Lettow-Vorbeck's army raiding and evading capture throughout the whole war. One of his strengths were the well-trained *askari* (African soldiers) that had served in colonial wars in the German Empire and who understood the terrain and the resources of the area, but these soldiers also absorbed the bulk of the casualties.

Finally, the Eastern Fronts featured different landscapes and challenges for warfare than any of the others. Inhospitable terrain and frigid temperatures in winter brought fighting almost to a standstill in parts of the Eastern Front in Russia, Poland, Galicia, and the Caucasus. Difficulties in maintaining reliable supply lines and the need to occupy many villages and towns in the combat zone added to soldiers' difficulties. Even the use of gas warfare was problematic because the low temperatures reduced the usefulness of this weapon. The sheer length of these battle fronts was difficult to fathom and to control—poor communication and breakdowns in transport meant coordination of attacks suffered. Added to this were linguistic problems in these multinational armies; the Habsburg army included more than a dozen different languages in its official numbers. Officers spoke German to each other, but they had to employ vernacular languages when working with ordinary conscripts.

In all of these situations, soldiers perceived the vast gap between their wartime homes and their civilian lives. They wrote home begging for food, clothing, games equipment (such as cricket bats or playing cards), and letters. Families responded with millions of letters and packages, but charitable organizations such as the Red Cross and Red Crescent also understood soldiers' need for comforts from home. Volunteers from around the world raised funds to send boxes of food, clothing, games, cigarettes, books, and other items to troops and prisoners of war. While the boxes did not always contain useful items, most associations made an attempt to tailor their offerings to the peculiarities of each combat zone. Soldiers in France received warm socks, while those in Mesopotamia often opened their boxes to find insect-repelling devices or clothing to help with mosquitoes. Some charities even tried to send separate boxes to religious groups with special foods or items used in worship such as pocket versions of the Bible or the Quran. Chinese laborers received gifts for the Chinese New Year, and American soldiers celebrated the Fourth of July in Europe with boxes from home. Such offerings cheered soldiers and helped them envision a world beyond their bivouacs.

For those spending their wars at sea, their combat zone was poorly defined. Many waterways served military functions during the war, so ships as diverse as river steamers and canal boats and battleships could become war zones. On board ships, mariners and naval personnel had little access to comforts from home, and often sailors spent months in foreign waters. Some even found themselves confined to ships or to inland concentration camps when their ships were captured in enemy ports or waters. Unlike soldiers on land, sailors and submariners fought a different battle with the elements, given the limited sanitary arrangements and often overcrowded conditions of some of the vessels. Those serving in submarines faced particularly hard conditions—lack of ventilation, intense heat and cold, and little protection from attack. Supply ships, battleships, and merchant vessels faced anxiety lest they fall prey to a torpedo from a hidden submarine, especially as accounts of such attacks multiplied in the media. No one was immune who traveled by sea, as the sinking of the HMS *Hampshire* in June 1916 demonstrated. More than 700 people died when the ship struck a German mine, including British Field Marshal Horatio Herbert Kitchener. The British used fast destroyers to accompany merchant and military ships to try to protect its shipping by 1916. Later a combination of air support and convoys cut down the effectiveness of German U-Boat attacks.

One other combat zone that became increasingly important as the war proceeded was the air itself. When the war began, pilots could not fire from their cockpits without fear of destroying their own propellers, but by 1915, Dutch airplane manufacturer Anthony Fokker created a machine gun synchronized to the propeller rotation and sold this mechanism first to the Germans. Other nations soon acquired the technology. This led to a new era of armed planes engaged in dog fights in the sky. With the development of better airplanes and firepower, pilots took to the skies for aerial bombing of military and civilian targets, but they also fought each other in the aerial equivalent of hand-to-hand combat. Death rates remained high for pilots throughout the war, and if they were not shot down by the enemy, they often crashed their rudimentary machines. Pilots did not face muddy trenches or mountainous slopes, but they did have to contend with extremes of heat and cold, foggy conditions, and of course, storms. Visibility defined their combat zone more than any fixed borders.

Therefore, when one talks of combatants in World War I, it is important to remember that combat took many forms. The landscapes and challenges that humans faced in combat varied widely according to their location, their status (rank), and the year of the war. A German soldier in 1914 in East Prussia would have experienced the war as one of movement initially and would have celebrated the German victory in the forests near Tannenberg, but that same soldier would have been freezing in a trench without proper winter equipment by early 1915. French troops assigned to a "quiet" sector in early 1915 faced the first successful German gas attack that spring when their section of the line became "active." Ottoman troops in December 1914 found themselves in sub-zero conditions and knee-deep snow in the Caucasus Mountains, but six months later some of these same soldiers held the heights over the Gallipoli beaches in searing heat. In 1914, British troops battled water shortages and sand in the Sinai desert, while the Japanese army and navy took control of China's Shandong peninsula with few difficulties and decent weather. This variety of situation and landscape makes it difficult to generalize about any one "experience" of World War I for combatants.

Occupation Zones

Near the combat zones, and sometimes synonymous with them, existed areas of formal occupation, where enemy or friendly armies held political power. Under military occupation, foreign officials suspended the normal rules of life in favor of martial law and wartime economic measures. For the most part, these occupation zones served as regions where the nations at war could increase their supplies and labor power, although some, such as the islands in the Pacific, existed far from any fighting. Regardless of location, the people living under occupation typically required policing and control because often occupied populations resisted their plight. Occupation could take several forms. Sometimes one nation occupied a region for nearly the whole war—as in the case of the German occupation of Belgium—and in such cases, bureaucratic structures and familiarity emerged. In other places, like Przemyśl in Galicia, opposing armies occupied and then evacuated the city, leading to multiple occupiers and widespread hardships. In active combat zones, villages and towns often moved between identities—behind the lines, in front of the lines, and as occupied zones. Sometimes whole towns disappeared from the map in World War I after suffering destruction during combat and occupation. For instance, nine monuments still stand today in commemoration of destroyed towns in the area surrounding the Verdun battlefield in France.

People living in occupied zones found their actions and movement scrutinized and controlled. Posters by occupying and civil governments demanded requisitions of animals, food, and other supplies, but they also warned of the dangers of espionage or resistance. Because armies needed draft animals, precious metals, and foodstuffs, people in occupied towns turned to black markets to obtain needed goods when their ability to feed themselves was threatened. In Belgium, civilians had to obtain passes from the German occupying authorities in order to travel anywhere in the country. In Poland and Galicia, vast quantities of resources were consumed by the occupying armies (Russian, German, and Austro-Hungarian), including timber, metals, and foodstuffs, altering the landscape and economic life. During the German and Bulgarian occupation of Romania, many of the foodstuffs and manufactured goods of the region were claimed for the war effort elsewhere. Children in occupied zones faced loss of their schools to military purposes. Schools that remained open often reformed to fit the needs of the occupier with classes in new languages and with new rules. People lashed out against occupying authorities by refusing compliance with rules, by smuggling, by sabotaging military installations, and by open resistance. Underground newspapers undermined occupying authorities and provided alternative sources for wartime information. Yet, despite signs of resistance, for those living under occupation it was difficult to avoid complicity. If a café owner served food to occupying soldiers, was this aiding the enemy? What if a household billeted soldiers—how could one keep from aiding unwanted houseguests? It was nearly impossible over a four-year war to completely avoid interaction with occupying forces.

Because of the blurred lines that existed in occupation zones during the war, collaborators and resistors became politicized postwar categories that complicated memory of the war in many nations for decades to come. Women suspected of fraternizing with occupiers experienced public shaming and ostracism in their hometowns, and some men and women even faced trial for war profiteering or collaboration. Others sought recognition of their resistance to enemy occupiers, often founding organizations or minting medals to recognize wartime service in occupied zones. Occupation certainly blurred the lines of war and created difficult situations for all involved.

Transitional Zones

Between the combat areas and the occupation zones, there existed territories that linked military personnel and civilians in other ways. These transitional zones could be staging areas for armies (*Etappen* in German), but they were also borders, ports, railheads, and waterways. The voracious needs of the armies at war meant maintaining almost constant movement of men and supplies into and out of the combat and occupation zones, so these transitional zones became vital links for continuing the fight. The foothills around Gorizia in northeastern Italy became a staging area for mountain fighting, while railheads in East Prussia amassed supplies for the German armies heading east. Such staging areas could also serve as rest and recreation centers for those at the fronts, giving them a different character than home fronts or even occupied cities. For instance, the Belgian town of Poperinge featured recreational clubs and huts, laundry facilities, and other pleasures for British troops, who called the town "Pops."

A good example of a transitional zone was Egypt, which served as a major British and imperial port for the embarkation of men, animals, and supplies for all the fighting in the eastern Mediterranean. Its first purpose was as a place to amass humans and materials for war in the eastern Mediterranean, but its cities also served as playgrounds for bored soldiers awaiting their orders. Countless ANZAC (Australian and New Zealand soldiers) reported in letters home about life in Cairo and Alexandria, sometimes omitting details of the wild side of their stays there. Alexandria, for instance, had a huge district given over to pleasures of the flesh, a neighborhood known for its multiple bars and brothels. Military officials worried about leaving soldiers in Alexandria too long because of high rates of venereal disease and drunkenness, but military logistics often required amassing armies in one place before moving them into a war zone.

In some ways the medical installations of the war also served as transitional zones. From the advanced aid stations where injuries were triaged to field ambulances to large medical centers behind the lines, facilities for the care of the wounded fit into the space between battlefront and home front. Even the personnel involved reflected the in-between nature of medical care. Medical trains, ambulances, and hospitals included personnel that were civilian volunteers, paid orderlies, military chaplains, army doctors and nurses, and Red Cross workers. The stretcher bearers who carried the injured and dead from the fields served in combat zones, but not as soldiers, giving their service a different meaning. The medical ships, rehabilitation homes, psychiatric wards, and hospitals on home terrain sat uneasily between military and civilian lines.

Other transitional zones became no-go areas because of the policies of armies at war. Brutal treatment of civilians who were considered disloyal created refugees in virtually every battlefield. In the so-called "pale of settlement" on the western border of the Russian Empire, military officials forcibly displaced hundreds of thousands of Russian citizens whose backgrounds were Jewish, Polish, Lithuanian, Roma, or German. These minority groups faced such scapegoating because of fears of espionage or disloyalty. Many found themselves without resources and stranded in the interior of the Russian Empire by summer 1915. Similarly, Habsburg armies deported nearly 80 000 Slovene civilians away from the Isonzo front in 1915 when fighting with Italy began. In what historians consider the first modern genocide, Ottoman authorities, beginning in spring 1915, used the assumed disloyalty of Armenian populations to beat, rape, torture, deport, and kill an estimated one million Armenians and hundreds of thousands of Greeks and Assyrians (who were also part of minority Christian communities in the empire). In other words, several empires used the upheaval of wartime and the paranoia that accompanied it to "solve" perceived minority problems with violence, and in the case of the Armenians, mass killing.

While camps for prisoners of war and interned civilians might not at first seem to fit the theme of transitional zones, these also served as marginal or liminal areas in times of war. For military prisoners, camp was neither home nor battle, yet POWs of military age were considered soldiers, still subject to military discipline and codes. POW camps in World War I were highly stratified, and it was not unusual to have divisions according to military rank, social class, and religion. Additionally, POW labor became significant for several of the combatant nations, so often bands of POWs could be seen working in French or Russian agriculture.

Each camp functioned as a small city with social activities, political organizations, and marketplaces, yet each was also patrolled and controlled. Prisoners, both military and civilian, described themselves as being in a strange transitional world between war and peace, between home and front. Some POWs spent nearly the entire war behind barbed wire, and as such, their war experience looked very different than that of their comrades after the war. Some faced mental or physical illness from the conditions of their imprisonment, others returned home to suspicions of cowardice or shirking. Like those in occupied zones, former POWs had a problematic postwar identity, and many had to prove their loyalties and their bravery to those at home when they returned. For civilian internees who had been imprisoned because of their status as enemy aliens, the war was even further distant. A large number of these prisoners had only been arrested because they were in the wrong country when war broke out.

Finally, it is important to note that some nations remained neutral during all or part of the war. These nations became home to refugee camps, espionage bureaus, and food production. They provided diplomatic services for the belligerent states in the form of prison inspectors, neutral locations for negotiations, and aid. Important neutrals included the Netherlands, where prisoners released in bilateral exchanges were sent for the duration of the war, and where large refugee camps housed Belgian and French families that fled wartime violence. Sweden and Denmark staffed crucial Red Cross medical centers and sent inspectors to prisoners' camps, most notably in the Russian Empire. Switzerland and Spain also became neutral transitional zones, through which personnel traveled from one side of the conflict to the other. The United States, which remained neutral until 1917, used its position on the edges of the conflict to consolidate its power in the western hemisphere and to shape the ideological terms of the conflict.

These shadowy zones between the fields of combat and the home fronts contained the seeds of revolution, sabotage, and espionage. Each nation maintained diplomatic personnel in the neutral nations, so these were hotbeds of information-gathering, conspiracy, and power during the war. Britain's major espionage agencies operated out of the Netherlands as did those of Germany. Vladimir Lenin famously spent much of the war in Switzerland alongside other dissidents and antiwar socialists who had sought refuge in this neutral country. Mata Hari, the Dutch-born courtesan and exotic dancer executed by France in 1917 as a spy, fell under suspicion while she was living in Madrid, Spain, a neutral zone. Because neutral zones were neither friend nor foe, the citizens of these nations had special privileges and their governments used their neutrality to their own advantage when possible. Herbert Hoover, an American businessman who led a humanitarian food aid program in Belgium during the war, used US neutrality to gain passes for travel and gasoline as well as special passports for moving across borders. Neutral citizens therefore had a place in the war, often as inspectors, aid workers, or medical personnel, but they remained slightly apart from the conflict as well.

Home Zones

Not least among the war zones of 1914–1918 were the home fronts of each belligerent state. In ways that governments had not entirely anticipated, home zones became most important for the continuation of the war effort. Through agriculture, industry, reproduction, and trade, the areas in the "back of the front" provided the necessary materials for combat. As such, the people inhabiting these fronts required strong persuasion that their activities and sacrifices were worthwhile. Huge propaganda machines emerged during the course of the war to help sell the conflict to its citizens. Citizens had to be convinced not just to fight but to ration food, make sacrifices, and accept increasing government intervention. Nations also used propaganda to raise money for the war effort and for the care of wartime victims. In order to motivate people to support this war, governments often sought to depict the enemy as barbaric or evil. Each belligerent used incidents from the war to make the case for enemy atrocities or poor behavior.

An excellent example is the Allied propaganda campaign surrounding the sinking of the ocean liner, the *Lusitania*, in May 1915, which had many neutral (especially American) civilians on board. Propagandists depicted scenes of drowning women and children against a backdrop of murderous German aggression. Such propaganda gave ordinary people a justification for warlike feelings and helped bolster morale.

Yet, when civilian morale did break down, it could be catastrophic, as in the case of the Russian Revolution. The fraying patience of civil populations created concern in all the countries at war. The Easter Rising of April 1916, in which Irish nationalists in Dublin tried to overthrow British Rule in Ireland, demonstrated how organized groups might take advantage of a wartime situation to push political demands. In the case of the Irish revolt, about 1600 rebels participated in the main action. For the British, this uprising in the midst of war (and just before a planned summer offensive on the Somme) required immediate and harsh action, especially since there was evidence that the rebels had coordinated their activities with German assistance. The leaders were tried and executed in May, and British martial law became the order of the day. As one historian has noted, "Almost everything that followed in the weeks and months after the Rising reflected poorly on the Government, converting public sympathy for the rebels into something more tangible." British repression and the continued presence of soldiers turned many wartime Irish patriots into nationalists. This did not go unnoticed by British authorities, and when conscription was introduced in Britain in 1916, Ireland was excluded from such policies.

Elsewhere, peaceful and violent disturbances challenged the authority of governments to conscript their citizens. Australians voted repeatedly against a mandatory draft, while anticonscription riots disrupted life in Quebec. In the Russian Empire, a massive anticonscription war broke out in central Asian provinces, which required the movement of armed forces to those regions in order to restore order. In Germany and Austria, workers increasingly took to the streets or engaged in debilitating industrial strikes in order to push for better wages and better access to food. French and American workers also used the war conditions to demand better pay. All of these events began to fray the edges of the social fabric.

As the war progressed, people living behind the lines were asked to make further sacrifices. Russians in the border zones lost everything, while Russians in Siberia housed refugees and prisoners sent to the interior. In some of the battle regions, soldiers lived off the land, meaning that civilians faced the loss of crops, food, supplies, and livelihoods through the violence and destruction of war. By 1915, rationing had become a reality for many civilians, and governments urged citizens to invest in war loans to help pay the enormous cost of maintaining massive armies. The old, the young, men, women, and children—all were recruited to the cause of victory in this war. Civilians, in great numbers, went to work in war industries or in replacement jobs in other sectors. In Britain, for instance, middle-class women worked in government offices, police and transport jobs, and in nursing or medical positions. German women travelled to occupied zones to serve as auxiliary clerks and service workers for the administrators in those regions. While all combatant nations called upon their citizens to support the war, home fronts varied considerably depending on their distance from the fighting. New Zealanders experienced war as a mostly distant event, while their English and French allies huddled in basements during air raids and heard the booming of artillery. This aspect of war on civilians became a celebrated reality after a raid by German naval guns on the English coastal towns of Scarborough and Whitby in December 1914. Only 25 people in the two towns died, but it established a new precedent for surprise bomb attacks on civilian targets.

What is important to remember is that war could not have continued for more than four years without the active participation of each of these zones of war. Combat soldiers required food and ammunition, which meant production at home and shipment through staging areas to the fronts. Occupied, neutral, and transitional zones allowed for the massing of men and munitions, while each zone created areas for medical care and treatment of war's casualties. It is easier to understand the length and scope of the war if one takes a holistic view of the ways in which the various zones depended upon each other. This helps explain as well the tendency toward total war that is evident in World War I. By 1915, these zones and the totalizing impulse were on full display.

Conclusion

By the end of 1915, two things were quite clear. This war had unleashed a Pandora's box of nationalist aspirations, ethnic cleansing, and expansionist ambitions. Second, the strategies that military leaders had been employing up to this point were not working. On the Western Front alone in 1915, the combined British, French, and German casualties topped 3.5 million. The Austro-Hungarian army had all but collapsed and was under German control on the Eastern Front, while the Russian Empire had suffered millions of casualties in its evacuation of Poland in 1915. The Serbian army had been devastated, and its surviving units sat in small camps scattered across the Greek islands. The number of battle zones had also expanded in 1915. The Turks had held Gallipoli but faced a new series of battles in the Caucasus Mountains. The two Italian fronts that bordered Austria-Hungary emerged in 1915, and when Bulgaria joined the war in October 1915, the Balkan front grew larger as well.

By the time that the Allied leaders gathered in the French town of Chantilly to discuss a coordinated offensive strategy in December 1915, stalemate had become a byword for the state of affairs in the war. As the Allies drew up spring plans, a new approach had also crystallized in the Central Powers' war planning meetings, one that focused on the idea of attrition. Attrition was the notion of launching a massive offensive against a target that held emotional and historical importance for the enemy in the hope that soldiers would defend that site to the death. The object of this approach was to "wear down" one's opponent. This notion of attrition required that military planners acknowledge the necessity for historic casualty rates on both sides, since the whole idea was to "outlast" one's foe. In each case, the two sides in the conflict had their sights on massive offensives that would end the stalemate and force the enemy to its knees. With this vision in mind, the planners set to work to make 1916 the year the war would end.

In short, the conclusion of 1915 brought a new deathly determination to the war. Each side sought to escalate the scope and violence of the conflict in an attempt to "knock out" the enemy through a major breakthrough. What it meant for the ordinary soldiers, the civil populations of the combat zones, and the industrial war complexes remained uncertain as people around the world celebrated New Year's Day 1916. The reality of what followed in fact became one cataclysm that helped to define the twentieth century, making 1916 a year that demonstrates more than any other the human cost of this particular war.

Citations

Page	Source

52 "in a week ..." quoted in Holger H. Herwig, *The First World War, Germany and Austria-Hungary 1914–1918*, 2nd Edition (London: Bloomsbury, 2014), 147.

52 "British fired more artillery shells ..." quoted in Michael Neiberg, *Fighting the Great War: A Global History* (Cambridge, MA: Harvard University Press, 2005), 75–76.

53 230 000 figure drawn from John R. Schindler, *Isonzo: The Forgotten Sacrifice of World War I* (Westport, CT: Praeger, 2001), 124.

53 "few had shoes ..." quoted in Herwig, 160.

54 "a formative experience ..." quoted in Hew Strachan, *The First World War* (New York: Viking, 2003), 173.

55 "on this insecure perch ..." quoted in Frederic Manning, *The Middle Parts of Fortune* (Melbourne: Text Publishing, 2001), 15.

56 "I can't recall ..." quoted in Svetlana Palmer and Sarah Wallis, eds., *Intimate Voices from the First World War* (New York: William Morrow, 2003), 151.

56 5000 civilians figure drawn from Jonathan Gumz, *The Resurrection and Collapse of Empire in Habsburg Serbia, 1914–1918* (Cambridge: Cambridge University Press, 2013), 58.

57 "war's largest internment camp" quoted in Neiberg, 2005, 110.

58 700 people figure drawn from "HMS *Hampshire*: 100th Anniversary of Sinking Commemorated in Orkney," bbc.com, June 6, 2016.

61 80 000 Slovene figure drawn from Schindler, 47.

61 Description and figures for Armenian genocide drawn from Alan Kramer, *Dynamic of Destruction: Culture and Mass Killing in the First World War* (Oxford: Oxford University Press, 2007), 148–152.

64 "Almost everything that followed..." quoted in Fearghal McGarry, *The Rising: Ireland: Easter 1916* (Oxford: Oxford University Press, 2011), 284.

Select Bibliography

Gooch, John. *The Italian Army and the First World War*. Cambridge: Cambridge University Press, 2014.

Gumz, Jonathan. *The Resurrection and Collapse of Empire in Habsburg Serbia, 1914–1918*. Cambridge: Cambridge University Press, 2013.

Hart, Peter. *The Great War: A Combat History of the First World War*. Oxford: Oxford University Press, 2013.

Herwig, Holger H. *The First World War, Germany and Austria-Hungary 1914–1918*, 2nd Edition. London: Bloomsbury, 2014.

Kramer, Alan. *Dynamic of Destruction: Culture and Mass Killing in the First World War*. Oxford: Oxford University Press, 2007.

Larson, Erik. *Dead Wake: The Last Crossing of the Lusitania*. New York: Crown Publishers, 2015.

Macdonald, Lyn. *1915: The Death of Innocence*. Baltimore: Johns Hopkins University Press, 2000.

Macleod, Jenny. *Gallipoli*. Oxford: Oxford University Press, 2015.

Manning, Frederic. *The Middle Parts of Fortune*. Melbourne: Text Publishing, 2001.

McGarry, Fearghal. *The Rising: Ireland: Easter 1916*. Oxford: Oxford University Press, 2011.

Neiberg, Michael. *Fighting the Great War: A Global History*. Cambridge, MA: Harvard University Press, 2005.

Palmer, Svetlana, and Sarah Wallis, eds. *Intimate Voices from the First World War*. New York: William Morrow, 2003.

Proctor, Tammy. *Civilians in a World at War, 1914–1918*. New York: New York University Press, 2010.

Schindler, John R. *Isonzo: The Forgotten Sacrifice of World War I*. Westport, CT: Praeger, 2001.

Stone, David R. *The Russian Army in the Great War: The Eastern Front, 1914–1917*. Lawrence: University Press of Kansas, 2015.

Strachan, Hew. *The First World War*. New York: Viking, 2003.

Strachan, Hew. *The First World War: Volume I – To Arms*. Oxford: Oxford University Press, 2001.

Suny, Ronald Grigor, Fatma Müge Göçek, and Norman M. Naimark, eds. *A Question of Genocide: Armenians and Turks at the End of the Ottoman Empire*. Oxford: Oxford University Press, 2011.

Travers, Timothy. *Gallipoli, 1915*. Stroud, UK: Tempus, 2015.

Tunstall, Graydon. *Blood on the Snow: The Carpathian Winter of 1915*. Lawrence: University Press of Kansas, 2010.

Appendix 3.1: Timeline for 1915

1915	*IMPORTANT EVENTS OF THE WAR*	*BATTLE*
January	Allied offensives at Champagne	
March 10	British offensive at Neuve Chapelle	Battle of Neuve Chapelle
April 22	German chlorine gas attack at Boezinge, Belgium	Second Battle of Ypres
April 24	Easter Rising in Ireland begins	
April 25	Landings at the Gallipoli peninsula	Battle of Gallipoli
May 1	Germans attack Russian front	Battle of Gorlice-Tarnow
May 7	Sinking of the RMS *Lusitania* by a German U-Boat	
May 15	Allied offensive on Western Front	Battle of Festubert
May 23	Italy joins the war on the Allied side	
June 29	First Battle of the Isonzo	Battle of the Isonzo
July 13	Combined German–Austrian offensive on Eastern Front	
July 20	French and German forces clash in the Vosges Mountains	Battle of Le Linge
August 5	Germans capture Warsaw	
September 5	Tsar Nicholas II assumes control of the Russian Army	
September 25	Allied offensives at Loos, Artois, and Champagne (to November)	
September 28	Battle of Kut (Mesopotamia) begins	Battle of Kut
October 9	Austrian troops occupy Belgrade	
October 11	Bulgaria joins the war on the side of the Central Powers	
December 7	Siege of Kut-al-Amara begins	
December 19	Sir Douglas Haig named Commander-in-Chief of British Armies	

4

1916. Who Participated in the War and How?

Figure 4.1 Conditions for soldiers and laborers varied tremendously depending on the Front. Here, members of the King's African Rifles and porters carry munitions across a river. In East Africa, travel was dangerous and difficult. *Source*: © Imperial War Museums (Q 67823).

World War I: A Short History, First Edition. Tammy M. Proctor.
© 2018 John Wiley & Sons Ltd. Published 2018 by John Wiley & Sons Ltd.

Imagine yourself as a 21-year-old university student in 1914. Your term is scheduled to begin in a few short weeks, and you are enjoying the summer holidays, perhaps at the beach or on a mountain hiking trip. Into your placid existence comes the news that your nation has declared war. If you are a male student, your immediate concern is whether you will be called up to serve under your country's general conscription policy or whether your friends will volunteer for the conflict. If you are a female student, your concerns will be different. You might be wondering how you may serve your nation in the coming war but you would also be considering the life and death implications of war for your brothers and friends. In either case, excitement and dread might coexist. Depending on your location, anxiety might win the day, especially if you fear invasion by the enemy. For young people around the world in 1914, the war served as a point of decision and a defining moment in their lives. War was an unknown for everyone, but perhaps the group most affected by the war and most caught up in its promise were young adults.

For older adults, war could be quite complicated. Married men and women faced separation from each other, and both worried about the impact of a prolonged absence of the male breadwinner on the family's livelihood. In agriculture, families knew that the disappearance of able-bodied men and the best draft animals from a neighborhood would mean a difficult or perhaps impossible harvest. In industry, men worried about losing good jobs to replacements. Parents whose children were of military age faced a different set of anxieties about the health and life of their loved ones. Elderly people feared the vulnerability they faced in a wartime world, and children struggled to understand what a war would mean. In each of these cases, the turn toward total war manifested itself, albeit in different ways.

In short, war did not elicit one reaction from the populations of combatant countries. The people drawn into war came from a multitude of backgrounds and brought with them attitudes, habits, political opinions, family situations, and religious beliefs that varied widely. While one young man in Britain might eagerly volunteer for the conflict, his best friend might hesitate to leave a good job, a girlfriend, or a family dependent upon his wages for the uncertainty of life as a soldier. Likewise, a young woman in Vienna might see the war as an opportunity to prove herself as a citizen, so she might train in first aid or volunteer for the Red Cross. Her neighbor and best friend could take an entirely opposing view and see war as an unwanted intrusion into her daily existence. Social class mattered enormously as did religious background and ethnicity in some cases. Citizens of an empire or state fell into a hierarchy of need during times of conflict, and thus categories of people who were seen as having suspicious loyalties or as less capable were assigned different roles than those considered necessary. In the United States, this meant the labeling of many African-American draftees as laborers rather than combat soldiers, while in the Russian Empire, it led to the forced expulsion of

Jewish families from border regions. Middle- and upper-class men and women could pay for the privilege of particular kinds of wartime service, and they could hire servants to attend to their personal needs while they performed this service.

Because of this diversity of experience and outlook, one cannot generalize about the ways in which people viewed the war. This chapter will instead examine some of the ways leaders sought to utilize their populations and to motivate them to participate in the war and will suggest ways in which the war shaped their lives and experiences, especially by 1916, a year of expansion and intensification of the conflict.

1916. Trial by Fire

January 1, 1916, brought a resounding victory for Allied (British and French) forces at Yaounde in Cameroon. The capture of the wartime German capital of the colony came after more than a year of fighting and led to a German retreat to the south. By February, the British counted the Cameroon campaign as a success and tallied up their victories in German-held African colonies. The British controlled three of these, with one remaining in German East Africa. This victory was duly celebrated in the British newspapers despite a widespread sense of depression about the war effort generally. By 1916 no one expected that any single victory would get the world closer to an end to this war. A sense of resignation ruled the day as it seemed that the war dragged on with no end and no real gains.

Civilian and military leaders felt enormous pressure for success in order to maintain morale both at the battlefronts and at home. None of the civilian leaders wanted to be responsible for more loss of life, and the United States—a neutral nation—even had an election in 1916 that centered around the question of war. Woodrow Wilson maintained the Presidency partly because of his campaign slogan, "He kept us out of war." In the nations at war, most had resorted to some form of shared governance or coalition system by 1916 to try to manage the wartime state and to bolster public confidence. Britain's Parliament moved to coalition government in 1915, first under Herbert Asquith and by late 1916, under David Lloyd-George. Germany also moved to a coalition system in the Reichstag by the middle of the war. France witnessed a series of leadership changes in 1916 and 1917 as civilian leaders tried to cope with the extreme stress of the Verdun campaign and worsening labor problems. In each of the countries at war, 1916 was the year of reorganizations. The Ottoman Empire, Russia, Germany, France, and Britain all instituted new administrations for delivery of needed munitions—some focused on industrial production, some on transport. All of these new offices sought to improve the situation at the battlefronts. Meanwhile, the flurry of government activity and its accompanying propaganda did little to assuage the fears of the populations.

To combat the sense of futility and lack of progress that many felt, commanders in all the major armies had plans ready to be deployed in 1916 in the hope that this year would be different and that a breakthrough would be possible. The combatants launched five massive offensives during the first seven months of 1916. The combined casualty rates for these battles numbered in the millions, gunners fired unprecedented numbers of artillery shells, and every new technology or idea that could be deployed was used. Every one of these offensives failed to create substantive change or to end the war.

1. February—The Germans and the Battle of Verdun

The first of the 1916 offensives came as a surprise to the French when the Germans attacked the heavily fortified region around Verdun in northeastern France. The Germans had prepared well, with 2.5 million shells stockpiled for the battle. Germany opened this attack on February 21 with a massive artillery barrage, creating what would become a transformed landscape over the next 10 months. The land is still scarred today, a century later, as shown in the photograph in the Preface. Erich von Falkenhayn, the German general in charge, had a clear vision of his goals at Verdun. He hoped to smash the French lines there, take its main forts, and destroy morale using a massive, coordinated (air, artillery, infantry) strike. The French suffered grievous casualties in the first few days of the battle, but they held important positions and later in the battle counterattacked to take back some of the land lost. When the initial breakthrough he sought failed, Falkenhayn began speaking of the policy called *attrition*, the notion of "bleeding the enemy white." Its cold-blooded waste of human life marked Verdun as one of the most devastating battles for both the German and French soldiers involved.

Over the course of the Battle of Verdun, the Germans attacked and created a salient (a bulge in the line), taking control of French fortresses like the one at Douaumont (which had been accidentally left undefended), levelling villages and forests. Yet despite the initial gains, the French line retreated and held, creating a different sort of stalemate in which the two armies would battle for almost a year. The French, under their commander in this region, Philippe Pétain, now relied on smart defense and limited offensives to hold their positions and slowly regain territory. One of the symbols of the French effort and the "spirit" of France became the supply road to the front, a tiny muddy road known as "*la voie sacrée*" or Sacred Way. Trucks carried men and supplies to the lines, keeping troops supplied. One of the consequences of the French effort in Verdun was that many soldiers were diverted to this front, leaving other planned offensives and fronts vulnerable.

Meanwhile, German leaders tried to hold their position at Verdun, hoping to outlast the French. Germans used small groups of specially-trained troops, later called stormtroopers, for the first time in this battle. These units formed an advance guard for a larger infantry attack to follow. In summer 1916, a second major fortress (Vaux) fell into German hands, but soon after the German advance stalled. The fighting was dreadful, with one village changing hands more than a dozen times during the battle, but slowly the French began to regain ground. For German leaders the need to dispatch troops to other fronts also weakened their position at Verdun, and by December 1916, the French had regained all the ground the Germans had taken. Both sides had suffered dearly: "the French lost 351,000 men, of whom 150,000 were killed; the Germans 330,000, of whom 143,000 were dead or missing." The sacrifice hardly seemed worth it; the lines on January 1, 1917 were nearly in the same place they had been in a year earlier.

2. March—The Italians and the Fifth Battle of the Isonzo

One of the assumptions that German military officials made in planning Verdun was that their Austro-Hungarian allies would attack or keep the Russian front busy, thereby allowing Germany to concentrate forces in the west. This did not entirely work because General Conrad von Hotzendorff saw more importance for the Habsburgs in the Italian Front. Instead of attacking Russia, the Austrians focused their energies on planning an attack in the Tyrol/Trentino region of northern Italy. Hotzendorff wanted to launch a battle in March but weather in the mountains delayed this assault until May. In the meantime, the Italian army, in keeping with its part of the coordinated Allied offensives planned for 1916, planned its own attacks on its Habsburg enemy. These objectives resulted in five different offensives in the Isonzo area alone during 1916, the first of which the Italians launched on March 9, 1916. The Isonzo (Soča), a river valley surrounded by mountains, represented a difficult terrain in which countless assaults led to limited results. Each of the 1916 Italian efforts in the region led to virtually no territorial change, but it did divert Austrian troops from other fronts. It was not until the Battle of Caporetto in late fall 1917 that significant change occurred on this front, when the Austro-Hungarian army overran Italian positions and decimated its opponent.

3. May—The Austro-Hungarians and the Battle of Asiago

One of the reasons that the Isonzo Front saw little change is that both Austro-Hungarian and Italian troops had to focus their energies on the Tyrol in northern Italy, where the Habsburg armies launched their major Alpine offensive in mid-May 1916. The fighting was treacherous here, with artillery creating rock projectiles out of mountain crags. The Austrians pushed the Italians back into the Asiago plateau (hence the name of the battle) near Trento leading the Italians to reinforce this area with more men and supplies. Ultimately, this offensive also stalled, and the Italian counterattack in June pushed the lines back toward the mountains. The two Italian Fronts, in the Trentino and in the Isonzo, remained intact, and both sides suffered major casualties through the repeated offensives of 1916.

4. June—The Russians and the Brusilov Offensive

As the French and Germans battled at Verdun and the Italian Front exploded into violence, the Russian army prepared for its own offensive in Galicia in 1916. On June 4, the Russian army, led by General Alexei Brusilov, broke through the Austro-Hungarian lines and captured 200000 men. The Russians relied on a new targeted "hurricane bombardment" that utilized aerial photography to pinpoint vulnerable sections for bombardment. This was in marked contrast to the long bombardment that had thus far preceded big battles. Brusilov also spent several months training troops in different techniques for assaulting trenches, and he created holding areas for reserve troops near the site of the attack. Initially this offensive was a great success with the Russians pushing the Austrian lines two dozen miles along a broad front. However, the Russians had to halt as they outpaced their supplies. The tide turned with the arrival of reinforcements—German soldiers from Verdun and Habsburg soldiers from Italy. Both the Habsburg and the Russian armies witnessed mutinies and desertion as exhausted soldiers refused to cooperate. By the end of 1916, the Habsburg army was a hollow shell, but the Russian army was also demoralized and dangerously unstable.

5. July—The British and the Battle of the Somme

The last of the major Allied offensives coordinated at Chantilly arrived in midsummer 1916. The British artillery began its weeklong barrage in late June, and the infantry advanced on July 1. This date became the single bloodiest day in modern British military history, with more than 19200 dead and nearly 58000 casualties in a 24-hour period. By the time the battle ended officially in November 1916, casualties on all sides (French, British, colonial, Belgian, German) topped 1.2 million. Like the other battles of 1916, the Somme in hindsight appeared misguided and brutal, and the futility of these offensives now seemed obvious.

Despite the seemingly overwhelming nature of the British barrage of July 1 (more than 1.5 million shells were fired), the Germans survived it. Even the deep mines packed with explosives that the British detonated under German lines didn't dislodge all the troops. The problem was twofold: 1) the attack was spread across such a large area that it was not concentrated enough to destroy the German defenses, which were solid; 2) an estimated one-quarter of all British shells were duds. Therefore, when the British army began their movement across

No Man's Land toward enemy lines, they were met by machine-gun fire and unhurt German troops in many sectors of the line.

Along with the other offensives of 1916, the Somme demonstrated quite clearly the difficulty of achieving military victory. Every piece of territory came at a terrible price, and even long advances did not seem to lead to any kind of political solution. For the Germans, the lesson of 1916 was that they needed a new approach. The Germans spent the winter of 1916–1917 building a fortified line back from their current positions on the Western Front, called the *Siegfriedstellung* (Hindenburg Line). Even though they were ceding territory, the Germans realized the advantage of creating a straight line of solid defenses on high ground. This new line shortened the front they had to defend, freeing up divisions for duty elsewhere. To cap this new plan, the Germans destroyed buildings and bridges as they retreated, poisoning wells and burning anything that could be of use to the enemy. The Allies, on the other hand, planned a new coordinated offensive for 1917 on the Western Front, which would focus on the Chemin des Dames (for the French) and the area near Arras (for the British).

6. Elsewhere

While offensives served as the focal point for military planning on all sides of the conflict in 1916, several other regions became hotspots in the war for other reasons. The use of naval power in traditional sea battles had been very limited up to 1916, and the only major naval engagement of the war (in 1916) offered little hope for a breakthrough using maritime strength. In May 1916, during a period when the Germans had suspended unrestricted submarine warfare because of international pressure over civilian casualties, a large battle force set out from German naval bases toward the north of Britain. British codebreakers working for the Admiralty sent advance warning of the strike, giving the British the opportunity to set a trap. The two opposing naval fleets fought a series of skirmishes in the North Sea over less than a 24-hour period. Both sides sustained losses and both claimed victory when the smoke cleared from the Battle of Jutland. The Germans had destroyed more British tonnage, but in the long run, the battle merely encouraged the German navy to avoid surface battles. Their naval focus had turned back to submarine warfare by 1917, which was not entirely a successful strategy. Britain's use of convoys and the entry of the United States into the war lessened the impact of the German U-Boat strategy.

Another place that seemed a likely candidate for some sort of breakthrough was on the southeastern or Balkan Front because Romania entered the war in August 1916 on the Allied side, lured by promises of postwar territorial gain. However, Romania's poorly trained troops, lack of firepower, and ineffective supply services were a recipe for disaster. As one historian has remarked: "The Romanian army mobilized in August 1916 was large in numbers but weak in training, experience, leadership and equipment, especially firepower at all levels." The Romanians' initial foray into battle led to small territorial gains against the Habsburg armies, whose troops were stretched thin by late summer. In addition, Romania's allies (France, Serbia, Britain) launched a limited offensive from the holding area of Salonika, but it went nowhere. Instead, an early winter and a quick response by the Germans, Ottomans, and Bulgarians led to the complete collapse of the Romanian war effort and the occupation of Romania by the Central Powers in December 1916. Romania's contribution, albeit unintended, was primarily in terms of resources. The German, Bulgarian, and Habsburg authorities stripped Romania of most of its grain and oil, using these vital supplies to continue the Central Powers' war. Eventually Romania negotiated a separate peace in spring 1918.

In the remaining German colony in Africa, today's Tanzania, the British brought in a new commander in 1916, South African Jan Smuts. Leading British imperial forces as well as Portuguese and Belgian troops, Smuts sought to cut off the German army under Paul von Lettow-Vorbeck and end the conflict. Instead, the armies maneuvered over vast territories all the while suffering terrible casualties from disease, parasites, and infections. Even the addition of more Kenyan troops (the King's African Rifles) who were acclimated both to the climate and to the terrain could not improve Smuts' chances of encircling Lettow-Vorbeck. No breakthrough seemed possible in this war theater.

The other major belligerent, the Ottomans, fought on several fronts in 1916, and like Germany and Austria-Hungary, launched offensives to try to break open the war. The Ottomans had significant forces in Persia (modern Iran), Mesopotamia (modern Iraq), Palestine (modern Israel and Jordan), Galicia (modern Ukraine and Poland), and the Caucasus (modern Georgia) in 1916. In Mesopotamia, the Ottomans besieged a British force at Kut-al-Amara in December 1915 and continued for several months until its surrender in late April 2016. The British troops, many of them from its colony in India, died in large numbers when they were marched to forced-labor prison camps. An estimated 70% of the soldiers from the surrendered garrison died in the aftermath of the surrender. One sergeant who survived later said, "we were beginning to think that the policy of the Turkish government was to have us marched around until we were all dead." Yet despite this victory at Kut, the Ottoman war was not the success that its leaders hoped, and military officials massed as many troops as possible in the Caucasus in order to hold their positions there.

Technological Advances

With the advent of new tactics and creative military planning in 1916 came the use of innovative technologies to try to create a breakthrough. Several important technologies played a role as new inventions or newly integrated tools for war in 1916. While chemical warfare had debuted in 1915, the offensives in 1916 featured use of a variety of poison gases in combination. Some of the variants that were developed in 1916 include more lethal concoctions known as "blue cross" and "green cross" gases. These combination chemical agents inflicted more damage by combining blistering and tear-inducing gases with asphyxiants. Despite these ugly innovations and the expansion of the use of poison gas by all belligerents, gas warfare never provided a breakthrough. Still all of the belligerents raced to create new, more lethal forms of poison gases at the same time that all of them sought effective protection in the form of masks and clothing. The most well-known and scary of the chemical warfare agents, mustard gas, did not make an appearance until 1917. Yet none of these gases brought a decisive victory in battle.

Two other battlefield tools saw initial or increased use in 1916, namely the flamethrower and the tank. The Germans used flamethrowers in several of their offensive actions, and first-hand accounts often discuss the sight of these walls of flame. In the Vosges battles of 1915, flamethrowers and gas had been used extensively in the close fighting of the mountain trenches. British forces introduced tanks in the Somme sector in September 1916, but mud and rain led to poor results for this first use. In fact, despite the potential of these new weapons of war, it was age-old technology that still dominated the scene—shovels. Soldiers dug in once again in 1916 and waited for the spring thaw.

Varieties of Experience

Men at War

One of the common sentiments expressed in war diaries of men during World War I is a worry about manliness. War frames men's lives as a test of masculinity with words such as strength, courage, and sacrifice at the center of debate. This language of masculine heroism places enormous pressure upon men to perform, and it certainly helps explain why men kept fighting, even when the situation was dire. Men who were not explicitly involved in the war, unless they were visibly too young or too old to fight, experienced shaming and peer pressure to become part of the war effort in combatant countries. Even men who went to war in other ways—as chaplains, stretcher-bearers, or diplomats, for instance—had to prove their mettle and felt the sting of others' disapproval. For laborers at the combat fronts, the stigma of being diggers not fighters could also rankle. Thus, any kind of men's war service should be understood in this larger gendered framework of "appropriate" masculinity. What constituted "appropriate" often depended upon the policies of the nation where men lived—the rules of volunteering and conscription helped define warriors, and, therefore, men at war.

Virtually all the combatant countries had a mandatory draft in place for some age groups of men by 1914. At the end of 1917, the only major nations at war who were *not* conscripting men into service were some of the British imperial states such as Australia and South Africa. Ireland was also excluded from the draft that went into full force in the United Kingdom in 1916 because of political unrest following the Easter Rising. In all other countries, men had little choice about whether to serve in the war if they were called up but some also volunteered in order to show their patriotism even before their names came up for the draft. The difference between the eager volunteer and the forced conscript played out in the trenches just as social class, age, and other factors defined war experience for men.

Evading service could be an option but it was not an easy one. Local draft boards issued waivers in many countries, especially on medical grounds. Men underwent physical inspection and if found unfit, they were sent home. However, dismissal on medical grounds could be humiliating, and many men kept trying to enlist until they could find a doctor who might overlook their medical problems. Men in some nations could also refuse military service if they were willing to risk prison, but the only nations that had official processes in place for so-called conscientious objectors were the United States and Britain. Even then, "COs" or the more derogatory term "conchies" faced prison and violence depending on their willingness to serve the nation in some capacity. Most conscientious objectors *did* serve in the war, typically in alternative war service roles such as ambulance drivers or clerks, as was the case with many Quakers, Mennonites, and other religious pacifists.

Once caught up in the war machine, men experienced the war in completely different ways. The old adage that "war is hell" did not apply universally to the soldiers at the combat fronts. Some enjoyed the camaraderie of military life, the rush of adrenaline that accompanied violence, and the adventure that war could represent. For others, war was an unwanted distraction from the business of their lives, and for these men, their service could not end soon enough. Still other men became ill as a result of the war, suffering from psychological and physical damage during their war service. Some men just got lucky in their military assignments, and for those units who spent their wars in quiet sectors, war was mostly boring. For the men caught in occupied territories, war brought loss of jobs and autonomy, and it sometimes meant forced labor or deportation. Location mattered. In the case of Belgium, a Belgian army soldier might be located just a few kilometers from his twin brother living in a town under German occupation. Each faced a different set of hardships and demands despite their proximity. One was given a gun, paid to work as a soldier and fed from government rations, while the other was forbidden to possess weapons, often unemployed, and fed from a charitable organization.

Men not serving as active duty fighting forces provided a variety of other necessary work for the war efforts. Every country involved in the war excluded men in occupations vital to the war from serving at the fronts. This work included government and civil service, mining, manufacturing, communications, and intelligence. Males of military age could be conscripted for labor as well, and men from non-combatant countries were hired as civilian contract laborers. Others could serve in volunteer corps in their home countries; in Britain, for instance, older men could sign up as "special constables" to keep order in the cities. Still other men spent their wars in prisoner camps, either as civilian or military prisoners, which placed them in a strange kind of limbo for the duration of the war. Finally, a number of men served in the medical services units of the war as doctors, orderlies, stretcher bearers, and ambulance drivers. In each case, war brought change, but it did not bring the same physical conditions nor the same dangers.

Soldiers had a hard time shedding their civilian lives and identities. As citizen-soldiers fighting for nation-states, they saw their military service not as a career path, as was the case in many earlier wars, but as a civic duty to be fulfilled. They planned to return to civilian occupations, families, and homes as soon as the war ended. Signs of civilian identities abounded in trenches, prison camps, and rest areas near the fronts. For instance, soldiers from Liverpool stationed in Vaux near Verdun recreated the city center of their home town in the village. Helen McCartney describes the scene: "The officers you will find billeted in the Angel and they look out on a very doubtful Exchange Flags. Then there is Dale Street leading to Abercromby Square…" This assertion of a civilian life was particularly visible in prisoner of war camps for civilian and military personnel. In the German prison camp at Ruhleben near Berlin, British POWs named the streets between their barracks with beloved names from home, such as Bond Street and Trafalgar Square. Likewise, German prisoners in British camps mounted theatrical and musical productions of their favorite shows from home in their native language.

Letters between soldiers and families emphasize the continued links between the men serving in the military and their home communities. For instance, children wrote to their fathers telling them about their daily lives at school, their help around the household, and any exciting events. Often families tried to reassure their loved ones at the front. In April 1916, George Butling wrote to his father, a British soldier from Liverpool, to assure him that the family was doing well: "Just a few lines to let you know how we are carrying on in 'Blighty.'… The rationing is in full swing here but Mother can get more than she can afford in every thing so you see we are A1. as regards the food item." Lovers and spouses often put into words their longing to be together again, but the realities of censorship of mails sometimes constrained and irritated these correspondents. When Martha Hanna analyzed several years of correspondence between Frenchman Paul Pireaud and his wife, Marie, she discovered that he mostly saw censorship of his letters as a minor irritation. The couple was still able to talk about important and small matters and to bolster each other's spirits. In one letter, for instance, Paul told Marie, "I live only for you while waiting to taste the happiness which is our due if that should be allowed us."

Correspondence contained all kinds of mundane and important information. In some cases a single letter brought despair or hope, as in the case of Habsburg officer Franciscus Sobolewski, whose family found out that he had been taken prisoner by the Russians through a letter written by another prisoner. Soldiers often reported to their families about neighbors and friends as well about themselves, understanding that information was vital for those waiting at home. Because friends, neighbors, and acquaintances also wrote to each other, not just to families, there was a thriving information network between home and front.

Regardless of location or status, men saw war as a formative experience that defined their sense of self, their relationship to nation and empire, and their gender role. As is clear in the variety of situations in which men could find themselves, there was no singular life for a man at war.

Women at War

War meant something different for women than for men. Just as a wartime world brought a particular gendered vision of masculinity into the light, this world also defined women's roles in gendered ways. Women were expected to do what was necessary for their societies in wartime, while also maintaining the nurturing home fires in preparation for a time when men would return. As part of this gendered vision, states fretted about women's sexuality and sought to control it through legislation and propaganda. A good example of this is the Defense of the Realm Act (DORA) in Britain, which continued to expand throughout the war and which provided many temporary measures for policing the home front. In addition to prohibitions on passing information to the enemy, the act imposed curfews, shortened pub hours, created price controls, and mandated blackouts in major cities. Additionally, several of the most important provisions of this act targeted women in the hope of controlling their public lives. Women accused of espionage were arrested under DORA provisions, and the Act sought to control women's sexuality through a number of measures that included raising the age of consent, outlawing advertising of abortifacients, and criminalizing women who contracted venereal diseases.

Women's sexuality defined many military and civilian discussions about protecting soldiers. Army officials erected systems of military brothels for controlling prostitution near training camps, front-line and staging areas, and occupied zones. Legislation in multiple nations also targeted women, making them subject to forced examinations for venereal diseases if they were caught loitering in public places and seemed suspect to officials. Women working for the militaries as auxiliaries or medical personnel faced restrictions on their lodging and travel. Most women's auxiliary units employed older female wardens, who lived in barracks or dormitories with the young women and who were assigned to protect their charges' virtue.

Despite these efforts to monitor and control women's activities, war brought additional freedom of movement and more job opportunities to many females, at least for the duration of the conflict. In front-line zones, women worked for the armies in service occupations such as transport and sanitation. Women staffed bathhouses and laundries near all the army outposts, and they carried food, medical supplies, and building materials to combat zones such as Italy and Galicia. The armies of East Africa and Mesopotamia had many women who accompanied their male loved ones, often exasperating European officers. In a global war, cultural traditions regarding warfare varied considerably, so women fought to retain the roles that they saw for themselves in military life as cooks, laundresses, and companions to their menfolk.

A few women broke through the gendered barriers of military service and fought as soldiers. One way for women to serve in a military capacity was to assume a male name and dress as a man in order to fight; this was particularly true in regions such as Serbia and Russia. A famous example of a female soldier was British-born Flora Sandes who served with the Serbian Army until an injury ended her career in the military ranks. Despite Sandes example, there are few documented cases of female soldiers in this war. Notable exceptions were all-women units formed in 1917 after the Russian Revolution. The best known of these units is the Women's Battalion of Death, which trained women as combat soldiers. It was more common for women to experience the violence of war through their labor as medical personnel, auxiliary workers, or military service workers (e.g., laundresses). Female porters, especially in mountain terrain, faced artillery fire and exposure to extreme weather conditions. Some women even set up medical units in active combat regions. The Scottish Women's Hospitals worked in Serbia in terribly dangerous conditions, and several female nursing or ambulance units saw war service in combat zones. Several such women wrote accounts of their evacuations with armies during retreats or of their time sheltering from artillery shells or aerial bombardment.

There were women who put themselves in the line of fire during World War I as well. They tried hard to volunteer for service as pilots, drivers, and news reporters. Others embraced lives of resistance to occupying authorities in such areas as Lithuania, Poland, Belgium, and northern France. Women ran underground information networks, they smuggled food and other supplies, and they served as intelligence agents. The electrified border between the Netherlands and Belgium, for instance, created a porous zone where women of all ages served as couriers, bringing information to intelligence bureaus (French, British, and German) in neutral Holland. Escape networks for protection of soldiers caught behind enemy lines often had female leadership as well. Edith Cavell, a British nurse managing a hospital in occupied Belgium, assisted with such an escape organization. Her institution housed Allied soldiers as they made the trip with volunteer guides to safety in the Netherlands. The German occupying authorities arrested Cavell and her collaborators, and Cavell was executed in October 1915, sparking an international outcry. In addition to official prosecution, women living in occupation or invasion zones also faced violence, especially sexual assault. Such cases were vastly underreported during and after the war, so it is hard to document how prevalent these attacks were.

Another way women were drawn into war was through paid and voluntary war service work. Millions of women around the world produced wartime goods and munitions, either in factories as paid war workers or in voluntary associations, where they knitted socks and sweaters, collected war materials, or produced parcels for soldiers, prisoners, and refugees. In northern France, where wartime fluctuations in the line had created vast swathes of destroyed villages, women volunteered their services to rebuild communities and to staff orphanages. One of the most famous of these organizations was Quaker-run, and it included production of prefabricated housing for displaced people. Other women served in neutral medical and social service organizations. Anne Morgan, for example, the daughter of rich banker J. P. Morgan, spent years running projects in France to rebuild devastated villages and to house orphans of the war. Swedish women, in another instance, served as prison camp inspectors in the Russian Empire, while British female doctors staffed a hospital in Serbia. In short, women were never absent from war zones, POW camps, occupied regions, or staging areas—their labor and their sacrifices helped make the war possible.

Because of their importance to military and civil officials, women used their power as citizens and workers to demand change during the war. Some petitioned their governments to complain about excessive requisitioning of animals or problems with rationing, while others took to the streets to protest working conditions, wages, and access to food. Particularly vulnerable were soldiers' wives and widows or families whose sole breadwinner had been conscripted. Women in these situations pushed governments to provide relief in the form of pensions, family allowances, and other aid payments in order to alleviate the symptoms of wartime deprivation. In the Ottoman town of İskilip (Çorum), for instance, women wrote to government officials demanding help, "While our husbands are toiling on the borders to protect the glory and honor of the nation, the compassion of our exalted government would not let their families die of starvation." These wives shared a sense of entitlement with wives in Berlin, St. Petersburg, Paris, and Belgrade, all of whom conceived of their service and sacrifice as citizenship. They expected recognition and assistance based on their roles in the nation.

Other women recognized war as an opportunity, either for paid work and opportunities never before open to them, or for political change. At a 1915 international women's peace conference held in the neutral Netherlands at The Hague, delegates discussed the need for peace but they also represented the major feminist groups internationally, all of whom were pushing for women's political rights, especially suffrage. These female activists varied considerably in their strategies and views of war, with some advocating resistance to wartime conscription. Members of Alice Paul's American suffrage group, the National Women's Party (1916), picketed the White House and, in 1917, went to prison for unpatriotic activities in opposing the war and promoting justice for women. Using a different strategy, Britain's major suffrage groups suspended their vocal campaigns for the duration of the war and successfully argued that women's wartime service made them particularly important members of the citizenry and deserving of the vote. Women in some nations did gain the vote in the immediate aftermath of World War I, but there is not a direct connection between women's war work and suffrage gains in most cases.

Like men, women experienced the war in vastly different ways depending on their social class, their proximity to battle, and their home situation. What is clear, however, is that women were highly invested in the war and saw patriotic service as an important part of their role as citizens as well.

Too Old or Too Young for War?

Perhaps one of the most important ways of defining war experience had less to do with gender and more to do with age. Children, especially very young children, were dependents, so their war was often contingent upon their family situations. Young people with intact families living in countries far from the actual fighting had the luxury of choosing whether to "do their part" in the war effort. Organizations such as the Boy Scouts or Girl Scouts provided safe options for children who wanted to raise funds for the war or to plant a victory garden. Other children got their war news through school, and again, distance from the front meant a more or less normal existence for some kids. The war did disrupt schooling in some states, particularly in regions where children's labor was required for agriculture. In the last two years of the war, a million German schoolchildren from urban areas were sent to rural areas to do farm work for six months of the year.

The situation was quite different for children living under occupation, who lived in destroyed villages, orphanages, or refugee camps. These children faced malnutrition, disease, and violence as a result of the war, which in turn led to public health crises in some locales. At home fronts in many of the hardest hit combatant nations, incidence of diseases such as tuberculosis soared, and physicians after the war found that children were often underweight for their ages.

Some of the most dire situations for children during World War I were in areas where minority populations had been targeted by imperial governments. For instance, some Armenian children who survived the 1915 genocide found themselves in orphanages or in Ottoman families. Adoptive parents of these kids changed their names and converted them to Islam, thereby erasing their past histories and identities. The situation for refugee or displaced children was also a difficult one, and many grew up in camps or in strangers' homes, sometimes in poor conditions. An example is the family internment camp in Bourke (Australia), which had terrible rations, incessant mosquitoes, and frequent outbreaks of disease that plagued the women and children housed there.

For teens, war brought increased job opportunities in many countries where replacement workers were needed in transport, retail, and industry. Adolescent girls and boys who had trained for domestic service or who expected to do so, now turned to other kinds of employment in greater numbers, creating a shift in the labor market in some nations. Teens also sometimes saw their educations cut short as families needed them for farm work or to provide monetary support. As the draft age expanded, teen boys sometimes found themselves in uniform or in labor battalions doing support work. Teen girls constituted a particular problem for local and national officials because they were seen as over-excitable, or worse, "khaki-mad." This latter condition filled the columns of newspapers because of the widespread impression that young girls were ruining their reputations running after men in "khaki" uniforms. Soldiers mention their encounters with teenaged girls quite frequently in letters and diaries, so officials did not entirely imagine the threat to public morality that came with concentrations of young men and women near military bases and recreational towns.

For the elderly, war could be a disaster. Many older people relied heavily on younger family members for financial assistance, food, and housing, and as family resources were strained, older family members could be isolated or cut off. Evacuees and refugees who were elderly encountered a particularly difficult transition, and heartrending photographs show the strain of war on the faces of older people. In a time when old age pensions (social security in the United States) were not universally available, many older people lived on the margins even prior to the war. The advent of rationed food meant standing in long queues in order to obtain limited supplies; for many elderly people, this was simply not possible. Those nations with the resources created assistance programs for older people who were dependent on the state.

Age also figured in the lives of those who were too old to serve actively but who were young enough to contribute to the war effort. Some middle-aged men and women worked tirelessly in war service, yet they were demonized as out of touch with the actual war. Returning soldiers often felt a generational gap between the civilian men and women at the home fronts, who had an ultra-patriotic approach to the war, and their own cohort who had experienced the violence and loss of combat. The generational tensions of war provide a recurring theme in postwar memoirs and in contemporaneous poetry, letters, and novels. For those at home, proving patriotism and sacrifice was a vital part of their understanding of the war, but it often clashed with the expectations of those who saw war at close range.

It is important to repeat that there was no singular experience of World War I. Sex, age, class, religion, nationality, disposition, luck—all these things helped determine what the war would mean to individuals and families. What was common to all by 1916 was a kind of fatalism about the war. Few could predict how or when it would end, and the strains of separation and sacrifice had begun to fray the bonds of communities. The year 1916 was marked by major offensives and major casualties on every front, but the hope that it might prove the turning point in the war was mostly an illusion. By December, soldiers and civilians alike were tired of war, and in some cases, they began to resist the demands of their states. This resistance exploded into full-fledged revolution in Russia in 1917, and it led to increasing propaganda and state policy to keep war efforts afloat in other nations.

Conclusion

In December 1916, military and political leaders faced up to the reality of entering another year at war. The year of massive offensives had failed to create the breakthroughs that had been expected. Labor shortages plagued the combatants and led to extreme solutions such as deportation of civilians, forced labor, and hiring of contract laborers from halfway across the world. Civilians and soldiers alike expressed discontent at the prolonged conflict. Shortages in vital war materials and foodstuffs made planning difficult and led to worsening conditions in some major cities and on certain fronts. Few leaders had any idea how to end the war.

Added to the distress of war generally by 1916, the winter of 1916–1917 proved to be one of the coldest on record. Many civilians were already living on reduced rations and ersatz (replacement) products, but this winter brought further fuel and food shortages. The situation was particularly bad in areas cut off by the British blockade, such as Germany, but Russian cities also felt the pinch. Lack of fuel meant the closure of factories, and terrible inflation led to cold, hungry, angry crowds. This terrible winter is usually known as the "turnip winter" primarily because of shortages of a staple food product, potatoes. In Germany, potatoes were replaced by a kind of turnip, the rutabaga, which has a much lower caloric content. With reduced bread rations and watery soup, civilians had to survive a bitterly cold winter. Increasingly it became clear that while battlefield offensives had not ended the war, social upheaval behind the lines might well prove to be the solution to this endless conflict.

Citations

Page   *Source*

71   "He kept us out of war" quoted in Michael S. Neiberg, *The Path to War: How the First World War Created Modern America* (Oxford: Oxford University Press, 2016), 162.

73   "The French lost ..." quoted in Keith Jeffery, *1916: A Global History* (New York: Bloomsbury, 2016), 57.

74   200 000 figure drawn from Hew Strachan, *The First World War* (New York: Viking, 2003), 190.

74   Figures for the first day of the Somme drawn from Peter Hart, *The Somme: The Darkest Hour on the Western Front* (New York: Pegasus Books, 2008), 11.

74   Total Somme casualty figure drawn from Hart, *The Somme*, 528.

74   1.5 million shells figure drawn from Strachan, *The First World War*, 192.

74–5   Background information on the failure of the Somme from Michael S. Neiberg, *Fighting the Great War: A Global History* (Cambridge, MA: Harvard University Press, 2005), 192–193.

75–6   "The Romanian army mobilized ..." quoted in Glenn E. Torrey, *The Romanian Battlefront in World War I* (Lawrence: University Press of Kansas, 2011), 21.

76   70% figure and sergeant's quote from Rob Johnson, *The Great War & the Middle East: A Strategic Study* (Oxford: Oxford University Press, 2016), 205.

79   "The officers you will find ..." quoted in Helen B. McCartney, *Citizen Soldiers: The Liverpool Territorials in the First World War* (Cambridge: Cambridge University Press, 2005), 78.

79   "Just a few lines ..." quoted from the Butling papers, Imperial War Museum.

80   "I live only for you ..." quoted in Martha Hanna, *Your Death Would Be Mine: Paul and Marie Pireaud in the Great War* (Cambridge, MA: Harvard University Press, 2006), 192–193.

80   Information about Sobolewski taken from Andrew Zalewski, *Galician Trails: The Forgotten Story of One Family* (Jenkintown, PA: Thelzo Press, 2012), 266.

80   Information on DORA taken from Tammy M. Proctor, *Female Intelligence: Women and Espionage in the First World War* (New York: New York University Press, 2003), 31.

82   "While our husbands are toiling ..." quoted in Yiğit Akin, "War, Women, and the State: The Politics of Sacrifice in the Ottoman Empire during the First World War," *Journal of Women's History* 26:3 (Fall 2014), 26.

83   Million figure drawn from Andrew Donson, *Youth in the Fatherless Land: War Pedagogy, Nationalism, and Authority in Germany, 1914–1918* (Cambridge, MA: Harvard University Press, 2010), 131.

Select Bibliography

Akin, Yiğit. "War, Women, and the State: The Politics of Sacrifice in the Ottoman Empire during the First World War," *Journal of Women's History*, 26:3 (Fall 2014), 12–35.

Broadberry, Stephen, and Mark Harrison, eds. *Economics of World War I*. Cambridge: Cambridge University Press, 2005.

Donson, Andrew. *Youth in the Fatherless Land: War Pedagogy, Nationalism, and Authority in Germany, 1914–1918.* Cambridge, MA: Harvard University Press, 2010.

Hanna, Martha. *Your Death Would Be Mine: Paul and Marie Pireaud in the Great War.* Cambridge, MA: Harvard University Press, 2006.

Hart, Peter. *The Great War: A Combat History of the First World War.* Oxford: Oxford University Press, 2013.

Hart, Peter. *The Somme: The Darkest Hour on the Western Front.* New York: Pegasus Books, 2008.

Hochschild, Adam. *To End All Wars: A Story of Loyalty and Rebellion, 1914–1918.* Boston, MA: Houghton Mifflin Harcourt, 2011.

Jeffery, Keith. *1916: A Global History.* New York: Bloomsburg, 2016.

Johnson, Rob. *The Great War & the Middle East: A Strategic Study.* Oxford: Oxford University Press, 2016.

Mayhew, Emily. *Wounded: A New History of the Western Front in World War I.* Oxford: Oxford University Press, 2014.

McCartney, Helen B. *Citizen Soldiers: The Liverpool Territorials in the First World War.* Cambridge: Cambridge University Press, 2005.

Morrow, Jr., John H. *The Great War: An Imperial History.* London and New York: Routledge, 2010.

Neiberg, Michael S. *Fighting the Great War: A Global History.* Cambridge, MA: Harvard University Press, 2005.

Neiberg, Michael S. *The Path to War: How the First World War Created Modern America.* Oxford: Oxford University Press, 2016.

Proctor, Tammy M. *Civilians in a World at War, 1914–1918.* New York: New York University Press, 2010.

Proctor, Tammy M. *Female Intelligence: Women and Espionage in the First World War.* New York: New York University Press, 2003.

Stoff, Laurie. *They Fought for the Motherland: Russia's Women Soldiers in World War I and the Revolution.* Lawrence: University of Kansas Press, 2006.

Strachan, Hew. *The First World War.* New York: Viking, 2003.

Torrey, Glenn E. *The Romanian Battlefront in World War I.* Lawrence: University Press of Kansas, 2011.

Zalewski, Andrew. *Galician Trails: The Forgotten Story of One Family.* Jenkintown, PA: Thelzo Press, 2012.

Appendix 4.1: Timeline for 1916

1916	IMPORTANT EVENTS OF THE WAR	BATTLE
January 1	British victory in Cameroon	
February 21	Germans launch offensive at Verdun	Battle of Verdun
March 9	Italians launch offensive in the Julian Alps	Fifth Battle of the Isonzo
April 24	Beginning of the Easter Rising in Dublin	
April 29	Surrender of British garrison at Kut	Battle of Kut
May 15	Austrians launch offensive in the Tyrol	Asiago Offensive
May 31	Britain and Germany face off in a naval battle	Battle of Jutland
June 4	Russian launch offensive against Austria-Hungary	Brusilov Offensive
June 5	HMS *Hampshire* sunk by mine (Kitchener died)	
July 1	British launch offensive against Germany	Battle of the Somme
August 27	Romania joins the war on the Allied side	

5

1917. How Did War Affect the Societies and People Who Participated?

Figure 5.1 In addition to millions of soldiers drawn into war service, millions of civilian women, men, and children performed war work at home and abroad. Here an American woman volunteer works behind the lines in France. *Source*: U.S. Army Signal Corps #21357, Record Group 111, National Archives and Records Administration.

World War I: A Short History, First Edition. Tammy M. Proctor.
© 2018 John Wiley & Sons Ltd. Published 2018 by John Wiley & Sons Ltd.

A ship's passenger alighting at the French port of Boulogne in the first week of September 1917 would have seen a surprising sight on the docks. Amongst the normal rush of carts, baggage, freight, and ship's personnel, the passenger would have observed a parade of Chinese laborers on their way to work unloading ships full of Argentinian beef. These Chinese civilian contractors might have passed another contingent of Egyptian laborers headed to their job sites, and it would not have been unusual for nearly a dozen other groups of laborers, organized by colonial or national status to be working on that September morning. Another thing might have caught the passenger's eye—damage to nearby buildings and streets from an aerial bombing raid just a few days before, which also killed some of the Egyptian and Chinese workers. Finally, the last thing our passenger might have observed were the large US ships now in port after the American entry into the war in April 1917. These ships had black and white zig-zag shapes or "dazzle paint" to camouflage them as they sailed in Atlantic waters.

This snapshot of a day in the life of a busy port such as Boulogne speaks to the deep impact of World War I on societies around the world. The long war, which was into its third year by 1917, had necessitated the reorganization of industry, transport, communication, and labor, both at home and at the various fronts of the war. Massive and costly government bureaucracies developed to manage these transformations, which by 1917 had expanded into a true modern war machine. This chapter outlines some of the major transformations of wartime societies in order to accommodate what seemed to be an endless war in three different kinds of settings, namely home fronts, battle zones, and occupied regions. Each faced a different set of challenges but each relied on an exploitation of resources and humans on a large scale in order to continue the war. By 1917, populations had grown weary of war, and the fraying social and political fabric had become readily apparent. Also, the main belligerents in the war were transformed as a result of the events of 1917—the United States entered the war, and the Russian Empire began a slow exodus that would culminate in a 1918 treaty.

Battles of Support 1917

For military and civilian leaders alike, 1917 became the year of shortages, where the endless question of how to provision and supply the fronts dominated conversations and policies. The rationing, labor shortages, and governmental demands for sacrifice and vigilance on the home fronts had a focus, namely supplying a seemingly endless conflict in the combat zones. By 1917, shortages in certain chemicals or raw materials led to backups in munitions production in multiple settings. Problems of transport of goods also became an issue, and it was necessary to find more labor for the combat zones as well as the staging areas, railheads, and ports. Four major strategies were developed to deal with labor shortages in the battle zones themselves.

First, civilian contractors were hired from around the world to travel in order to work for the war efforts. In addition to the Chinese and Egyptian laborers mentioned at the beginning of the chapter, colonial citizens from European empires were hired or sometimes impressed for war work. The French contracted laborers from Indochina and Algeria, but they also recruited guest workers from nearby neutral nations such as Spain. British imperial laborers came from all parts of the world including tiny islands such as the Seychelles and major population centers in India. On other fronts, millions of African civilians worked as carriers for the armies in East Africa (on both sides), while the Ottomans and the British both hired porters and casual laborers from among local populations living near to the fronts. In the Russian Empire, ethnic and religious minorities were drafted as laborers, and the armies at every front employed local civilians for tasks such as laundry, food preparation, and other services.

The second strategy for finding enough workers for the fronts came from expanding the ages and restrictions on conscripts. Many states raised their draft age to include older men, who were then assigned as laborers or to policing in occupied and combat zones. The addition of new allies, such as the United States, also brought new workers. The United States drafted men directly into labor battalions, known at the Service of Supply; many of these recruits were racial minorities such as African-Americans or men considered unfit for combat because of illiteracy or other problems. Children were given holidays from school to help with harvest or to do other war collection (e.g., scrap metal or wool drives). In some cases, auxiliary armies of women were recruited to provide labor at the fronts so that more men could be released for combat. Examples of such auxiliaries include the Women's Army Auxiliary Corps (Britain), the Australian Women's Service Corps, and the Women's Auxiliary Labor Force in the Field (Austria-Hungary), just to name a few.

Third, states used captive populations as labor. Millions of able-bodied men were confined to POW camps, so by 1916 and 1917, most of the combatant governments released some of these men for labor in agriculture and industry. Prisoners worked under a number of arrangements, usually in day-labor groups from the camps or in residential assignments at farms, villages, or industrial zones. POW laborers wore uniforms, caps, or identifying bands to show their status, and they often received pay for their work.

Finally, some states used forced labor to meet their production needs, and, if necessary, deported men and women to other regions for work duties. One of the most highly publicized deportations of laborers occurred in 1916 when roughly 25 000 men, women, and teens were relocated from Lille, France, to other regions by the German occupying authorities. While only about a third of the deportees were women, they became the focus of Allied propaganda regarding German morality and war practices. Most of the Lille deportees did road work or helped with agriculture, but Allied media lingered on the impropriety of taking young women and girls from their homes. Other deportees in Poland, for instance, also worked in gangs to clear forests, repair roads, or tend crops, but their plight was not highlighted in the same way. Forced labor and deportations were on the whole a temporary phenomenon in World War I, but the use of civilian populations for forced labor did set a precedent that would be exploited on a much larger scale in World War II.

Germany provides a good example of the massive mobilization of labor in World War I. By 1917, Germany employed more than 300 000 foreign contract laborers in industry and approximately 60 000 forced laborers from occupied zones. A public outcry led to the return of most of the forced laborers by the end of that year. The bulk of agricultural and industrial labor, however, had moved to prisoners of war. Roughly 1.7 million prisoners worked in industry and agriculture in Germany and their occupied zones by 1917.

The problem of labor, both at home and in the battle zones, was never really solved. The needs of wartime exceeded the human capacity of many of the nation-states in the war, and this led to difficulties in supply, which in turn led to morale problems. In addition to shortages of human labor, increasingly states experienced shortages in suitable animals for labor. Millions of horses, camels, mules, donkeys, oxen, dogs, pigeons, and other animals also got "drafted" for service in the war. Repeated requisitioning of animals at the home front left civilians without the service of animals for farming or transport. In some cases, livelihoods were destroyed as small vendors were left without an animal to pull a cart, or a small farm could find no suitable animal for hitching to a plow. All of these animals needed to be fed, housed, and cared for, and as the war dragged on, the losses mounted of both animals and their human handlers. One of the real headaches of managing animals at the front lines was finding enough fodder. At the fronts, animals saw extensive service hauling artillery and guns as well as supply wagons, but as the war continued and resources became more scarce, armies turned to more mechanized vehicles out of necessity.

Mechanized transport, in fact, may have been the most important technological innovation of the war. Motor cars, trucks, motorcycles, railways, and trams all featured in transport at the fronts. Of course, a number of these modern machines required a raw material as well—gasoline, which was rationed in many countries. They also depended upon the work of mechanics who could repair and maintain their tricky internal workings. A good example of the use of both animal-drawn and motorized vehicles to supply front lines is *La Voie Sacrée*, or the Sacred Way that linked the French effort at Verdun with its nearest railhead, 50 miles away. This one tiny road supported a constant flow of motor vehicles, munitions, food, supplies, animals, and men throughout the battle. Trucks, motorcycles, and bicycles moved alongside horse-drawn artillery and men on foot from rail hub to trenches. Other fronts featured similar supply trains—in the Palestine campaign, British supply lines broke down and had to be reestablished with tracks carrying goods from the railheads to camel convoys, who delivered them to the fronts. Innovations in logistics, transport, and supply were important to the war's development.

Sometimes logistical triumphs emboldened the efforts of military leaders as was the case with French General Robert Nivelle, who launched a disastrous 1916-style offensive at Chemin des Dames in April 1917, which proved to be one of the most momentous battles of 1917. Nivelle envisaged a coordinated British attack at Arras, a different part of the front, which he hoped would surprise the Germans. The British moved thousands of men and amassed soldiers and supplies in underground caverns before the attack. In terrible wet weather, the British attacked and pushed back the German lines, recapturing key areas such as Vimy Ridge. However, the attack soon stalled, and the trenches reformed and stabilized so that no further progress was possible after the first week of movement. The initial British success might have allowed for broader success had the French made progress, but instead the Germans had prepared much more fully for the French assault at Chemin des Dames.

Nivelle's grand idea had been that the British would divert German attention and allow the French to make a breakthrough in the lines using improved and speedier transport, supply, and protection. Nivelle stockpiled ammunition, built new rail links and fortified positions in preparation. However, the Germans had already retreated from a large area in front of the French lines to their newly-fortified Hindenburg Line of trenches, leaving nothing but devastation in their wake. They also had good intelligence on the French plans, so they had planned for the attack with reinforced machine gun nests. As one historian has noted, "If the Germans had been surprised at Vimy-Arras, it was to be the other way about on the Aisne, where evidence of a great offensive in preparation had alerted the Germans to what Nivelle intended." The first day was a debacle for the French army, and by the end of the opening week of the battle, the situation had only worsened. More than 30000 French soldiers died and another 100000 were wounded in that week alone. Despite this disaster, Nivelle ordered a continuation; it took an order from President Poincaré to end the offensive. Public outcry led the president to replace Nivelle with a new general, Philippe Pétain.

The end result of this failure at Chemin des Dames was a series of incidents of both "collective indiscipline" and outright mutiny in French army units in April and May 1917. Groups of soldiers, perhaps as many as 35000 in total, refused to enter front-line trenches and issued lists of demands. Some of these mutineers took trains to French cities and left the frontline areas altogether during the incident; others sat down and refused to move. Authorities acted quickly to arrest ringleaders and to make promises of change in leadership and strategy. Most of the demonstrations ended by June, but this scenario remained a frightening possibility for the armies at war. In fact, by 1917, the maintenance of soldiers' morale became a paramount concern for military planners.

Soldiers concerned themselves with more than their own lives at the front. They were not cut off from what was happening at home, and the letters from family and friends created a pretty clear picture of life in the cities and countryside. Soldiers knew about shortages, censorship, work requirements, and civilian morale, and sometimes they resented the complaints of their loved ones at home and expressed frustration. More often, however, soldiers began to question the war, understandably wondering if their presence at home might not be more beneficial to the nation and certainly to their families. The mutineers of 1917, for instance, were more likely to be married men chafing at their enforced absence from loved ones and their lack of leave. Home was a potent motivating factor for those fighting in the war, which exercised a strong pull. Vasily Mishnin, a soldier in the Russian Army encapsulates this sentiment in a diary entry on December 31, 1916: "Let such a year as this die for ever and never come back ... I want to be happy. Instead, there are tears in my eyes. Oh Lord, what is this and when will it end?" As this quotation suggests, civilians were not the only ones who felt the war was dragging on too long. Like civilians, soldiers waited for news of a breakthrough that might lead to an end to the conflict.

Unfortunately, for most soldiers, the war only intensified in 1917. The British began a quest to retake control of Mesopotamia after their defeat at Kut in 1916, and Russian forces fought on even after the first Russian Revolution in spring 2017. However, some of the worst combat experienced during the war took place in the autumn of 1917. In the Julian Alps, Italian forces suffered a devastating defeat in October when a combined German–Habsburg force launched an offensive in the mountains near Caporetto (now named Kobarid, Slovenia). The attackers moved soldiers, guns, and ammunition into position slowly and secretly over several weeks before beginning the battle with an artillery barrage of chlorine and phosgene gas shells on October 24. Italian gas masks were inadequate, and the first casualties of the campaign were gas victims. The ensuing battle was a disaster for the Italian army, who were totally unprepared for the assault. One particularly famous action was the capture of a high mountain summit by Erwin Rommel and his German detachment, who with only 100 men captured a whole Italian brigade and took control of the Matajur peak in "fifty-two hours of almost nonstop advancing." Altogether the Italians were pushed back more than 100 miles and "lost 10,000 killed, 30,000 wounded, 293,000 taken prisoner, and another 400,000 to desertion—733,000 men, over a third of the entire army" at Caporetto. The news could hardly have been worse for the Allied forces.

Yet more bad news continued to plague all the armies on the Western Front. The French, of course, had suffered mightily at the Chemin des Dames, but both sides faced abominable weather conditions and high casualties in the waning months of 1917. Two events, part of one massive British offensive at Messines and Passchendaele (also known as the Third Battle of Ypres), created a horrifying landscape for all the soldiers involved. The British artillery barrage, underground mine explosions, and aerial bombing combined to create massive craters and shell holes that turned into death traps for men, animals and vehicles as weeks of torrential rain commenced. One British officer described the scene thus: "We splashed and slithered, and dragged our feet from the pull of an invisible enemy determined to suck us into its depths … the swamp swallowed its scream-ing victims, and we had to be ordered to plod on …" Despite fatigue, heavy losses, and poor morale, the fighting continued into December. One large battle at Cambrai launched on November 20 featured a glimpse into the future of fighting. The British employed a new technology in force at Cambrai by using more than 300 armored tanks followed by infantry. The Germans fell back when their bullets failed to penetrate the tanks' armored surfaces. A German officer noted their shock at the ranks of metal tanks: "We could have dealt with men of flesh and blood like ourselves, but we were defenceless against these armoured machines." What looked initially like a British victory with this surprise tactic disappeared with a German counterattack a few days later. These campaigns, particularly the sodden nightmare of Passchendaele, made it clear for all to see that neither the strategies of the past nor technologies of the future were working in this war.

Fighting the War at Home

One of the first concerns of any of the nations involved in fighting was control of industrial production and military supply. It was immediately clear in 1914 that many important industries such as fuel, transport, munitions production, and communication would need to be highly regulated or even nationalized in order to supply the war effort. Particular areas of the economy became "neces-sary" for national defense, so munitions workers, miners, railway personnel, and other industrial laborers found themselves enmeshed in the war through their regular occupations. For example, in December 1917, US President Woodrow Wilson announced his government's plans to assume federal control of the nation's railways as a wartime measure, telling the nation in his speech that "this is a war of resources no less than of men … and it is necessary for the complete mobilization of our resources that the transportation systems of the country should be organized and employed under a single authority …" Similarly, Germany assumed complete control of its coal industry in July 1915 and announced the creation of a syndicate to regulate this wartime necessity. In fact, most of the belligerents to some extent nationalized key industries in the name of war expediency and necessity.

Another area that governmental officials sought to organize and control was food production, pricing, and distribution, using a variety of systems. Germany and Austria, for instance, moved in 1915 to establish a series of *Zentralen* (central commodities bureaus) for each area of food production and for many other raw materials as well. These "Centrals" were really cartels based around particular industries. What this meant in practice was that a Central, such as the Potato Central, would regulate farm production and transport of potatoes. The Centrals would also fix prices and oversee rationing of the potatoes to the civilian and military consumers. Britain and France also controlled prices and production, but through less centralized mechanisms than the Centrals. Most countries also set up limited or full-scale rationing of goods such as potatoes, bread, sugar, and fuel, which required supervision of production and distribution of goods at the local level. Supplies of these basics varied widely during the war and possession of a ration card did not always mean that local supplies were ample to meet all the demands.

Given this situation, black markets for food became a feature of daily life in home fronts. Arrest reports in European cities document people of all ages smuggling butter, potatoes, sugar, and other staples. Fights broke out in food queues, farmers reported the pillaging of their crops, and officials tried to regulate hoarding. As war deprivation and shortages mounted, officials created substitute or altered foods. One well-known example was German K-Brot or *Kriegsbrot* (War Bread), which was a dark, heavy bread made with multiple grains and sometimes with other fillers and adulterated ingredients, such as sawdust. During the European-wide potato shortage in the winter of 1916–1917, known as the "turnip winter," many civilians ate rutabagas and turnips as potato substitutes. Local officials tried to help households in preparing new or substitute products by publishing recipes in newspapers or in some cases by producing war cookbooks. In the United States, which did not ration food during the war, Food Administrator Herbert Hoover urged housewives to conserve food for the war effort by practicing "wheatless" and "meatless" days at least once per week. The United States had plentiful supplies of agricultural goods, but Hoover also thought that American voluntarism was strong enough that rationing was not necessary.

One of the reasons why civilian populations faced food and commodity shortages is that the war machine required a tremendous supply of goods for its men in the field, but the other important factor is that by 1917 shortages of labor had severely limited production. Particularly hard hit were agricultural areas. Conscription of the male population combined with requisitioning of draft animals (horses, oxen, mules) brought many towns and villages to crisis conditions.

Those who managed to get crops into the field sometimes were not sure how they would find the personnel to harvest the food. Shortages of chemical fertilizer exacerbated the farming problems when many of these chemicals were requisitioned for use in munitions. One of the solutions used by states such as the Russian Empire, Germany, and France was to employ prisoners of war in agricultural work behind the lines. Prisoners worked and often lived with farm families in conditions that in many cases were better than the camps to which they had been confined. Other ways of dealing with the problem of agriculture included brief furloughs during harvest times for soldiers at the fronts, release of schoolchildren for field work, and employment of women. All of these solutions upset the normal operation of life in rural areas.

Agricultural and industrial production were key to any state's war effort, but so too was war financing. Each of the nations involved in war went to their citizenry to ask for donations to the cause, usually in the form of taxes and war bonds. These so-called war loans supported the necessary wartime expansion but they also insured that everyday people were invested in the war—literally. From children in Germany who could buy an iron nail and then knock it into a wooden cross in the center of town to those living in Austria who could purchase a "child bond," people of all ages had a financial stake in the war itself. Girl Scouts in the United States sold Liberty Loans on street corners, and kids in Britain purchased Victory Bonds at school. Adults, of course, invested even more heavily in war bonds. Even those who did not willingly purchase a war bond felt the financial pinch of the war, usually through higher taxes. When shortages of funds threatened, some combatants, such as the Ottoman Empire, printed money to meet its costs, thereby creating an inflationary price spiral by late in the war.

Government-sponsored propaganda played an important part in all of these efforts to involve the population in wartime efforts to increase industry, agriculture, and financing. Civil officials produced posters, films, consumer items, recipe guides, books, games, and artwork to encourage a patriotic spirit of sacrifice among its citizenry. Often this state-sponsored propaganda called for people to remember their civic duty, as with a French poster that told civilians "To not waste bread is your duty" or an American poster that admonished, "Food is ammunition—don't waste it!" Those who did not contribute were depicted as shameful shirkers of their responsibilities as citizens. These official efforts at drumming up support for the war effort were supplemented by private organizations who also solicited money and time from civilians in support of refugee assistance, prisoner of war work, and other war charities. It is not surprising that a certain war weariness marked civilian letters and diaries by the last year of the war.

Government officials worried and watched civilian morale, and wartime censorship allowed most states to read private mail of soldiers and also of civilians. Using massive postal censorship offices, officials monitored everyday sentiment in the cities and at the fronts. States also aimed to control the messages that circulated regarding the war, so many newspapers and other forms of media were subject to censorship as well. State propaganda organizations created appropriate messages for distribution to the public at home, in some cases using well-known authors, artists, and actors to publicize the message. For those seeking to subvert or undermine the official message regarding the war, governments passed legislation that allowed imprisonment for sedition and unpatriotic language. These sweeping governmental powers led to the arrest of socialists in the United States, pacifists in Britain, religious and ethnic minorities in the Russian Empire, Armenians in the Ottoman Empire, and Indian nationalists in the British Empire, just to name a few of the groups targeted by war emergency measures.

Civilians also could face espionage charges for passing information to people in other countries or for suspicious activity at home. As early as 1914, there were spy panics in the combatant countries. Vigilant citizens accosted foreigners, reported their neighbors, and spread rumors about the spies living in plain sight. Especially as the war dragged on into its third and fourth years, those identified as dangerous could find themselves imprisoned or even killed. In France, the officials overseeing the 1917 trial of Mata Hari, an exotic dancer and courtesan accused of espionage, condemned her as an "enemy within" as much for her perceived social deviance as for any real information she was able to impart to the Germans. A similar case emerged in Britain in 1918 where a libel trial also featured an actress/exotic dancer, Maud Allan, who was accused by an ultra-nationalist Member of Parliament of both perversity and passing secrets to the enemy. Allan, a Canadian, faced accusations of espionage, perversity, and moral degradation after she performed the play *Salome* in London in 1918. The subsequent trial showcased societal fears about the impact of war on public morals and on safety of the nation. Both the Allan trial and the execution of Mata Hari also highlighted how gender roles in wartime became magnified; both women were marked as "unfeminine" and "improper."

Certainly critics of the war did exist. An increasingly vocal minority living in the belligerent states began clamoring for an end to the bloodshed. Some of these voices were political radicals, such as Vladimir Lenin, who led the Bolshevik Revolution in the Russian Empire in fall 1917, or Rosa Luxemburg in Germany, a Marxist who sought unity of workers across national lines. Others were families who had suffered great losses and whose grief spilled into public calls for an end to the violence. Still others were soldiers who risked their lives in order to denounce the war. These calls for an end to war also reverberated in the halls of power. Woodrow Wilson made it known in a famous January 1917 speech that he would help broker a "peace without victory" if the warring nations would be willing. When that plea did not work and the war continued, some nations sued for peace separately by March 1918, including Romania and the former Russian Empire (soon to be known as the USSR).

One final area that is important for understanding the civilian experience of war in 1914–1918 is that those on the home front were subject to injury, illness, and death due to war. High-minded talk of the rights of victims and the founding of international peace organizations in the years prior to World War I made it seem as if civilians might have some protection in time of conflict. In fact, civilians faced great privation, loss of livelihood, and in some cases, violence from the war. Aerial bombing, an innovation of World War I, meant that civilians living quietly at home, far from a fighting front could still die from a bomb dropped out of the skies by an airplane or zeppelin. Others died in munitions explosions, such as the massive blast at Halifax, Nova Scotia (Canada) in December 1917 when a munitions ship collided in the harbor with a Belgian food relief ship. In addition to these violent deaths, the rise in infectious diseases as a result of wartime mobility and shortages of staples of daily life such as fabric, food, and soap led to epidemic rates of tuberculosis, skin diseases, sicknesses associated with malnutrition (such as rickets and scurvy), and later, influenza.

The escalation of civilian problems is most apparent by 1917. Food shortages and rationing led to black markets and smuggling, which broke down the social fabric of communities. This breakdown of trust and responsibility in turn fueled fear of internal threats—the enemy within—creating public condemnations that solidified this anxiety. Ultimately, these strains destroyed some political and social entities entirely, especially when public trust gave way to civil unrest and revolution. These civil difficulties also tied into problems at the battlefronts, where soldiers knew from letters and visits what was happening at home. These soldiers also faced some of the same anxieties, shortages, and problems.

Behind Barbed Wire

Soldiers and civilians had some measure of control over their wartime lives, at least in the small decisions. However, prisoners of war had no control over their lives. An important feature of World War I was the creation of complete prison societies around the world for military personnel and civilians. These wartime complexes ranged in size from a few hundred people to tens of thousands living behind barbed wire as prisoners of war. Some had been captured in battle and spent the rest of their war as military prisoners in camps for officers or ordinary soldiers. Others never saw any fighting, but instead were arrested as civilians for being of an "enemy" nationality. Finally, men and women who were considered dissidents, spies, or disruptive influences on the wartime populace also found themselves behind bars or barbed wire. This last group was comparatively small, but it included pacifists, socialists, spies, saboteurs, and prostitutes.

For prisoners, the war was both distant and immediate. They suffered from lack of information and chafed at the immobility of their lives. Many of the

POWs and internees wrote in letters and diaries about the boredom and confinement they were experiencing, but a good number participated as well in the creation of prison societies. Camps that had been temporary shelters for prisoners turned into cosmopolitan and even sophisticated dwellings. Prisoners came from all walks of life and from different occupational backgrounds, so these prison cities featured the skills and talents of their inhabitants. Henri Pirenne, a well-known scholar of European history who was arrested by the Germans as a dissident in 1916, held university lectures in economic history for men at Holzminden, an internment camp in Germany filled with civilian internees from France, Belgium, Poland, Russia, and Britain. This camp also had a women's sub-camp, so a few weeks later, Pirenne also began lecturing in the women's university, which featured courses in history and language (German, Flemish, French, and English). Pirenne also recorded the life of the camp—noting the presence of sporting events such as tennis and football (soccer), as well as concerts and theatrical productions. Like Holzminden, other internment and POW camps had a range of activities and educational offerings, but they also featured vendors and service providers. Cafes, shops, canteens, and restaurants emerged along with booths for engravers, cobblers, dentists, and tailors. Men set up tables in courtyards in order to play chess and other board games.

Many of those living in the camps, despite having guards and commandants in place, created political systems for themselves. Barracks or buildings had captains who then worked to negotiate with camp authorities for better food or conditions; these captains also served as an important liaison with inspectors sent from neutral countries to make sure international guidelines for humane treatment were observed. Barracks captains also played a political role as mayors for the camps or sub-camps. In some cases, inmates held elections complete with political campaigns. One important feature of these camps that was quite different in World War I from the concentration camps of World War II, was that most were organized along national and class lines. Officers had separate facilities from enlisted men, and in civilian camps, some barracks or areas were set aside as "privilege camps" for those with the money to pay for better facilities. Privileged prisoners could access bank accounts and officers received pay from their countries, so both groups had the ability to hire other prisoners as servants and to buy luxuries. Divisions also occurred because of race and religion, with practicing Jewish or Muslim prisoners, for instance, living in separate facilities with kosher or halal kitchens in many of the camps.

The prison societies of World War I had swelled in size by 1917, and while accurate statistics are hard to calculate, the number in captivity certainly exceeded six million. For those living behind barbed wire, 1917 brought new fears as shortages in foodstuffs led to reduced rations in the camps themselves. Even worse, those in captivity in the Russian Empire found that they were given their freedom in fall 1917 in the wake of the Revolution, only to realize that they had to find transport home. Harrowing stories of POWs making their way back to the Ottoman Empire or to Austria on foot from camps deep in the heart of Russia abound from late 1917 and early 1918. Some people took pity on these POWs and provided food, shelter, or transport, but for many, the release from captivity was probably worse than their imprisonment, given the uncertainty of finding food and shelter during their journeys.

One final thing is important to remember about those who went through the war as prisoners and internees. Their status in a postwar world was difficult. Enemy aliens faced two equally terrible scenarios—returning to their adopted homes to find their houses and possessions gone, or being repatriated to countries where they no longer had ties. For military prisoners, their return home often led to questions about their courage in battle and about their sacrifices for the nation. Were they heroes or cowards? Had they served their countries? Such questions complicated homecomings for those who had lived behind barbed wire.

Under Foreign Occupation

If internment and prison camps were the ultimate in constructed wartime societies, occupied regions also competed for the title of most artificial creation of the war. People who lived under occupation faced a strange mix of normal everyday political, social, and community structures with a layer of bureaucracy imposed by their foreign overlords. For many, this created a cognitive dissonance between the uncertainty and false "life" of wartime and the normal ordinary facts of everyday existence. The vacuum in which occupied societies existed, where information and movement was highly controlled, contributed to a sense of unreality. The level of control by occupying authorities varied widely depending on how long an area was occupied, its location in relationship to the battle zones, and the resources the region brought to the struggle.

One of the common experiences for occupied populations in wartime was the experience of requisitions. Occupying authorities expected all of the regions under their control to contribute to their war efforts, whether they wanted to do so or not. This meant massive requisitioning of crops, manufactured products, and raw materials. A woman in Brussels described such requisitions in her diary, noting that everything from copper teapots to woolen mattresses to family dogs could be claimed by the Germans for the war effort. Likewise, in Poland, civilians suffered from relentless requisitioning of household items (especially metal), and they faced real scarcity in food by the end of the war. In Romania, quinine was seized and distributed to German troops stationed in malarial zones, leaving the civil population without this drug. All occupied regions suffered from shortages of soap (which contributed to disease), leather for boots and shoes, fabric for clothing, and basic foodstuffs because of widespread requisitioning.

For most occupied areas, the war brought hardship. Many people lost their livelihoods through unemployment or requisitioning, and food shortages were common throughout occupied regions. In Belgium, the creation of the Commission for Relief in Belgium, an American-led food aid project, meant that most families in Belgium and Northern France had access to food, clothing, and supplies during the war. This organization used young male American delegates to supervise food and clothing distribution to needy Belgians of all ages, insuring that both the German guarantee not to seize the food and the British guarantee to allow the food through the blockade were honored. In other regions, most notably Serbia and Romania, conditions were terrible. Epidemic disease, malnutrition, and lack of fuel created misery for civil populations in those areas. As the war efforts of each occupier waxed and waned, occupied populations felt the pinch of increased surveillance or the loosening of restrictions. Perhaps what most marked these societies under occupation was the sense of loss of control and uncertainty. The whims of the occupying officials marked the lives of those living in their care, and those whims could be terrifying.

Some occupied regions became the subjects of social experiments by the authorities charged with their control. Most of these occupations had the potential to become permanent colonies for the occupiers, so they began reshaping the areas under their control to meet postwar needs. A good example is the Japanese occupation of Micronesia (*Nan'yo*) from 1914 to the end of the war. The Japanese, who expected to make these islands permanent parts of their empire, sent experts to map, photograph, and study the island. They also built infrastructure and industry, including roads, harbors, and sugar plantations. Micronesian children took Japanese language class, and Japanese settlers moved to the islands during the war. By 1920, more than a quarter of the population of Saipan was Japanese, and the islands had undergone several years of Japanization. These efforts paid off for Japan as most of Micronesia remained under nominal Japanese control as a League of Nations mandate after World War I. Japanese settlement and business enterprises continued in the postwar period and until the islands were transferred to US control after World War II.

Another occupation zone molded by social experimentation was the German-occupied *Ober Ost* in modern Latvia, Estonia, Belarus, and Lithuania. While nearby Poland was under civil occupation and kept many of its local officials and structures in place, the *Ober Ost* became a kind of "military Utopia" for officials, who sought to reshape this land for German settlement. As in Japanese-controlled Micronesia, the German *Ober Ost* quickly populated with experts who studied the region and made recommendations. The authorities systematically stripped the region of resources for the war effort, taxed its citizens, and established a punitive regime that featured massive requisitions and forced labor battalions of up to 60 000 people. Local residents resented the high-handed intervention of occupiers in their lives. Germans mapped and redistricted, moved populations, reshaped farmland and forests, and forced city-folk to attend mandatory bathing events at public baths. These policies led to underground resistance, strikes, and famine conditions in some areas, and this experiment in creating a new land for German settlement ultimately failed.

Even when large-scale social experiments were not the objective of occupiers, they still undoubtedly shaped and changed the societies that they controlled. In Belgium, the German authorities sought to find sympathetic people among the Flemish speakers of the land, seeing them as Germanic-speakers who shared a culture and identity with Germans. The occupiers closed French-language universities such as the University of Ghent and reopened them with Flemish-only classes. They also enforced pro–Flemish policies (*Flamenpolitik*) that fanned the flames of Flemish nationalism, contributing to the growth of a vocal Flemish activism in the twentieth century. Likewise in Poland, the German Governor-General, Hans Hartwig von Beseler, also created new entities when the Germans assumed control after the Russian retreat. The Germans reopened Warsaw University as a Polish-language institution and seemed to be supporting limited Polish self-governance, but the Germans didn't reap the benefits they expected in terms of goodwill and cooperation.

One other feature of occupied societies was resistance. People living under the control of foreign authorities used everything from passive resistance techniques to outright violence as tools for coping. Spy networks in occupied zones passed information to outside nations, either out of patriotism or for money, and these intelligence networks often served as resistance groups as well. In Belgium, civilians relied on underground newspapers and postal systems as informal information networks, often mocking the German officials for their inability to locate the couriers or the printing presses. Famously, Belgian resistors delivered the underground newspaper *La Libre Belgique* to the German Governor-General's office without detection. Belgians also refused to abide by "German time," insisting on showing up at official appointments on "Belgian time," which was an hour different.

In other areas, resistance turned to conflict. The *Ober Ost*, with its harsh military regime, witnessed serious violence as partisans assassinated German soldiers, sabotaged German installations, and tried to disrupt the plans of occupiers. Occupying authorities posted warnings against partisan activity and even offered rewards for information on subversive activity, but these strategies had little effect. In the Balkans, Serb guerillas known as *Komitadjis* attacked local officials and occupation troops in 1918 when the countryside turned toward lawlessness and civil war. In short, a whole range of responses emerged during the war to the experience of occupation.

Societies at war were diverse places. People faced uncertainty and shifting centers of authority, whether they were in front-line trenches or in an occupied region in the Pacific. The war made normal life difficult as families worried about their loved ones, fretted about where to obtain food, and tried to adjust to the changing political and social restrictions of wartime life.

The Impact of the United States

While the United States did not formally enter the war until April 1917, the nation was not entirely a bystander in the conflict. Beginning in November 1914, Americans undertook a project to provision Belgium as a neutral nation. Led by an unknown but wealthy engineer, Herbert Hoover, the Commission for Relief in Belgium arranged shipping, inspection, distribution, and accounting for a large-scale food project assisted by representatives from Spain and the Netherlands (also neutrals) and from Belgium and France. The United States also arranged loans, particularly to Allied forces, and it provided arms, food, and supplies to both sides, beginning in 1914. By 1915, most of the munitions, food, and other trade items went to the Allies because it became increasingly difficult to transport them to Germany through the British blockade. These wartime demands for goods led to a US economic boom during its "neutral" period, which meant that the American economy had already ramped up its production even before the nation formally entered the war.

Beginning in 1914, some private US citizens volunteered for war service as well, often in medical or humanitarian endeavors. Anne Morgan, the daughter of banker J. P. Morgan, established a charitable foundation to help rebuild devastated villages in France known as the American Fund for French Wounded. Other Americans from the Society of Friends (Quakers) joined British "Friends" in doing similar work with refugees in destroyed French villages. Doctors, nurses, and volunteers spent time working for the American Red Cross and other organizations such as the YMCA. A few Americans even joined foreign military formations such as the Lafayette Escadrille (a French-led American air squadron) or the Canadian Army. Recent immigrants to the United States sometimes returned to their homes to fight as draftees as well, as was the case with many Italians who had been living in the United States when Italy joined the war in 1915.

The United States also provided inspection and diplomatic services for the nations at war, brokering deals and facilitating conversations between belligerents. As a neutral nation, one valuable service the United States provided was in negotiating exchanges of prisoners, and American diplomats played an important role in conducting independent inspections of prison camps. Civilian and military prisoners from multiple countries petitioned US diplomats for better food or housing conditions, others protested what they saw as unjust imprisonment. In each case, American officials conducted investigations. These positive roles for the United States as a neutral country were counterbalanced by the American government's exploitation of the wartime problems of competing nations to further its own agenda and concerns. A good example of this is the US strategy of expanding its trade presence in Latin America in the face of British blacklisting of German companies.

Although the United States was not at war, neither was it entirely at peace in the period before formally entering World War I. Under the terms of the Monroe doctrine, the United States had increasingly found reason to intervene in the nations of Central and South America. So when political instability threatened in Haiti in 1915, President Woodrow Wilson dispatched Marines to protect US strategic and economic interests in the region. He also wanted to forestall any European intervention. This US occupation and policing of Haiti continued until 1934, when troops left, but US companies and officials remained. Wilson also became involved in the revolution going on in Mexico after repeated strikes on US civilians in border zones by Pancho Villa, one of the rebel leaders. John J. Pershing, later commander of the American Expeditionary Force in World War I, led a so-called "punitive expedition" into Mexico in 1916 that lasted until January 1917. Both of these military actions may have prepared the American public for war overseas in Europe, and both certainly trained leaders for the eventual forces headed to the Western Front.

Propaganda also lured the United States into a war mentality before official entry into the war. Both sides saw the United States as a possible ally, given its diverse population base and its large proportion of English speakers but also its sizable German-speaking minority. Germany and Britain sought to influence US citizens to support their respective sides, and heated accounts of atrocities, bravery, and justifications for war appeared as early as fall 1914. This battle for American hearts shifted considerably in 1915 with two events. First, the sinking of the RMS *Lusitania* in May with the loss of more than 100 American lives led to a wave of anti-German sentiment in the United States. Second, the execution of British nurse Edith Cavell by German occupying authorities in Belgium in October became a major British propaganda tool for depicting the Germans as heartless murderers. From 1915 until the actual entry into war in 1917, sentiment shifted toward the Allied cause. Voices in favor of entering war on the Allied side appeared more frequently in the American media in this period.

The actual sparks that led to an American declaration of war were deliberate German actions. First, despite an international outcry against unrestricted submarine warfare, the German navy resumed this practice. German military officials perceived this strategy as a necessity, given the British blockade. President Wilson protested the decision and demanded an end to the practice before breaking off diplomatic ties. Second, German foreign minister Arthur Zimmermann hatched the idea of trying to get Mexico to invade the United States in return for help from Germany in regaining territory lost in the nineteenth century to American expansion. Zimmermann thought this action would distract the United States from events across the Atlantic and prevent US entry into the war. Thus the "Zimmermann telegram" instructed the German ambassador to make an offer to Mexico, but the missive was discovered by British intelligence and turned over to US authorities. The telegram was leaked to the media in March 1917, enflaming American public opinion. Wilson, clearly reluctant to commit troops to this costly overseas war, went to the US Congress and received permission with a clear majority in each chamber to declare war on Germany on April 6, 1917. It was not until December 1917 that the United States formally joined the war against Austria-Hungary. The slow process of raising a foreign expeditionary force began. It was nearly a year before substantial numbers of American soldiers traveled abroad, so although the United States entered the war in 1917, the impact of its presence was not fully felt until 1918.

Warnings of Discontent

By 1917, populations throughout the belligerent nations felt the strain of the war. This was particularly true in areas that had been involved in conflict prior to 1914. For instance, those living in the Balkans and the Ottoman Empire had already been involved in two wars—in 1912 and 1913—and they would continue to fight into the early 1920s over borders and ethnic politics. In the belligerent nations, minority groups faced additional strain in the war as their loyalty was repeatedly questioned; in some areas, they were persecuted, deported, imprisoned, or killed in the heightened atmosphere of wartime paranoia. The social impact of this growing strain and stress of life is most noticeable in the Russian Revolutions of 1917, where ordinary women joined together with male workers, sailors, and soldiers in an act of refusal in spring 1917. This upheaval toppled the Tsar and led to a provisional government but did not immediately end the war. The officials charged with the transition to a new regime did not sue for peace and continued to fight, leading to a second Revolution in the fall of 1917. This October Revolution, spearheaded by the Bolshevik faction of communists in the Russian Empire, succeeded partly because its leader, Vladimir Lenin, promised an end to war. The peace treaty of Brest-Litovsk in March 1918 between Germany and the Bolsheviks ended Russia's formal role in the war. It also led other national leaders to look fearfully at their citizenry, hoping that no similar revolution would emerge.

A wave of revolutions and disturbances descended upon the wartime world in 1917 and after; the signs of deteriorating morale were clear. Civilians complained in letters to the front about shortages in food, and soldiers fretted about the loss of homes and livelihoods as they continued to serve far from their families. Paranoia reigned with false accusations of espionage and treason, persecution of minority groups, and attacks on those considered non-patriotic. For instance, in July 1917 in Bisbee, Arizona, a copper-mining town, local vigilantes rounded up nearly 1200 unionized male workers who were on strike and deported them to New Mexico, where they lived in a makeshift detention camp. When asked why he ordered the deportation by local citizens deputized for the occasion, Sheriff Harry E. Wheeler said, "It became a question of 'Are you an American, or are you not?'"

Elsewhere nations also attempted to quell anticonscription sentiment, using force if necessary, as it was in the central Asian provinces of the Russian Empire and in French West Africa. Perhaps most worrisome for government officials, organized groups acted against their nations in 1916, taking advantage of the opportunity to create change. In Ireland, continued agitation as a result of the 1916 Easter Rising led to clashes on the streets between British army forces and civilians. This strained the loyalty of Irish soldiers, who were being asked to fire against their own nation. Adding to the tensions this situation created, when Britain sent in former soldiers as forces of order in the form of the so-called "Black and Tans" at the end of the war, Ireland erupted into a brutal civil war. The last year of the war witnessed even more unrest, with widespread strikes, riots, and outright rebellions. In Canada, troops had to return home to help control "Easter" riots in 1918 by Quebec's nationalists who were protesting their nation's role in a foreign war.

Within the armies themselves, discontent and desertion had become issues. The 1917 French army mutinies had signaled the distress of ordinary soldiers and officers, and while such serious disobedience did not surface again during the war, tensions continued to simmer. Italy's disastrous losses at Caporetto in 1917 also led to a rash of desertions. Anti-conscription protests in the British Empire affected troop morale as did the terrible winter conditions on the Western Front in late 1917 and early 1918. In the multinational army of Austria-Hungary, soldiers from minority nationalities in the empire began deserting in greater numbers. Polish, Czech, and Slovak draftees deserted, and some of them even created legions to fight against their former states. Even the German rank-and-file demonstrated their desire for an end to the war. Crown Prince Rupprecht registered his despair in August 1918, noting that "Poor provisions, heavy losses and the deepening influenza have deeply depressed the spirits of the men." That same month large numbers of German soldiers surrendered to French forces, pointing to a collapse in morale. The psychological impact of the arrival of large numbers of Americans only added to the sense of doom felt by Germany's soldiers.

Conclusion

By the end of 1917, those fighting the war had learned the importance of morale—both at home and at the front. Signs were abundant that all was not well with civilian and soldierly morale by the winter of 1917–1918. Military officials knew that a breakthrough of some kind was necessary. Terrible scenes from the war had made their way into public consciousness by the end of 1917. Perhaps none was worse than the stories of British soldiers drowning in mud in the fields of Flanders or of German soldiers being buried alive by underground mines exploded in Belgium. If the devastation in Belgium was not enough to argue for some change in approach, the Italian losses at the Twelfth Battle of Isonzo (Caporetto) in the fall of 1917 provided more evidence. Not only did the Austro-Hungarian offensive push Italians far back into their own territory with great loss of position and territory, but this Italian disaster also forced the movement of British, French, and later, American units to Italy to bolster the war effort there. Only the removal of the unpopular Italian military leader, Luigi Cadorna, helped stabilize the Italian war effort in 1917. The blow to morale, both in Italy and on other fronts, was considerable, and military leaders knew that 1918 had to feature a different approach. Meanwhile, all looked anxiously at Russia, where revolution continued to reshape not only the Russian Empire but the whole wartime alliance system.

Citations

Page	Source
91	Figures and description of Lille deportation drawn from Margaret H. Darrow, *French Women and the First World War: War Stories of the Home Front* (Oxford: Berg, 2000), 118.
92	Figures on Germany's labor mobilization drawn from Albrecht Ritschl, "The Pity of Peace: Germany Economy at War, 1914–1918 and Beyond," In *The Economics of World War I*, edited by Stephen Broadberry and Mark Harrison (Cambridge: Cambridge University Press, 2005), 52–53.
93	"If the Germans had been …" quoted in John Keegan, *The First World War* (New York: Vintage, 2000), 326.
93	Figures for French casualties drawn from Michael S. Neiberg, *Fighting the Great War: A Global History* (Cambridge, MA: Harvard University Press, 2005), 244.
93	Figures for the French mutinies drawn from Leonard V. Smith, *Between Mutiny and Obedience: The Case of the French Fifth Infantry Division during World War I* (Princeton, NJ: Princeton University Press, 1994), 183.
94	"Let such a year as this die …" quoted in Svetlana Palmer and Sarah Wallis, eds., *Intimate Voices from the First World War* (New York: William Morrow, 2003), 286.
94	"Fifty-two hours …" quoted in John R. Schindler, *Isonzo: The Forgotten Sacrifice of the Great War* (Westport, CT: Praeger, 2001), 255–256.
94	"lost 10,000 killed …" quoted in Eric Dorn Brose, *A History of the Great War: World War One and the Crisis of the Early Twentieth Century* (Oxford: Oxford University Press, 2010), 275.
95	"We splashed and slithered …" quoted in Peter Hart, *The Great War: A Combat History of the First World War* (Oxford: Oxford University Press, 2013), 365–366.
95	More than 300 tanks figure drawn from Keegan, 370.

95 "We could have dealt with men ..." quoted in Hart, 371.

95 "This is a war of resources ..." quoted in the *New York Times* (December 27, 1917).

96 Description of Hoover and US food conservation drawn from Tammy M. Proctor, *Civilians in a World at War, 1914–1918* (New York: New York University Press, 2010), 89.

97 Information on Austrian "child bond" taken from Maureen Healy, *Vienna and the Fall of the Habsburg Empire: Total War and Everyday Life in WWI* (Cambridge: Cambridge University Press, 2004), 244.

97 "To Not Waste Bread" poster is available at the University of Illinois Archives, http://imagesearch.library.illinois.edu/cdm4/item_viewer.php?CISOROOT=/wwposters&CISOPTR=83

97 "Food is Ammunition" poster is available at the Library of Congress, http://www.loc.gov/pictures/item/94514370/

98 Maud Allan and Mata Hari information drawn from Tammy M. Proctor, *Female Intelligence: Women and Espionage in the First World War* (New York: New York University Press, 2003), 40–41, 126–131.

101 Requisitions described by a woman in Brussels drawn from Sophie de Schaepdrijver and Tammy M. Proctor, *An English Governess in the Great War: The Secret Brussels Diary of Mary Thorp* (Oxford: Oxford University Press, 2017).

102 Information on the Japanese in Micronesia drawn from Hermann Joseph Hiery, *The Neglected War: The German South Pacific and the Influence of World War I* (Honolulu: University of Hawaii Press, 1995), 187.

102 "military Utopia" quoted in Vejas Gabriel Liulevicius, *War Land on the Eastern Front: Culture, National Identity and German Occupation in World War I* (Cambridge: Cambridge University Press, 2000), 54.

103 Background on *Komitadjis* drawn from Jonathan Gumz, *The Resurrection and Collapse of Empire in Habsburg Serbia, 1914–1918* (Cambridge: Cambridge University Press, 2009), 193.

107 "It became a question of ..." quoted in Christopher Capozzola, *Uncle Sam Wants You: World War I and the Making of the Modern American Citizen* (Oxford: Oxford University Press, 2008), 126–128.

107 "Poor provisions ..." quoted in Hew Strachan, *The First World War* (New York: Viking, 2003), 315.

Select Bibliography

Brose, Eric Dorn. *A History of the Great War: World War One and the Crisis of the Early Twentieth Century*. Oxford: Oxford University Press, 2010.

De Schaepdrijver, Sophie, and Tammy M. Proctor. *An English Governess in the Great War: The Secret Brussels Diary of Mary Thorp*. Oxford: Oxford University Press, 2017.

Englund, Peter. *The Beauty and the Sorrow: An Intimate History of the First World War*. New York: Vintage, 2012.

Gregory, Adrian. *The Last Great War: British Society and the First World War*. Cambridge: Cambridge University Press, 2008.

Gumz, Jonathan. *The Resurrection and Collapse of Empire in Habsburg Serbia, 1914–1918.* Cambridge: Cambridge University Press, 2009.

Hart, Peter. *The Great War: A Combat History of the First World War.* Oxford: Oxford University Press, 2013.

Healy, Maureen. *Vienna and the Fall of the Habsburg Empire: Total War and Everyday Life in WWI.* Cambridge: Cambridge University Press, 2004.

Hiery, Hermann Joseph. *The Neglected War: The German South Pacific and the Influence of World War I.* Honolulu: University of Hawaii Press, 1995.

Kauffman, Jesse. *Elusive Alliance: The German Occupation of Poland in World War I.* Cambridge, MA: Harvard University Press, 2015.

Liulevicius, Vejas Gabriel. *War Land on the Eastern Front: Culture, National Identity and German Occupation in World War I.* Cambridge: Cambridge University Press, 2000.

Lyon, Bryce, and Mary Lyon, eds. *The Journal de Guerre of Henri Pirenne.* Amsterdam: North Holland, 1976.

Neiberg, Michael S. *Fighting the Great War: A Global History.* Cambridge, MA: Harvard University Press, 2005.

Paddock, Troy R. E., ed. *World War I and Propaganda.* Leiden: Brill, 2014.

Palmer, Svetlana, and Sarah Wallis, eds. *Intimate Voices from the First World War.* New York: William Morrow, 2003.

Proctor, Tammy M. *Civilians in a World at War, 1914–1918.* New York: New York University Press, 2010.

Proctor, Tammy M. *Female Intelligence: Women and Espionage in the First World War.* New York: New York University Press, 2003.

Ritschl, Albrecht. "The Pity of Peace: Germany Economy at War, 1914–1918 and Beyond." In *The Economics of World War I*, edited by Stephen Broadberry and Mark Harrison, 41–76. Cambridge: Cambridge University Press, 2005.

Smith, Leonard V. *Between Mutiny and Obedience: The Case of the French Fifth Infantry Division during World War I.* Princeton, NJ: Princeton University Press, 1994.

Strachan, Hew. *The First World War.* New York: Viking, 2003.

Watson, Alexander. *Ring of Steel: Germany and Austria-Hungary in World War I.* New York: Basic Books, 2014.

Appendix 5.1: Timeline for 1917

1917	IMPORTANT EVENTS OF THE WAR	BATTLE
January 19	Zimmermann telegram sent to German ambassador in Mexico	
February 1	Germans resume unrestricted submarine warfare	
March 7	Russian "February" Revolution begins (Feb. 23 on Julian calendar)	
March 11	British occupation of Baghdad	
April 6	United States joins the war on the Allied side	
April 9	British launch offensive against Germans	Battle of Arras
April 16	French launch Nivelle offensive against Germans	Chemins Des Dames
April–June	French Army mutinies	
June 7	British launch offensive against Germans; detonate 19 mines	Battle of Messines
October 12	British launch offensive against Germany	Battle of Passchendaele
October 15	Mata Hari executed in Paris	
October 24	Habsburgs launch offensive against Italy	Battle of Caporetto
November 6	Bolshevik "October" Revolution in Russia (Oct. 24 on Julian calendar)	
November 20	Battle of Cambrai	Battle of Cambrai

6

1918. What Circumstances Led to the End of the War?

Figure 6.1 One result of the First World War was the destruction of historic empires, including the Russian Empire in the Revolution of 1917. This photograph depicts enthusiastic revolutionary crowds in St. Petersburg. *Source:* Library of Congress Prints and Photographs, LC-USZ62-31831.

World War I: A Short History, First Edition. Tammy M. Proctor.
© 2018 John Wiley & Sons Ltd. Published 2018 by John Wiley & Sons Ltd.

Helsinki, Finland, in the dead of winter, seems like an inauspicious place to start a revolution. Yet, in the aftermath of the 1917 Russian Revolution, the debate over the shape of a new Finland led to a bloody and bitter civil war, which broke out in January 1918 over the future of this former corner of the Russian Empire. An armistice in December 1917 between Vladimir Lenin's Bolshevik government and Germany had led to a power vacuum in Finland as Russian troops began to withdraw and German occupying forces began to arrive by spring 1918. Divisions between rural and urban populations, between conservatives and socialists, and between working-class and middle-class populations spilled over into violence. Finland, which had been a comparatively quiet corner of the war, now faced a murderous civil war with an "extraordinarily high death toll of over 36,000 within six months" as the so-called Reds and Whites battled. Sporadic violence continued into the early 1920s.

This unique and relatively short example of civil war signals the fundamental change wrought in the geopolitical balance by three years of war and by the Russian Revolution. When considering how and why the war officially ended in 1918, these two factors play a crucial role. The nature of war and the revolutionary upheavals it spawned also help explain why, for many people, violence did not end with an armistice or even a peace treaty. As 1918 dawned, a series of important shifts had taken place in the nature of the war. First, Lenin's Bolsheviks signed an armistice ending the fighting in the Russian Empire in December 1917, and they made plans for treaty negotiations in the spring. This removal of the Russian front from the war freed up a number of German units for service elsewhere and convinced Allied planners that new strategies needed to be pursued. Second, the entry of the United States into the war meant a boost in supply of almost everything for the Allies (food, munitions, soldiers), but the mobilization of the Americans was slow. Without a standing army of any size and with its distance from the battle, most American soldiers and goods could not arrive until sometime in 1918.

Finally, war weariness was taking a toll on morale in every sector. Financing the war was difficult and rates of desertion had risen. In major cities, labor disputes and strikes rose in both quantity and severity, and serious problems with discipline and morale at many front-line zones also worried officials. Most everyone involved in the war, from politicians to military planners assumed that 1918 would be decisive in some way. Everyone knew that it would be impossible to continue this war much longer without the complete destruction of the social fabric of the societies at war.

In fact, it was clear to most observers that the war had become a race to achieve victory while supplies and a semblance of morale remained. As early as January 8, Woodrow Wilson delivered a speech to Congress laying out his vision of a postwar settlement. Known as the "Fourteen Points," this series of principles excited the interest of many national and colonial liberation movements with its emphasis on the concept that populations in a state should have a voice in the creation of nations. Importantly, this speech was quite vague about whom might qualify for determining their own fates as nations, and it provided both hope and disappointment when the text was published in the international press. Major points included specific demands such as the creation of an independent Poland and broader ideological claims for self-determination and a "League of Nations" as an international mediation force in the postwar world. Wilson doubled down on these ideas in subsequent speeches, including one in February where he explained self-determination as a core ideal, noting that "every territorial settlement involved in this war must be made in the interest and for the benefit of the populations concerned."

Like Wilson, other Allied leaders sought to frame the war and the eventual peace in their public messages. In a speech to union delegates on January 5, 1918, Prime Minister David Lloyd George made it clear that the war was poised at a turning point:

> When men by the million are being called upon to suffer and die and vast populations are being subjected to the sufferings and privations of war on a scale unprecedented in the history of the world, they are entitled to know for what cause or causes they are making the sacrifice. It is only the clearest, greatest and justest of causes that can justify the continuance even for one day of this unspeakable agony of the nations. And we ought to be able to state clearly and definitely not only the principle for which we are fighting but also their definite and concrete applications to the war map of the world. We have arrived at the most critical hour in this terrible conflict...

Lloyd George went on to outline once again Britain's war aims for the public, noting that this was not about aggression against or destruction of the enemy. Instead, this was a war to protect the rights of others such as Belgium and Serbia. By laying out these aims, the Prime Minister called on the public to steel itself for more bloodshed, echoing calls that leaders in other nations were also making as the world prepared for yet another year of war.

In most nations, officials began actively to plan for peace without really knowing when the end of the war would come and who would emerge on top. Meanwhile, the battles continued, and perhaps the most difficult thing to understand about World War I is how and why it continued for so long in 1918 when all those involved felt that a ceasefire was both necessary and desirable. This chapter will examine the impact of the Russian Revolution and the ensuing treaty with the Central Powers (Treaty of Brest-Litovsk) while also explaining the impact of US troops in 1918 and the important events that led to the official end of the conflict. The war disintegrated into a series of armistices and civil revolts, ultimately setting the stage for a bloody and painful postwar period. Some scholars even argue that these armistices sowed the seeds of World War II well before the treaties were signed.

The Impact of Russia's Revolution

It is difficult to underestimate the importance of the two-pronged Russian Revolution and its aftermath on the eventual postwar world. When the revolution began in 1917, it was a surprise to many people, not least the Russian Imperial Government. As agitation and political maneuvering continued for months, Russian forces remained in combat, which meant that none of the grievances that had sparked revolution had yet been addressed. This lingering crisis created the opportunity for a second revolution in the fall of 1917, and this time the new leaders, the Bolshevik party, sought an armistice with Germany to end the fighting. The Russian armistice and its later peace treaty had a profound impact on the war, especially for Germany's war effort, so it is important to understand the basic underlying motives for revolution in 1917.

Although military morale was poor in the Russian Army in March 1917 (February Revolution on the Russian calendar), it was not the soldiers that initiated popular revolution. Instead, the revolutions were sparked by food shortages in the cities. Particularly problematic for the Tsarist government were the bread shortages, which plagued the country throughout the winter of 1916–1917. Workers went on strike against high prices and lack of food in the early weeks of 1917, but matters escalated by March. Civilian anger spilled over into the street, which in turn radicalized soldiers, sailors, and workers, leading to a toppling of tsarist authority. Governing now became the function of a series of interconnected groups—peasant committees, local *soviets* (or revolutionary councils) in the armed forces and in cities, and a provisional central government intent on continuing the war. Despite the excitement and optimism that many reformers felt for this new future, the war—which had sparked the Revolution—continued. More casualties, more price problems, enduring food shortages, and a somewhat indecisive provisional government meant that the grievances of the people did not disappear. Eventually this led to the second Russian Revolution in November 1917 (October Revolution on the Russian calendar), led by Vladimir Lenin. Here too, the war played a role, since Lenin only returned to Russia from exile in April 1917 with the collusion of the German Empire, who wanted an end to war on the Eastern Front. German officials arranged for the rail transport of several exiled Russian revolutionaries back to their home country in the hopes of further destabilizing Russia.

Just two weeks after seizing control of Russia and its former empire from the earlier revolutionary government, Lenin ordered the army to seek a ceasefire with Germany in November 1917. When the high command showed reluctance to obey this order, Lenin merely sidestepped them and went straight to the soldiers at the front, now organized into revolutionary councils. As Joshua Sanborn notes, "the end of fighting on most of the front was accomplished not by central edict or by diplomats in a chandelier-filled hall, but by repeated instances of mud-caked Russian soldiers coming to terms with relieved German officers under a flag of truce." These negotiations took a few weeks, but the entire Russian–German–Austrian front had reached a general ceasefire by mid-December. From the time of the armistice until the peace treaty was signed in early March, the Bolsheviks sought legitimacy and control of this empire they had claimed. To gain a measure of stability, the Bolsheviks knew that an end to war was necessary, regardless of cost. The treaty that Lenin's government signed was disastrous—the new Soviet Union lost a third of Russia's prewar population, half of its industrial strength, and a third of its agricultural land.

The effect of the Russian armistice on the war fronts and on those involved was electric. In the former Russian Empire and its borderlands, civil war erupted with claims from a variety of ethnic and national groups. Some groups declared independent states, such as in Finland and the Ukraine. Others began lobbying for states that fit their national ambitions, such as the inhabitants of the Baltic states and Poland, but since Germany was occupying so much of their territory, many of these activists had to wait for German defeat before making their claims for nationhood. In short, the Russian Empire's dissolution opened up the possibility of major boundary change. Armed with Wilson's concept of self-determination, nationalist leaders used this opportunity to press their cases in the court of international opinion.

War over control of the government between Bolsheviks and their political rivals also consumed time and energy, even with the end of formal hostilities with the "enemy." Amidst this unstable and dangerous atmosphere, the army attempted to demobilize soldiers, a monumental and slow task. Civilians, who assumed that relief from shortages and wartime sacrifice would soon follow an end to war, found that they had been misled. Wartime deprivation continued, especially in areas where fighting raged. Unfortunately, ordinary people experienced severe hardship in many areas of the former Empire well into the 1920s. Like civilians, prisoners of war thought the war would bring a quick liberation and return to normalcy. Prisoners of war in Russian camps were indeed released, but they faced an arduous trek home with little assistance from the new Soviet Government. Some managed to find motor or rail transport, but the majority had to make their way home on foot, depending on scavenging or handouts for food. Finally, deportees and refugees who had been evacuated from front-line regions during the war experienced further displacement by postwar civil disturbances. Their suspect loyalties made them targets for a new Soviet regime in the midst of heightened paranoia that accompanied the violent postwar period. It was during this same period of fear and unruly violence that Soviet secret police (*Cheka*) executed the former tsar and his whole family at a house near Ekaterinburg (Ural Mountains) in July 1918.

In a larger sense, the Russian armistice also unleashed a new set of war plans for those still involved in the conflict. All the calculations by the nations involved in war up to 1918 were predicated on the idea that Germany had to maintain two fronts in this war (at least). With the withdrawal of Russia from the conflict and the signing of the Treaty of Brest-Litovsk on March 3, 1918, those realities shifted, leaving Germany with a large territory to occupy and administer but also providing it with the opportunity to concentrate its attention on the Western Front. Germany had won the war on the Eastern Front, so now it turned its eyes to the west.

The Western Front in 1918

Germany's victory in the east in 1918 spurred its military push to achieve the same on the Western Front. With the end of hostilities against Russia, Germany now had more men, more munitions, and more resources to bring to Belgium and France, despite still having to reinforce and bolster forces in the Balkans, Italy, and the Ottoman Empire. In March 1918, German officials knew that morale was low at home and that revolution might be a possibility, but they gambled on their military power, hoping that a hard, fast offensive on the Western Front would break the Allies before the United States could deploy its forces. This offensive was a last-ditch effort by the German High Command to end the war for good.

By this point in the war, Erich von Ludendorff had assumed control of the German armies in the west. The series of offensive actions he launched on March 21, 1918, began with frontal assaults on British troops at the Somme, then shifted east to French lines near Chemin des Dames. Almost simultaneously, the Germans also called upon their arsenal to shell the French capital with the so-called "Paris Gun" beginning on March 23. This huge gun had a barrel that was nearly 130 feet long and was designed to terrorize the French capital. German leaders hoped that together, these dual assaults on military and civil targets would bring the Allies to the point of surrender on all fronts. More than 250 died and several hundred were injured in the Paris bombardments, while the German military advance gained ground in the first few weeks by pushing the British lines back 40 miles. The Germans retook regions they had yielded in 1917 and pushed within striking distance of Paris with innovative use of targeted "hurricane" artillery bombardments and elite heavily armed "storm troop" formations as a vanguard for the attack. Part of the initial success of the German push was its coordination of artillery, infantry, and aerial combat during the spring 1918 offensive, which was a harbinger of what we know as "blitzkrieg" warfare in World War II.

One of the key factors in the German plan for 1918 was the more sophisticated use of new technologies in their offensives, which was a feature of most army strategy on the Western Front after Verdun. Some of the largest and most decisive aerial dogfights of the war occurred in 1918, with both sides using their best machines and pilots. The planes also functioned almost as artillery, flying low over exposed troops and strafing them with machine gun fire and bombs. German Pilot Ernst Udet described an attack: "Tearing along at a height of about 30 feet above the ground, [his captain] peppered the marching troops with his two guns. We followed close behind him and followed his example. The troops below us seemed to have been lamed with horror…" It was during these spring battles that Udet's captain, who was Germany's best-known pilot, Manfred von Richthofen (the Red Baron), died. Richthofen led the most famous of Germany's fighter groups (called *Jagdeschwader*) from 1917 until his death; he remains one of the most recognizable "aces" of the war. During his career he shot down 80 Allied planes.

In addition to the greater use of airplanes in offensives, armies had begun using another technology with more accuracy and to deadly effect, the tank. Germany had by 1918 developed a tank (known as the A7V) to combat Allied tanks (such as the British Mark IV and the French CA1) on the Western Front, and the first battle where tanks were utilized by both sides occurred on April 24, 1918. Despite this clash between tanks, Germany never really developed sufficient numbers of tanks in order to use them to good effect. Their A7V tanks were slow (top speed of eight miles per hour) and required large crews of 18 men. More importantly, the Germans only produced 20 of these tanks; the British, French, Belgians, and Americans produced 6000 tanks. While tanks did achieve limited success in some zones, they were not a factor in the ultimate Allied victory on the Western Front.

In spring 1918, over the course of five offensives, the Germans did advance, retaking territory lost earlier in the war and punching holes in the Allied lines. Yet, despite massive artillery power, new technologies, and "storm troop" formations, the Germans could not achieve a decisive breakthrough at any point in 1918. Peter Hart describes the desperation that German leader Ludendorff felt by late spring: "He had captured large swathes of despoiled ground, ruined villages, shattered copses and blasted roads, but he had failed to knock the British out of the war." By June, the advantage on the Western Front had begun to shift, and rather than achieving victory, German efforts began to fail.

Both sides suffered hideous losses (roughly 800 000 Germans and 900 000 Allied forces in three months), and it was in the wake of these devastating battles that the so-called "Spanish" influenza arrived at the Western Front from its origins in the American Midwest. While numbers are hard to determine and death rates varied by location, at least 50 million died worldwide, or nearly 4% of the global population in 1919. The flu decimated populations around the world, but it was a flu strain that killed more young adults than it did small children or elderly people. In fact the demographic that was hardest hit, young people aged 18 to 30, mirrored the makeup of many of the group of men and women serving at war fronts. Therefore, when flu made its way from the training

119

camps of the United States to the Western Front, units of soldiers and medical personnel began getting sick, destroying fighting capacity.

Hundreds of thousands of men in each army ended up incapacitated, in hospital, or dead by late spring and summer. Another break for the Allies came when the French gained crucial intelligence of German plans for a summer attack from interrogation of recently captured prisoners of war. This information allowed French units to evade the German artillery barrage and to position themselves to defend territory. Coordination of ground forces, artillery, and air power by the Allied leaders stopped the Germans and forced a retreat by the end of July 1918. So it is not surprising that by August 1918, German military leaders knew that their offensives had not achieved their goal.

While Germany licked its wounds after the failed spring offensives and combated morale problems in its cities, the Allies had spent months working on new methods of employing artillery. They also began trying more sophisticated forecasting of the locations of enemy artillery based on weather readings and sound ranging with microphones. Other technologies had matured; for instance, Allied tanks had become more reliable if still slow. Another advantage that turned the tide of war for the Allies was the influx of resources and men from the United States, which boosted capacity and morale. The British and French were still able to fight, and American soldiers had begun to arrive in large numbers. More than 300 000 US soldiers joined existing British and French units in early summer 1918, and by the time of the November 11 Armistice, the all-American units stationed at the Western Front topped 1.5 million men. By late summer 1918, the forces of Britain, Belgium, France, and the United States had the confidence to launch a major counter-offensive aimed at ending the war. Their objective was the destruction of the German Hindenburg Line, a well-fortified line of trenches placed on high ground. Each ally had a different sector from which to work, with the Belgians and British in Flanders and the Somme, the French near Chemin des Dames, and the Americans on the eastern part of the front near the Argonne Forest.

It is important to note that this was to be the first real test of an independent US army in France because when the American Expeditionary Force first arrived, they had been integrated into existing French units and used French weapons. Some US soldiers also served with the British in the spring and summer of 1918. One of the most famous of these joint efforts was at Belleau Wood, located 35 miles from Paris, where a US Marine Corps brigade held off a German attack at great cost. Historian Michael Neiberg explains that this was an important action in terms of halting the German advance, but it also spawned a Marine Corps story that became legendary, in which the Marine commander told his French comrades who were urging them to retreat: "Retreat, hell! We just got here." These early stories of American bluster helped fuel the image of American fighting forces as fearless just as they entered the war in large numbers for the first time.

However, despite some success in these joint operations, General John Pershing demanded a separate American army with US officers as a goal, even as he quietly sent men into British and French lines during the crucial period when the Allies were trying to stop the German offensive. He thought that Americans would fight better as an independent unit and as a citizen army. So the counter-offensive of fall 1918 was a test of Pershing's claims for the superiority of an all-American force. Beginning in September 1918, an independent US army launched its own offensives, first at St. Mihiel (12–16 September) and then in the Meuse-Argonne campaign (26 September). In the first offensive, half a million American soldiers attacked a German salient (bulge in the line) that had been established in 1914; they were facing well-built and fortified trenches and other defenses. Despite this problem, the Americans were successful in capturing territory because the Germans had fallen back to other fortified positions prior to the attack.

The Meuse-Argonne was a much different campaign for the US army. The Argonne forest was dense and had high ridges, where the Germans had built sturdy fortifications. Over the course of the campaign, which only stopped with the November 11 Armistice, the Americans had moved forward 34 miles using 1.2 million troops, which was "more soldiers than the entire Confederate army during the Civil War." These soldiers, as historian Jennifer Keene has noted, represented the diversity of the American population, with African-Americans, recent immigrants from around the world, and Native Americans all serving as laborers and combatants along with white, native-born Americans. This American force, alongside its allies, turned the tide of the war by October 1918. More accurate and deadly artillery helped make this offensive a success; German soldiers faced an unprecedented number of shells from enemy guns. The Hindenburg Line was broken on October 5, 1918. From that moment on, the end of the war on the Western Front was inevitable.

The coordinated fall counter-offensives by the United States, France, and Britain ended German chances for victory in the west and pushed them into a retreat. However, as they retreated, German forces used a scorched-earth policy of total destruction. Not only did the Germans destroy transport lines and bridges, but they also deliberately ruined harvests and pillaged or burned villages in order to render them useless to their pursuers. Some areas were booby-trapped with gas canisters or mined with explosives. Many historians argue that this deliberate devastation of the French land during the 1918 retreat may have contributed to the French insistence on harshness at the treaty table a few months later.

Alongside the failure of the German spring offensive in 1918, four years of war had also taken a toll on the home front. Like Russia, Germany combatted severe problems with civilian morale in its cities because of high prices and food shortages in 1917. Massive industrial strikes plagued major population centers;

121

in 1918 alone, factories lost more than five million days of production to strikes, which affected more than 7000 factories. Black markets sprang up around the country, and police tried to stop hoarding and stealing in rural areas. Endless food queues drained the energy of women, many of whom were soldiers' wives or widows, and it was clear that the mood had become quite ugly by early 1918. Protests, strikes, and petitions did not bring change, and in October 1918, German cities also experienced revolution. Nearly a dozen major cities in Germany faced revolutionary violence, forcing the military to divert troops to Germany's hinterland in order to contain the fighting.

Political structures disintegrated in the face of these challenges to authority, and the Kaiser abdicated and fled from German army headquarters in Spa, Belgium, to the Netherlands on November 10, 1918. Wilhelm was not the only ruler to abdicate; Emperor Karl of the Habsburg Empire also gave up his throne on Armistice Day, November 11. All the nationalist minorities under German control now seized the opportunity to declare independence as well; exiled elites announced provisional governments and sought access to the negotiations that would follow the war. Allied nations fueled these ambitions by recognizing the nascent nation-states in several cases, most notably Czechoslovakia. The war had opened a Pandora's box in the historic empires of Russia, Austria-Hungary, and the Ottomans. For Germany, all the gains of the war and their occupation regimes disappeared in 1918. They had won the monumental battle in the east against the Russians, but they had lost the war itself.

Other Battlefronts by 1918

As the end of the conflict loomed in the west, the other fronts also began crumbling. On December 11, 1917, General Edmund Allenby's Egyptian Expeditionary Force entered the city of Jerusalem, claiming it for Britain and its allies. Allenby himself entered on foot, head bare. Supported by Faysal ibn Husayn's Arab forces who had risen in revolt against their Ottoman overlords, Allenby had begun this advance a few months earlier in Palestine and the Arabian Peninsula. Supply and transport were tricky in this inhospitable environment, making water one of the key ingredients to success in battle. Allenby's forces relied on railways, animals, and pipelines to maintain a water supply. After taking control of Jerusalem, his army gradually wrested control of major cities from Ottoman and German forces. By the summer of 1918, Allied troops had advanced into Syria and pushed Ottoman armies into retreat or surrender. With the fall of Damascus on October 1, 1918, the Ottomans knew they faced an end to their war in the Middle East. All the major Ottoman cities were in Allied hands—Mecca, Baghdad, Jerusalem, Damascus—and the British had control of both Persia (modern Iran) and Mesopotamia (modern Iraq). The armistice that went into effect at noon on

October 31, 1918 (known as the Armistice of Mudros) served as a harbinger for a series of truces in the next few weeks, as the Central Powers collapsed into revolution under the weight of a long war.

The situation in the Middle East mirrored the deteriorating wartime efforts of the combatants in other theaters of war in several ways. First, people living under Ottoman and then British occupation in the Middle East felt the severe pinch of food shortages and in some cases outright famine by early 1918. The combination of requisitioning, disruption of agriculture, and wartime destruction had decimated the food supply chain, leading to dire conditions. Other Central Powers saw less severe hardships, but nonetheless soldiers and civilians in the empires of Austria-Hungary, Germany, and Russia also suffered under reduced rations and food shortages. In Britain and France, rationing regimes ramped up to handle scarcity of certain foodstuffs but shortages still occurred, and people queued in long lines for basic goods. In many occupied zones, disease and malnutrition raged. These accumulated hardships took a toll and led to a profound sense of war weariness at all levels of society in each combatant country.

Second, the long war effort and the sacrifices this war demanded opened up the possibility for opposition from political and ethnic minorities which took the form of agitation, riots, and even revolutions. War conditions created a perfect storm in which imperial governments saw a rise in demands for national independence by minorities and for an end to inequality amongst subject peoples. These revolts began as early as 1916 with the Easter Rising in Ireland and anticonscription fights in Central Asia, but by 1918, most of the nations at war encountered agitation at home. Finally, the exit of the Russian Empire and the entry of the United States in force by early 1918 changed the war fronts and raised the stakes. The Ottomans no longer had to maintain forces in the Caucasus with Russia's exit, but the presence of the United States on the Western Front helped spur new Allied offensive efforts in the Middle East and in Italy.

In Italy, soldiers had been mainly defending their line against further attack since their crippling defeat and retreat from Caporetto in October 1917. However, by spring 1918 the Austro-Hungarian army lacked manpower and resources, so they launched one last offensive in June 1918 in order to force an armistice or surrender on this front. Italian forces held their ground, and in turn, counterattacked in late October 1918. Austria-Hungary surrendered in early November 1918 to the Italians, both sides reeling from their losses. As the Austro-Hungarian war effort dissolved, revolutionary activity broke out in the cities of Austria and Hungary. By the beginning of November 1918, then, hostilities had ceased on the Italian Front, the Ottoman Front, and the Russian Front (albeit earlier), so the Armistice of November 11, 1918, on the Western Front was as much an expected outcome as it was a necessity.

When considering the collapse of the Central Powers in the fall of 1918, historians argue about the primary reasons for their defeat. One consensus is that lack of resources, men, and supplies doomed the Central Powers in the end. Another common argument is that these big multinational empires, especially the Habsburg and Ottoman empires, were already poised on the edge of internal chaos in 1914, and the war helped bring nationalist claims to the forefront. Some scholars contend that Allied forces learned more from the war by 1918 and utilized motorized transport and combined strikes (infantry, artillery, tanks, air) more effectively. However, the topic that is perhaps most contested is the role the United States played in ending the war. Historians argue about whether or not US entry tipped the balance toward the Allies by 1918. When the Armistice arrived in November 1918, many American soldiers had just arrived in France or had only just recovered from the flu. It is hard to say whether their battle presence was indispensable to victory, however, their presence in the war gave the United States the right to participate in the shaping of the postwar world.

Americans felt they had earned the right to help reshape global politics in the aftermath of the war because of their sacrifices and their unique status in what they considered the most democratic civilization on earth. Not only did American troops serve on the Western Front, but two small contingents also served in Russia, playing a role in holding back Bolshevism, another key goal that would emerge in the 1920s. About 8000 US soldiers joined a combined British, Japanese, Italian, Chinese, and French operation in Siberia that was designed to guard the railway there and to help stranded Czech fighters make their way west. In a real sense, this action aimed to monitor and stabilize territory and resources as civil war raged in the region; also, the allies wanted to keep an eye on each other's ambitions in Siberia. Americans remained in this fight until 1920. Another force, mostly from Michigan and Wisconsin (roughly 5000 men), fought alongside the British against Bolshevik troops in Archangel, an important port city. Little was achieved in either action from an Allied point of view, and these expeditions have been overshadowed by the narrative of Americans in France. Yet, in Russia as well as in France, the untested American army contributed to the Allied victory in 1918 by their sheer numbers, if for no other reason.

In addition, few dispute that one valuable role the United States played in 1918 and 1919 was as a threat to force Germany to come to terms at the treaty table. With millions of bored young American soldiers hanging out in camps in France after the armistice, most German civil and military officials did not want a resumption of the war. While the US army waited for a treaty, its personnel also served a role in battlefield salvage, repair of transport and communication lines, and as part of an occupying force in postwar Germany. The US Government worried about its soldiers' morale and their morals, so money poured into recreational facilities run by wholesome organizations such as the YMCA. The allies even had a sort of soldiers' Olympics in 1919 with the Inter-Allied games, which were held in a purpose-built stadium outside of Paris. The funding and labor for the arena, christened Pershing Stadium, came from the US military and the YMCA. Finally, in understanding the impact of the United States entry into World War I, it is important to remember that morale had fallen to critical levels among soldiers and civilians in the combatant nations by spring 1917. Wilson's declaration of war in April provided hope for the Allies with the promise of more men and supplies, but it also provided a spur to the Germans to try to end the war before American industrial might could be fully utilized.

Assessing the Damage

Regardless of the American intervention, the war appeared to be winding down in 1918. The combined impact of a raging influenza epidemic both in the combat zones and in the civilian areas with the high casualties of four years of fighting and sacrifice had taken a toll. Desertion rates rose, as did self-inflicted wounds as a way of avoiding further fighting. At home, workers demanded better pay and conditions, and the social fabric that held the nations at war together was tearing.

Religious belief, which plays such an important role in maintaining social cohesion and in shaping individual identity, both informed the experience of war and sometimes faced a challenge from that war. For some, faith was a comfort to those affected by war and a motivational force for enlisting in and enduring the war. Yet, organized religions also confronted severe challenges from those who felt betrayed by the war, many of whom questioned religious leaders and sought meaning in the experience. Certainly some people lost faith entirely, and alternative forms of belief saw a surge, especially practices such as spiritualism. Stories of miraculous escapes, appearances of ghosts of dead comrades, and other supernatural occurrences made frequent appearances in personal letters and public accounts of the war. These sightings aligned with established religious traditions, but often stretched or challenged them. For example, the Virgin Mary appeared in various places to Christian soldiers, and in one famous incident, the Virgin appeared monthly (beginning in 1917) in Fátima, Portugal. As political regimes that had been intimately tied to religious authorities toppled, such as the Ottoman Empire and the Russian Empire, people living in these former empires had to recalibrate both their political and their spiritual identities, which contributed to a sense of anxiety at the end of the war. Through this turmoil the picture that emerged was of a weary world hoping for peace, even an imperfect negotiated peace.

By 1918, the damage to societies and individuals had become clear, and scientists had begun to study the effects of the war. From these studies and medical experimentation came a series of diagnoses and new treatments designed to counter the devastating injuries of war. Many areas of medical care saw major advances: surgery (including plastic surgery), prosthetics, infectious disease treatment, and cardiac care. Physicians made major advances in surgical techniques out of necessity during the war. Just a few examples of the development of specialized treatments help demonstrate the changes that occurred in virtually every aspect of surgery and wound care. In 1914, a serious abdominal wound meant a death sentence for most soldiers, yet hospitals saw floods of these patients. To deal with the problem by 1918, in the Allied hospitals, special abdominal surgeries with sophisticated blood transfusions saved countless lives. Similarly, New Zealander Harold Gillies saw horrible facial injuries in France early in the war and managed to put together a special unit in England designed to treat catastrophic facial damage. Dr. Gillies pioneered life-saving skin graft technologies to help repair men's faces for a postwar world. His work helped create the modern field of plastic reconstructive surgery. In Italy, scientists created new treatments for the large numbers of soldiers who suffered from frostbite in mountain warfare. In all these cases and countless more, medical practitioners and scientists sought new ways to repair the physical damage of war from gas, artillery, machine guns, exposure to harsh climates, malnutrition, and disease.

Another experience that seems to mark most soldiers' experiences, regardless of what front they were on, was the noise and fear of bombardment by modern artillery. If any one thing marks the front-line societies built by war, it was probably the noise of munitions. Few men forgot the feeling of being under fire, whether it be heavy artillery, bombs from a passing plane, or a gas barrage. Yet they could scarcely convey this experience to those at home because it was too foreign and visceral to put into words. As US soldier Nels Anderson noted in his diary, "I wish I could write down just how it feels to be under fire for four or five hours…. At this game a fellow never knows when he puts on his shoes whether they will ever be taken off again." Some soldiers broke under the strain of the noise and fear of artillery bombardment, earning the label "shell shock" for the varied symptoms they displayed. This English term was coined by Charles S. Myers in 1915 in an article in the *Lancet*, and it became the preferred way to describe the psychological effects of the war. Symptoms of shell shock varied widely from psychological distress to memory loss to delusions to what we might label post-concussive syndrome. Physicians and psychologists struggled to diagnose and treat such symptoms, and they worried that perhaps such soldiers were merely "shirking." Historian Jay Winter has perceptively noted: "This tendency to resist the view that terror could cripple a perfectly healthy, sober, God-fearing man, either temporarily or permanently, had significant consequences for the treatment of psychologically disabled men and for the status of their claims for pensions…" While some men did get treatment for shell shock, the stigma attached to it never really disappeared, and many men struggled alone with no medical intervention.

Taken together, the toll of psychological strain and physical injury led to a situation where many men just wanted the war to end. Civilians, too, felt the strain, both in worry about their loved ones in harm's way and because of their own problems with getting sufficient food and fuel for their families. As 1918 continued, the clamor for an end to hostilities rose in volume.

Conclusion

In a small clearing in the Forest of Compiègne in France, General Ferdinand Foch received German representatives in his private railway carriage to discuss the terms of an armistice. The Allies had a list of demands for German demilitarization and a continuation of the blockade, which they presented to the German representatives who had 72 hours to sign. During this period of discussion, word came from Germany that the Kaiser had abdicated and fled the country. The Wilhelmine Empire had ended even before the armistice had been signed. With turmoil at home and despite their concern over the harsh terms of the armistice, the German delegation signed the document. It went into effect at 11 a.m. on November 11, 1918.

With this agreement, hostilities ceased on the Western Front. The German navy was entirely in Allied hands by the next day. It took two more weeks for all official surrenders to occur—General Paul von Lettow-Vorbeck, the German leader in East Africa, laid down arms on November 25. In Germany itself, people expressed relief but also anger and incredulity at the terms of the Armistice. Revolution erupted and spread in Germany until the new provisional government violently crushed the most insistent of the revolutionaries in Berlin. Well-known international Marxists Karl Liebknecht and Rosa Luxemburg were murdered on January 15, 1919, for their role in the so-called "Sparticist" uprising in the German capital city. By 1919, civil rebellion, revolution, and popular protest had arisen in many of the former combatant countries. In Ireland, a civil war broke out in January 1919 and revolutions occurred in Austria, Hungary, and former Ottoman lands in late 1918. In short, World War I was perhaps the greatest spark for revolutionary political and social change in the twentieth century, and its reverberations destabilized the decades that followed. While the official fighting ended in late 1918, the violence continued as world leaders sought a series of negotiated treaties that they hoped might bring lasting peace to the world.

The toll of war could scarcely be absorbed in 1918 nor can we comprehend it easily now. Roughly two million German soldiers and another 1.8 million Russian soldiers died. The war dead in other nations and empires proved staggering as well: 1.1 million Habsburgs, nearly one million British imperial troops, and 1.3 million French. Even the United States, with its shorter period of actual fighting, suffered more than 114 000 dead. Exact figures are hard to come by but 10 million combat deaths and another 21 million casualties approximate the damage. An estimated 6 to 10 million civilians perished from war-related causes, and all these numbers fail to take into account most of the worldwide deaths from influenza. So, while the armistice of November 11 brought joy and relief, it also signaled a sober time for reflection on just what had been lost. These losses led to feelings of revenge and new grievances, which in turn helped shape the peace treaties and postwar political environment that developed.

Citations

Page	Source
114	"extraordinarily high death toll…" quoted in Pertti Haapala and Marko Tikka, "Revolution, Civil War, and Terror in Finland in 1918," in Robert Gerwarth and John Horne, eds., *Paramilitary Violence in Europe after the Great War* (Oxford: Oxford University Press, 2012), 72. Additional background information from pages 78–79.
115	"every territorial settlement…" quoted in Erez Manela, *The Wilsonian Moment: Self-Determination and the International Origins of Anticolonial Nationalism* (Oxford: Oxford University Press, 2007), 41.
115	"When men by the million…" quoted in *The Times*, January 7, 1918.
116–7	"the end of fighting…" quoted in Joshua A. Sanborn, *Imperial Apocalypse: The Great War and the Destruction of the Russian Empire* (Oxford: Oxford University Press, 2014), 227.
117	Information on the results of the treaty drawn from Adam Tooze, *The Deluge: The Great War, America and the Remaking of the Global Order, 1916–1931* (New York: Viking, 2014), 108.
117	Information on the tsar's execution drawn from Amanda Carter, *George, Nicholas and Wilhelm: Three Royal Cousins and the Road to World War I* (New York: Vintage, 2011), 409.
118	Figures on the Paris Gun are drawn from Michael S. Neiberg, *Fighting the Great War: A Global History* (Cambridge, MA: Harvard University Press, 2005), 314.
119	"Tearing along…" quoted in Peter Hart, *The Great War: A Combat History of the First World War* (Oxford: Oxford University Press, 2013), 422.
119	80 aces figure drawn from Ian F. W. Beckett, *The Great War*, 2nd Edition (Harlow: Pearson, 2007), 256.
119	Information on tanks drawn from Michael David Kennedy, "Tanks and Tank Warfare," In *1914–1918-online. International Encyclopedia of the First World War*.
119	"He had captured…" quoted in Hart, 438.
119	Figures on influenza drawn from John M. Barry, *The Great Influenza. The Epic Story of the Deadliest Plague in History* (New York: Viking, 2004), 169, 450.
120	Figures on US soldiers drawn from Christoph Mick, "1918: Endgame," in Jay Winter, ed., *The Cambridge History of the First World War, Volume I: Global War* (Cambridge: Cambridge University Press, 2014), 169–170.

120 "Retreat, hell!..." quoted in Neiberg, 328.

121 "more soldiers than..." quoted in Jennifer D. Keene, *The United States and the First World War* (Harlow: Pearson Education, 2000), 59.

122 Figures on German strikes drawn from Chris Harman, *The Lost Revolution: Germany 1918 to 1923* (Chicago: Haymarket Books, 2003), 143.

122 Information on the abdication of the German and Habsburg rulers drawn from Carter, 413–414.

122 Information on Allenby and the Jerusalem campaign drawn from Robin Prior, "The Ottoman Front." In *The Cambridge History of the First World War, Volume I: Global War*, 317.

124 Information on the US expeditions in Russia available in Benjamin D. Rhodes, *The Anglo-American Winter War with Russia, 1918–1919* (New York: Greenwood, 1988).

125 Information on Fátima drawn from Patrick J. Houlihan, "Religious Mobilization and Popular Belief," in *1914–1918-online. International Encyclopedia of the First World War*.

126 Information on abdominal surgeries drawn from Leo van Bergen, in *1914–1918-online. International Encyclopedia of the First World War*.

126 Background on Harold Gillies and examples of his work available from http://www.gilliesarchives.org.uk/

126 Information on Italian frostbite drawn from Andrea Scartabellati and Felicita Ratti, "Science and Technology (Italy)," in *1914–1918-online. International Encyclopedia of the First World War*.

126 "I wish I could write down..." quoted in Allan Kent Powell, ed., *Nels Anderson's World War I Diary* (Salt Lake City: University of Utah Press, 2013), 131–132.

126 "This tendency to resist..." quoted in Jay Winter, *The Cambridge History of the First World War, Volume III: Civil Society*, 315.

127–8 Figures for the dead drawn from Antoine Prost, *The Cambridge History of the First World War, Volume III: Civil Society*, 587–588.

Select Bibliography

Barry, John M. *The Great Influenza. The Epic Story of the Deadliest Plague in History*. New York: Viking, 2004.

Beckett, Ian F. W. *The Great War*, 2nd Edition. Harlow: Pearson Education, 2007.

Bergen, Leo Van. "Medicine and Medical Service." In *1914–1918-online. International Encyclopedia of the First World War*, ed. by Ute Daniel, Peter Gatrell, Oliver Janz, Heather Jones, Jennifer Keene, Alan Kramer, and Bill Nasson, issued by Freie Universität Berlin, Berlin, 2014. doi: 10.15463/ie1418.10221

Broadberry, Stephen, and Mark Harrison, eds. *The Economics of World War I*. Cambridge: Cambridge University Press, 2005.

Capozzola, Christopher. *Uncle Sam Wants You: World War I and the Making of the Modern American Citizen*. Oxford: Oxford University Press, 2008.

Carter, Amanda. *George, Nicholas and Wilhelm: Three Royal Cousins and the Road to World War I.* New York: Vintage, 2011.

Davis, Belinda. *Home Fires Burning: Food, Politics, and Everyday Life in World War I Berlin.* Chapel Hill: University of North Carolina Press, 2000.

Fawaz, Leila Tarazi. *A Land of Aching Hearts: The Middle East in the Great War.* Cambridge, MA: Harvard University Press, 2014.

Haapala, Pertti, and Marko Tikka. "Revolution, Civil War, and Terror in Finland in 1918." In *Paramilitary Violence in Europe after the Great War,* Robert Gerwarth and John Horne, eds., 72–84. Oxford: Oxford University Press, 2012.

Harman, Chris. *The Lost Revolution: Germany 1918 to 1923.* Chicago: Haymarket Books, 2003.

Hart, Peter. *The Great War: A Combat History of the First World War.* Oxford: Oxford University Press, 2013.

Houlihan, Patrick J. "Religious Mobilization and Popular Belief." In *1914–1918-online. International Encyclopedia of the First World War,* ed. by Ute Daniel, Peter Gatrell, Oliver Janz, Heather Jones, Jennifer Keene, Alan Kramer, and Bill Nasson, issued by Freie Universität Berlin, Berlin, 2015. doi: 10.15463/ie1418.10716

Keene, Jennifer D. *The United States and the First World War.* Harlow: Pearson Education, 2000.

Kennedy, Michael David. "Tanks and Tank Warfare." In *1914–1918-online. International Encyclopedia of the First World War,* ed. by Ute Daniel, Peter Gatrell, Oliver Janz, Heather Jones, Jennifer Keene, Alan Kramer, and Bill Nasson, issued by Freie Universität Berlin, Berlin, 2016. doi: 10.15463/ie1418.10905

Manela, Erez. *The Wilsonian Moment: Self-Determination and the International Origins of Anticolonial Nationalism.* Oxford: Oxford University Press, 2007.

Mick, Christoph. "1918: Endgame." In *The Cambridge History of the First World War, Volume I: Global War,* edited by Jay Winter, 133–171. Cambridge: Cambridge University Press, 2014.

Morrow, Jr., John H. *The Great War: An Imperial History.* London: Routledge, 2005.

Neiberg, Michael S. *Fighting the Great War: A Global History.* Cambridge, MA: Harvard University Press, 2005.

Powell, Allan Kent, ed. *Nels Anderson's World War I Diary.* Salt Lake City: University of Utah Press, 2013.

Prior, Robin. "The Ottoman Front." In *The Cambridge History of the First World War, Volume I: Global War,* edited by Jay Winter, 204–233. Cambridge: Cambridge University Press, 2015.

Prost, Antoine. "The Dead." In *The Cambridge History of the First World War, Volume III: Civil Society,* edited by Jay Winter, 561–591. Cambridge: Cambridge University Press, 2014.

Rhodes, Benjamin D. *The Anglo-American Winter War with Russia, 1918–1919.* New York: Greenwood, 1988.

Roshwald, Aviel. *Ethnic Nationalism & the Fall of Empires: Central Europe, Russia & the Middle East, 1914–1923.* London: Routledge, 2001.

Sanborn, Joshua A. *Imperial Apocalypse: The Great War and the Destruction of the Russian Empire.* Oxford: Oxford University Press, 2014.

Scartabellati, Andrea, and Felicita Ratti. "Science and Technology (Italy)." In *1914–1918-online. International Encyclopedia of the First World War*, ed. by Ute Daniel, Peter Gatrell, Oliver Janz, Heather Jones, Jennifer Keene, Alan Kramer, and Bill Nasson, issued by Freie Universität Berlin, Berlin, 2015. doi: 10.15463/ie1418.10624 Translated by Noor Giovanni Mazhar.

Strachan, Hew. *The First World War*. New York: Viking, 2004.

Tooze, Adam. *The Deluge: The Great War, America and the Remaking of the Global Order, 1916–1931*. New York: Viking, 2014.

Ward, Alan J. *The Easter Rising: Revolution and Irish Nationalism*, 2nd Edition. Wheeling, IL: Harlan Davidson, 2003.

Winter, Jay. "Shell Shock." In *The Cambridge History of the First World War, Volume III: Civil Society*, edited by Jay Winter, 310–333. Cambridge: Cambridge University Press, 2014.

Appendix 6.1: Timeline for 1918

1918	*IMPORTANT EVENTS OF THE WAR*	*BATTLE*
January 8	Woodrow Wilson's "Fourteen Points" speech	
March 3	Treaty of Brest-Litovsk	
March 21	German offensive on the Western Front	
June 15	Italians stop Habsburg offensive	Battle of Piave
July 16–17	Execution of Tsar Nicholas and his family	
July 18	Allied counter-offensive on Western Front	
September 12–16	American "independent" army offensive	Battle of St. Mihiel
September 26	Americans launch offensive against Germans	Battle of Meuse-Argonne
September 29	Armistice with Bulgaria	
October 31	Armistice of Mudros (Ottomans)	
October 31	Hungary dissolves its union with Austria	
November 3	Italians defeat Habsburgs in a wide offensive	Battle of Vittorio Veneto
November 4	Hostilities end on Italian front with Habsburg surrender	
November 11	Armistice on the Western Front	
November 21	Surrender of German naval ships under terms of armistice	
November 25	Surrender of the German army in East Africa (Lettow-Vorbeck)	

7

1919. How Did the Peace Treaties Shape the Postwar World?

Figure 7.1   The peace treaties that followed the war created almost immediate conflict despite a celebration by the media in postcards such as this one. Wilson's moment of glory at Versailles disappeared in the political firestorm he faced when he returned home. *Source*: Library of Congress Prints and Photographs, LC-DIG-stereo-1s04279.

On March 21, 1919, a small group of seven former Italian soldiers met in the northern city of Milan to draw up a new political manifesto. Three of these men began their political careers as ardent socialists. One of them, Benito Mussolini, even worked as a journalist and editor for a major socialist newspaper prior to World War I. All of them had become disillusioned with Italian political leaders

World War I: A Short History, First Edition. Tammy M. Proctor.
© 2018 John Wiley & Sons Ltd. Published 2018 by John Wiley & Sons Ltd.

and with their own political parties. In particular, they worried that the working classes could not or would not rise in revolution without a spark. For Mussolini, that spark was war. Their new party, soon to crystallize into the National Fascist Party, aimed to fuse the revolutionary groundswell and potential of Marxism with a new ultra-nationalist dynamism that would be led by an elite vanguard of men. Headed by Mussolini and backed by a paramilitary squad of enforcers known as "squadristi," Mussolini's new party drew ex-soldiers, disillusioned socialists, and radicalized students. Mussolini's group sought to unify Italy and to expand its boundaries while also promoting the nation as a world power. Italy's secondary role in the peace negotiations that followed the war had disappointed and disillusioned many of those who had championed the war as an opportunity to make Italy great.

In addition to Mussolini's fledgling organization, ex-soldier, airman, and poet Gabriele D'Annunzio also challenged the postwar settlements. Along with a few hundred men of regular and irregular forces, D'Annunzio occupied Fiume, a port city in the Adriatic, in September 1919, proclaiming it part of Italy. This former Austrian possession was supposed to become part of the new Yugoslavia, so the incident became a diplomatic drama for Italy, Yugoslavia, and the great powers. Months of negotiation led to the expulsion of D'Annunzio from the city by force in 1920 and the creation of a "Free State" in Fiume. Continuing political instability and maneuvering by nearby states finally led to a treaty ceding the city of Fiume to Italy in 1924. The whole incident demonstrated not only the power of the idea of reclaiming lost territory for postwar nations but it also pointed to the emerging populist politicians and their reliance on force. In Italy, the birth of fascism was a clear indication of the ways in which these post-war sentiments were merging into new political parties.

For both D'Annunzio, a well-known poet, and Mussolini, the so-called "mutilated victory" of World War I had brought shame to Italians as their demands for land and negotiating power were ignored by the other Allies. In fact, this widespread frustration in Italy with the peace treaties and postwar settlements helped fuel the growth of the fascists, who took power in Italy after a threatened "March on Rome" in October 1922. To avoid violence and unpleasant publicity that such a march might bring, King Victor Emmanuel (a constitutional monarch) met with Mussolini and invited him to name himself as prime minister on October 29, opening a new era in Italian and European politics. The March that occurred became a celebration of the legal takeover of power rather than a violent show of force. Mussolini accomplished what d'Annunzio could not.

Italy was not alone in its discontent with the peace treaties that followed World War I. Dozens of nations, ethnic and nationalist groups, and a multitude of individuals felt disappointed and betrayed by the postwar world. From China and Japan to Hungary and Italy, political leaders protested the gap that had emerged between the promises of a transformed future and the realities of the postwar gains. This was especially true in defeated nations and destroyed empires, where the war "left 'shatter zones', or large tracts of territory where the disappearance of frontiers created spaces without order…" Stateless people and citizens of new states acted to try to influence their own fates. Their protests took on a variety of forms, ranging from all-out war to peaceful protest. From the end of the war in 1918 to the signing of the last of the peace treaties in 1923, a new global order emerged that would help instigate World War II just one generation after World War I. This chapter examines the peace treaties and negotiations that followed the war and explains some of the lingering problems of the post-World War I world. The lack of resolution for those problems created an opening for demagogic leaders and a new world crisis by the 1930s.

Making Peace: Treaties and the League of Nations

Perhaps the best known of the postwar peace treaties, the Treaty of Versailles, also faced the most opposition. This treaty emerged from the negotiations at the Paris Peace Conference, which opened in January 1919 and concluded six months later. Even before the conference began, the Allies had begun planning for the postwar world. Acute food shortages in former enemy and occupied countries worsened under the blockade, leading Herbert Hoover to create a pseudo-governmental aid organization to feed children in these regions. The American Relief Administration, which began operating with a Congressional appropriation in spring 1919, transformed into a private humanitarian aid group that fed children and adults in more than a dozen countries into the 1920s. This food relief meant an American presence in Europe even at the same time that the US Congress rejected other initiatives such as the League of Nations.

In addition to food, fuel, and housing shortages, revolutions in Germany, Austria, and Hungary continued to simmer, while the founding of several new republics in places like Czechoslovakia, Poland, Yugoslavia, and Finland created diplomatic headaches. Britain was precoccupied by outright political defiance from Irish nationalists elected to the UK Parliament, from Arab nationalist leaders, and from members of the Indian National Congress. War, border skirmishes, and spontaneous violence plagued the Russian borderlands, the Baltic, the Balkans, and the former Ottoman Empire. In short, the peace conference began in the midst of violence and chaos, leading Allies to prioritize protection and stability in many of their initial conversations. Events outside of the closed negotiation sessions sometimes overtook diplomacy, which meant that political borders and national sentiments were in flux even before the treaties were signed.

While the negotiators in January included representatives of 10 Allied nations, the real powers emerged later in the spring. By that time, most of the decisions were in the hands of delegations from Britain, France, and the United States, who were led respectively by David Lloyd-George, Georges Clemenceau, and Woodrow Wilson. These nations controlled the fates of millions of people, and they knew the stakes were high. Yet each had national priorities that guided their actions, leading to terrible showdowns when those priorities clashed. The three disagreed profoundly on several practical matters, including the questions of reparations, redrawn borders, occupation of enemy territory, and disarmament. All these matters had to be negotiated in minute detail at the Paris conference in the midst of petitions from minority groups, small nations, allies, and former enemies. The decision, made in 1918, to exclude the losers from the table, amplified the outcry against the treaty when its unpopular terms became public in Germany. Finally, the question of the Soviet Union, which had negotiated a separate peace and now had territorial demands of its own, only complicated matters further.

In the end, the Treaty of Versailles strongly favored French concerns, with the result that the US Senate refused to ratify the treaty and the obligations it would have imposed on the United States. With this rejection, the United States later negotiated its own separate peace treaties with its enemies. Despite this difficulty, the Treaty of Versailles came into force in Germany in 1920. Its terms reorganized the borders of Europe, established a strict reparations schedule, disarmed Germany, demilitarized a huge territory on the Rhine River, forced German leaders to take complete responsibility for the war (the so-called War Guilt Clause), and created a League of Nations, an international mediation organization that Woodrow Wilson had described a year earlier in his Fourteen Points speech. By taking each of these issues in turn, the guiding principles of the treaty become apparent and help explain the problems that plagued the postwar world.

Borders

All the Allied leaders agreed that German territory should be reduced, but they did not always agree on how that territory should be apportioned. On the western borders, France sought control of its former provinces of Alsace and Lorraine (which it got) but also the Rhineland region (which it only partially controlled). The French were appeased by an agreement to have a 15-year Allied occupation along the left bank of the Rhine, while the right bank was designated a demilitarized zone. After the severe destruction of mines and railways by retreating German armies in 1918, the French also wanted to take control of the Saar region on the French–German border, with its rich mining and industrial resources. In this case, a compromise was struck—the Saar would be administered by a newly created League of Nations for 15 years during which time the French could exploit the mines. As part of the deal, German territory in the border zones of Eupen and Malmedy, also rich industrial areas, became part of Belgium.

In addition to trimming Germany's boundaries in the west, the treaty also adjusted German territory in the east. First, the settlements made with the Bolsheviks in the Treaty of Brest-Litovsk were nullified, creating an opportunity for many aspiring nations in the region (Poland, Ukraine, the Baltic states). Second, the creation of an independent Poland led to treaty boundaries that separated German territory into two pieces—the bulk of the state and a small East Prussian region surrounding the city of Königsberg (today Kaliningrad). The major port city of Danzig (Gdansk) became an independent city-state under League of Nations nominal control, and another port, Memel, eventually became part of a new Lithuania. In the end, Germany lost 260 square miles of territory in the east to the new Polish Republic as well as more than three million of its population. (See Map 3.)

These territorial and population losses hit the German populace hard, especially since, in 1918, Germany had won the war in the east. Germans had begun making plans for use of the "eastern" lands that their armies occupied in Poland and Baltic areas, so the forfeiture of these gains from war with Russia seemed especially harsh. The reduction of territory meant loss of agricultural and industrial capacity for the rebuilding of Germany, but in addition to this economic loss, the treaty was a blow to German nationalism and morale. Almost from the moment of the signing of the treaty, German politicians set their sights on restoration of eastern territories. Certainly, the Nazi policy of Lebensraum (seeking additional space for the nation) that Adolf Hitler promoted was centered in this longing for the territories east of Germany.

Disarmament and Demilitarization

On the question of disarmament, Germany stood little chance of keeping much of its defense capability. Its navy was reduced to a handful of coastal defense ships and naval bases were decommissioned. The treaty barred Germany from possessing submarines at all. On land, Germany's army was reduced to a volunteer force of 100 000 men (conscription was prohibited), and the Rhineland region was demilitarized in a 50-kilometer strip on the east side of the river. All fortifications and military installations west of the Rhine were forbidden. The treaty even limited activities of German police, veterans' associations, and private youth groups in order to stop surreptitious military training. Finally, the Allies prohibited Germany from possessing an air force, a general staff, and weapons such as poison gas and tanks. To police these provisions, Allies placed occupying forces in the Rhineland and monitored the destruction of military capabilities.

War Guilt and Reparations

Perhaps the most hated features of the Treaty of Versailles in Germany were the clauses concerning war responsibility and reparations. With the inclusion of Article 231, the "War Guilt Clause," Germany was assigned sole responsibility for World War I and given the task of paying for the damage of the war in Europe. Therefore, beyond its territorial losses, Germany faced the repayment of wartime debts and the payment of crushing reparations to its former enemies and occupied zones. The Allies demanded reparations in the form of immediate cash gold reserves, future payments on a long schedule, and goods "in kind" that included everything from books and artwork to farm animals and industrial machines. Allied occupiers planned to make sure reparations appeared by remaining in Germany until regular payments were made for several years. Interestingly, the treaty did not mandate an exact total for reparations but instead left that task to a post-treaty reparations commission.

To pay its reparations bill, Germany needed to borrow money, which would add to the debt it had already incurred as a result of war. Of course, it was not the only country that had to finance war-related debt. Some of the borrowing had come through war bonds, but much of the borrowing by the Allied powers had depended on loans from the United States. By 1922, the total net debt to the United States was $10.5 billion (equal to roughly $143 billion in 2016). So beyond the big question of Germany's ability to pay its crushing debt, there was a larger economic instability at the heart of the postwar settlements. As the 1920s turned to the 1930s, not only did the question of Germany's war guilt become a motivational cry for the political parties of that nation but American control of large parts of the global economy also created further tensions.

League of Nations

Finally, a central feature of Woodrow's Wilson's Fourteen Points speech and an important idea at the heart of his vision of the treaty was the League of Nations, an international council dedicated to conflict resolution and collective security. The original covenant for the League aimed to create a general assembly of member states that could administer the provisions of the postwar treaties, settle disputes, and create international committees to deal with the world's most pressing problems. Most of the Allied powers agreed to the general outlines of the League, but they differed greatly in their understanding of the details. What emerged from the negotiations was an organization based in Geneva that lacked a real security force to mediate disputes. The League also failed to establish a concrete definition of what a self-governing state would look like in the postwar world. Since self-governing states could apply for membership, this was an important omission. Most importantly, Wilson was not able to gain the support of the US Senate for the League; in fact the Senate refused to ratify the Treaty of Versailles at all. Many Senators worried that the League would entangle the United States in European problems in a way that was antithetical to US security and foreign policy. The Senate's rejection of the treaty and the League meant that Wilson's signature idea would henceforth be a European-only League of Nations, with no US participation.

In the end, the Treaty of Versailles made no one completely happy, and it faced opposition and denunciation even before it was signed. Famously, Ferdinand Foch, the supreme Allied commander at the end of the war refused to attend the signing and denounced the treaty: "This is not peace. It is an armistice for twenty years." From the British ranks, young economist John Maynard Keynes wrote a devastating critique of the treaty entitled *The Economic Consequences of the Peace*, which appeared in December 1919. Keynes's book became a bestseller in multiple countries with its criticism of the treaty for excessive demands on Germany's economic resources and its warnings about debt to the United States. With Foch and Keynes denouncing the treaty and with the rejection of the settlement in the US Senate, a sense of the problems of the postwar peace pervaded Allied media as early as 1919. On the German side, the anger at the terms of the treaty could hardly be contained. Clever politicians were able to shape and feed this anger in the 1920s and 1930s. Politicians such as Adolf Hitler funneled general anger into an elaborate story about a "stab in the back" delivered to Germany by internal enemies of the nation who had been responsible for the signing of the treaty. Hitler identified these enemies as socialists, communists, Jews, and other "undesirables," and used the war in his speeches to target these populations. The "stab in the back" concept contributed greatly to a sense of German victimhood and shame that would prove useful in whipping up a new nationalism in the interwar period.

Other Treaties

Like the Treaty of Versailles, many of the other 1919 treaties were built on compromises that did not really appease any of those involved. In some cases, treaties had to be renegotiated when no political leaders would sign them. Each of the treaties led to territorial loss, reparations payments, and reduced military might for the Central Powers. At the Treaty of Neuilly in November, Bulgaria lost territory and population (including access to the Aegean Sea), while the other Balkan states gained. Romania doubled its population and the new Yugoslavia tripled Serbia's prewar population and territories as a result of postwar treaties. Greece also gained land at the expense of Bulgaria. The Treaty of St. Germain in September demanded that Austria pay reparations, which were beyond the means of this new nation without the Habsburg treasury and after the devastating economic impact of war. Austria was promised League of Nation membership and received that status in 1920. Its former partner, Hungary, experienced a pro-Communist *coup d'état* by Bela Kun in 1919 and a short war with Romania, which occupied Budapest that same year, effectively ending the Kun regime. The Treaty of Trianon, signed in June 1920, struck a familiar note—loss of territory (Hungary gave up two-thirds of its prewar land), reparations, and admission of responsibility.

While violence continued in Central Europe and the Soviet Union, the negotiations for a treaty with the former Ottoman Empire stalled, and large questions loomed about the former German colonial holdings around the world. The question of colonies was largely decided by the creation of a new system of "mandates" under the oversight of the League of Nations. Mandates were not technically colonial possessions, but instead they were under the tutelage of another nation in a framework of international accountability. Each mandate was classified according to its readiness for self-government (A, B, C), and each region was assigned a "protector" who would help the colony along the way to self-sufficiency. These mandates were loosely guaranteed by the international League of Nations as a trustee against outright annexation by their mentors. Former German and Ottoman territories, especially overseas, became mandates after World War I under the control of France, Belgium, Britain, Japan, South Africa, New Zealand, and Australia. Postwar mandates included the following modern states:

Class A: Israel, Jordan, Syria, Lebanon, Iraq
Class B: Tanzania, Cameroon, Togo, Rwanda, Burundi
Class C: Samoa, New Guinea, Nauru, Micronesia

Each class represented perceived readiness for self-rule, so those in Class A were defined as being most ready for independence.

Meanwhile, the Allies tried to impose a settlement similar to those signed by the other Central Powers on what would become modern Turkey with the Treaty of Sèvres (August 1920). Allied forces occupied Istanbul in order to pressure the Turks to ratify the treaty, but under the leadership of former Ottoman officer Mustafa Kemal, the Turks resisted. Kemal and his supporters instead declared an uprising and set up a new government in the city of Ankara. Meanwhile, open warfare continued between Greek and Turkish factions, which led to a disastrous series of battles, atrocities, and vengeance attacks between 1920 and 1922. In fact, this violence capped 10 years of almost continual unrest along the Greek, Turkish, and Balkan borders that began with the First Balkan War (1912) and continued into the 1920s.

The Aegean coastal town of Smyrna (modern Izmir in Turkey) demonstrates the ferocity of the feelings of ethnic nationalism sparked by this war and the long Balkan conflicts of the previous decade. Smyrna, formerly a multiethnic town, was occupied by the Greeks with the backing of the Great Powers. Troops targeted Turks for violence and humiliation, inciting Turkish sentiments. This led Kemal to order the Turkish army to march on the city; Smyrna was burned nearly to the ground by Turkish forces who sought to retaliate by singling out

Greek houses and inhabitants in the violence. Large numbers of Greek-speaking citizens of the region fled on British and American ships to escape the violence, by the end of September 1922, one official wrote: "The Turks claim to have solved the problem of minorities." This action set a precedent for the idea of deportation and homogenizing populations that fundamentally transformed the Middle East. In July 1923, Turkey, under Kemal's leadership, signed a treaty with the Allies (the Treaty of Lausanne), ending Allied occupation and providing decent terms for Kemal's new nation. This treaty gave Turkey independence and "solved" the minorities issue by instituting a mass population exchange of Greeks and Turks between the two nations.

In hindsight, the most disappointing thing about all the postwar treaties is how limited they were in solving the real crises that had emerged as a result of the war. Many of the territorial disputes remained open wounds, and the war itself had created new grievances in border regions. Crushing economic debt and inflation plagued postwar nations. The movement of refugees and displaced peoples who sought recognition and homes added to the strain on governments that had only recently been created. Minority populations in the new nations demanded redress of their grievances, and colonial populations decried their betrayal by the Great Powers and Wilson's promises of self-determination. In the end, the legacy of the treaties are these big questions that marked the interwar period, helped spark World War II, and persisted into the latter years of the twentieth century.

Big Questions—Crises of the Immediate Postwar

Between the time of the armistices of 1918 and the peace treaties of 1919 through to 1923, the political and social status of large groups of people in Europe, Africa, and Asia remained in flux. Borders dissolved, creating problems of national identity and citizenship, while factions fought over the constitution of new nations and governments. Amidst chaos and uncertainty, the seeds of the interwar world were planted. Wilson's promise of "self-determination" for peoples had stirred up a burgeoning ethnic and cultural nationalism that divided villages, cities, and nations upon lines that had before the war remained blurry and undefined. The hardening of lines of race, religion, language, and ethnicity led to violence throughout the former territories of the Ottoman, Habsburg, Romanov, and Hohenzollern empires and pervaded the ideologies of the postwar political factions forming in these regions.

In the Soviet Union, civil war raged from 1918 to 1921, and a revolutionary terror that rivalled or surpassed The Terror of the French Revolution broke out. Enemies of the state, minorities, former landlords, and tsarist officials found themselves targeted for torture and execution. Whole groups of people or villages could be deemed traitors, and violence and fear plagued the new nation. While this so-called Red Terror proceeded, opponents created their own White Terror and allied with nearby nations. As Joshua Sanborn notes, "Both Reds and Whites utilized extralegal, arbitrary and merciless violence to achieve political ends." The numbers killed in this period of wild violence are still debated today, but what is clear is that the death toll disproportionately affected civilians. The end of the Civil War did not curtail the struggle for former Russian subjects; the 1920s brought a vicious famine in the Volga region. Vladimir Lenin's death in 1924 led to a reshuffling of Soviet Leadership, and the emergence of Josef Stalin in the late 1920s brought his brutal campaigns for collectivization and industrialization. Total war ideology pervaded the Bolshevik state, and Stalin's attempt to create a totalitarian state between the 1920s and World War II owed much to the lessons of World War I.

One new nation where the politics of identity loomed large is Poland, where the end of the war brought both an extended war with the Soviet Union and the Ukraine as well as sustained and brutal attacks on perceived outsiders within the nation. In November 1918, Polish leaders, most important among them Józef Piłsudski, declared an independent Poland with a provisional government and then set about trying to make this statement a fact through diplomatic maneuvering internationally and through outright war with its neighbors (such as the Soviet Union). As these high-level negotiations and battles proceeded, local attacks spontaneously broke out, many of them aimed at Jewish populations. These anti-Jewish riots spread to various communities with the worst attack occurring in the large city of Lemberg (Lviv) in late November 1918. After fighting in the area during which Jewish leaders had maintained neutrality, Ukrainian forces withdrew and Polish troops occupied the city. Accounts about how the violence began vary widely, but in the end more than 70 people were killed, nearly 500 were wounded, and a large portion of the Jewish section of Lemberg had burned, including three synagogues. None of those who were primarily responsible for this outbreak of violence ever faced trial. Soon after, Poland held its first free elections and began the work of establishing its borders and creating a national citizenry out of the fragmented population that emerged from war.

Minority Questions

Given the fluid boundaries of postwar nations and the violence against minorities in many of the postwar states, the negotiators at the Paris Peace Conference sought to protect minorities who might be disenfranchised or abused by the political deals being struck. Nearly 30 million people in Europe found themselves part of nations in which they were not the dominant nationality or ethnicity. Many of these minorities were Jews, but other minority groups included Germans,

Ukrainians, Slovaks, Ruthenians, and Russians, just to name a few. Eventually two different solutions emerged to the "minority problem" and each carried its own set of challenges.

The first solution, negotiated at the Paris Peace Conference in 1919, was the creation of a series of minority treaties. New nations had to agree to the terms of these treaties before they could receive formal recognition of their governments. The treaties contained broad guarantees of legal equality, religious freedom, and freedom of life and liberty. The treaties also provided vague assurances of the ability of minorities to gain naturalization as citizens while protecting the minorities' ability to operate their own charitable, religious, and educational associations. However, many of the treaties declared official languages and provided little protection for minority language instruction or use. Finally, much of the enforcement of these treaties was left to the states themselves with some oversight from the new League of Nations. The minority treaties were most prevalent in eastern and central Europe, where multiple ethnic, religious, and linguistic groups lived side by side.

An example of one of these agreements is the minority treaty signed between the Allied powers and Romania, which had doubled in population after the war. In December 1919 when the treaty was signed, Romania's borders enclosed a minority population of almost 30%, which included Hungarians, Jews, Germans, Ukrainians, Bulgarians, Turks, Russians, Gypsies, Serbs, Poles, Slovaks, Greeks, and Armenians. This suggests great diversity of the interwar population in an expanded Romanian state and also explains why many of these groups pushed for protection of their rights. Romania agreed to provisions for choice of nationality, civil and legal equality, and protection of minority status, but what emerged here and in other states was a problem of enforcement. The League of Nations had little real power to guarantee or police nations who chose to violate their minority treaties, and in Romania, minority rights eroded in the 1930s especially for Jews, who became targets of a Romanian antisemitic, fascist-style political party.

A second approach to the so-called minorities problem was most apparent in Anatolia and Greece, where the 1923 Treaty of Lausanne, which ended the war with modern Turkey, established a mandatory population exchange. In this region where the war had continued to rage between Greek and Turkish forces and where 50 000 had died since 1919, postwar officials sought a new solution. Rather than create rules to protect minorities, the signatories decided to end the minority problem by separating the populations, forcibly (if necessary) in a way reminiscent of the actions in Smyrna. The treaty called for the "compulsory exchange of Turkish nations…and of Greek nations" that affected more than a million Greek Christians living in Turkey and nearly 400 000 Turkish Muslims residing in Greece. While some had already fled because of the violence of the Greco-Turkish war that erupted in 1919, many had to be forcibly relocated to nations where they did not know the language and had no ties. In a sense, the postwar nations of Greece and Turkey had ended their minority problem by eliminating their minorities.

Even with the "solutions" to the minority problems in place in the conquered territories there were still a number of displaced people and refugees who had been uprooted by war and its aftermath. Many of these individuals and families now were officially "stateless," as they had lost their countries of origin, and they had no permanent residence. A large number of these long-term refugees were people who had fled from the Russian Civil War and now found themselves in the capitals of Europe: Paris, Berlin, Vienna, London. The League of Nations recognized the distress of these individuals, many of whom faced abject poverty. In order to provide this group with some ability to gain jobs and become mobile in a postwar world, Norwegian diplomat Fridtjof Nansen, who was serving as High Commissioner for Refugees for the League of Nations, oversaw a commission to design special passports for refugees, especially Russian émigrés. The first of these appeared in 1922, but they were used throughout the interwar period, and the so-called Nansen Passport was extended to Armenian refugees as well. Although holders of this passport gained the ability to travel to some nations, the Nansen passport also marked them as stateless. Most became homeless refugees or permanent guests in a country other than their own.

Economic and Political Challenges

In addition to the ongoing challenges facing minorities and refugees in the postwar world, there was an economic crisis in the years immediately following 1919. Many of the nations that had been involved in the war struggled with inflationary spikes, devaluation of currency, trade problems, and shortages in major commodities in the early 1920s. This economic instability led to acute hardship for families and to a wave of anger, especially among industrial workers, that fueled strikes and labor actions. Even the United States, which had come out of the war with increased trade prospects and agricultural surplus, experienced an inflationary/deflationary cycle from 1919 to 1921 that constituted what we would call a recession today. More damaging were the hyperinflations (flooding of the market with money, making that currency virtually worthless) that plagued postwar Germany and Austria. The worst year was 1923, when inflation rose so quickly that German currency lost its value entirely. Prior to the war, the dollar was worth a little over four German marks. By late 1923, the dollar was worth about four trillion marks. To deal with this crisis, the German government created a temporary scrip, the *rentenmark*, which effectively stabilized money until a new *Reichsmark* came into usage in 1924.

Finally, political extremism of a new form flourished in the interwar period, and its origins owed much to the war and its veterans. In Italy, Mussolini's Fascist Party drew heavily from former soldiers of World War I with nearly 60% of its members in 1921 identifying themselves as ex-combatants. Many of these early fascists had retained or claimed weaponry from the war itself, so they were armed with cannons, machine guns, and hand grenades in addition to regular rifles and handguns. As Alan Kramer explains of these weapons, "The war had bequeathed not only a political, but a very tangible physical legacy." Personnel and weapons were not the only legacies of the war in the creation of interwar fascism. Mussolini and other fascist leaders conceived of their ideology as an extension of wartime comradeship, ultra-nationalism, and violence as a motivating force. Prewar socialists such as Mussolini perceived how a totalizing war could make people sacrifice for the nation, and they fused this idea with notions of creating a collective ethos. Class struggle gave way to a mythic and sacrificial nationalism. In short, fascism is a political invention that emerges from war not as an inevitable result but as an ideology that crystallized several political strands in a crucible of violence and postwar disappointment. It grew quickly as well. In 1919, Mussolini's group had 800 members; by November 1920, the fascists had 20 615 members.

Other nations also embraced versions of fascism, and virtually every nation in Europe had some form of home-grown fascist-style right-wing party by the 1930s. Each of these parties varied considerably and reflected local conditions. Oswald Mosley's British Union of Fascists had little of substance in common with Romania's Legion of the Archangel Michael, yet their reliance on uniforms, national myths, and an elevated view of violence united them nonetheless. Another important element uniting fascist-style parties and authoritarian right-wing dictatorships in the period was a rejection of liberalism and parliamentary democracy as outdated and weak. As such, reasoned political argument and debate disappeared in favor of emotion-laden propaganda, mass rallies, and nationalist rhetoric. The combination of this modern political rhetoric, expanded media outlets such as radio and film, and the devastating economic depression led more people to consider the merits of right-wing parties by the 1930s.

No country demonstrates this trend more thoroughly than Germany, which, in the postwar period, had developed a multi-party republic known as the Weimar Republic. The new Germany emerged from the shadow of postwar defeat and deflation by the 1920s, becoming what appeared to be a stable and strong force in Europe. The blow of the Great Depression in the aftermath of 1929 shattered this stability and exposed weaknesses in the parliamentary system, creating an opening for a small, radical, right-wing political party to take power in 1933. Adolf Hitler's National Socialist Party (Nazi), like Mussolini's fascists, had emerged after World War I with a core group of ex-soldiers. Like Italy's fascists, Hitler's Nazi's wore uniforms, relied on a group of paramilitary enforcers (the SA), and glorified violence. Unlike Mussolini, however, Hitler got little traction in Germany until economic depression led to a crisis in confidence in the mainstream political parties. The Nazis relied on promises of erasing the shame of World War I and the humiliation of the Treaty of Versailles in order to gain votes by 1932. When Hitler was named Chancellor in January 1933, the most

145

successful of all the interwar fascist-style parties took power over the most important country economically in Europe and launched a campaign that led to World War II. Hitler's politics embodied the ultimate ethos of what Modris Eksteins calls the "doctrine of conflict," where war is a perpetual state, violence and coercion are institutionalized, and there is no room for pity or compromise.

Woodrow Wilson's idea of a war to end wars and a war to make the world safe for democracy proved an illusion. Economic instability and depression as well as the rise of authoritarian and totalitarian regimes in the interwar period demonstrated that the forces unleashed by World War I continued to destabilize the world. What had become apparent in the interwar period was the extraordinary power of ethnic nationalism and the lure of violent and extreme solutions to disputes. As Aviel Roshwald persuasively argues, "Where formerly a wide range of nationalist visions—ranging from narrowly ethnic to pan-nationalist, from liberal to chauvinistic—had competed for attention and popular support, there had now come into being...a new post-imperial political geography."

Conclusion

In many ways 1922 to 1924 were the decisive years in understanding the postwar impact of World War I for diplomatic, political, social, and economic reasons. These were the years of the Soviet famine, the German hyperinflation, and the consolidation of power for Mussolini's Fascist Party in Italy. Adolf Hitler experienced his first brush with fame in an ill-advised and failed Beer Hall *Putsch* (*coup d'état*) in 1923 that nonetheless gave him a public platform for his ideas during the trial that followed. In the British Empire, Ireland concluded its war for independence with the creation of the Irish Free State, and Mahatma Gandhi, who was leading an anticolonial campaign in India, spent those two years in prison on a charge of sedition. Britain elected its first Labour (socialist) government. Vladimir Lenin, leader of the Soviet Union, died in January 1924, sparking a power struggle in which Josef Stalin would emerge as leader. In other words, these were pivotal years in the shaping of postwar politics and societies.

Significant events occurred in 1923 and 1924. First, in January 1923 the French along with Belgian and Italian allies occupied the Ruhr region of Germany, which was rich in coal. The occupiers claimed that Germany had reneged on its treaty obligations to pay reparations. Germany, facing hyperinflation and crushing economic debts, had stopped payments temporarily. The French occupation of the Ruhr led to a massive German campaign of resistance to French authority with work stoppages and minor sabotage. The French retaliated with deportations and harsh discipline. This incident threatened to destabilize Europe and create a new crisis. Germany appealed for international intervention to the League of Nations and the United States.

The League hoped for a negotiated diplomatic solution to this showdown over the Ruhr, and a series of commissions met to deal with the crisis. It was in this environment that the Dawes Plan took effect in 1924, with the purpose of renegotiating debt and reparations agreements for Germany. This plan, largely brokered by the United States, provided loans directly to Germany as well as a new payment scheme for its war obligations. The French, who were still occupying the Ruhr region, had to agree to a withdrawal timeline in order to receive their own renewed loans from US banks. These negotiations led to bitter disappointment and enmity between Germany and France, setting the stage for renewed conflict once the spark of economic depression was lit.

As this chapter has demonstrated, the war did not conclude with a sense of closure or with an end to violence. Instead, the postwar treaties brought solutions to the issues of borders, minorities, and reparations, but these solutions contained their own problems. Hostility and bloodshed continued, and in some regions the postwar years proved more frightening and deadly than World War I itself. One of the big lessons that World War I made clear was the difficulties that global, total war created. Wilson's vision of a "war to end wars" proved to be impossible.

Citations

Page	Source
133–4	Background information on Mussolini and D'Annunzio drawn from Zeev Sternhell, *The Birth of Fascist Ideologies*, Translated by David Maisel (Princeton, NJ: Princeton University Press, 1995).
135	"left 'shatter zones' …" quoted in Robert Gerwarth and John Horne, "Paramilitarism in Europe after the Great War: An Introduction," in *War in Peace: Paramilitary Violence in Europe after the Great War*, Gerwarth and Horne, eds. (Oxford: Oxford University Press, 2012), 4.
137	Figures showing Germany's lost territory are drawn from Alan Sharp, *The Versailles Settlement: Peacemaking after the First World War, 1919–1923*, 2nd Edition (Houndmills: Palgrave Macmillan, 2008), 131.
138	Figures showing net debt to the United States drawn from Adam Tooze, *The Deluge: The Great War, America and the Remaking of the Global Order, 1916–1931* (New York: Viking, 2014), 302.
139	"This is not peace …" quoted in Michael S. Neiberg, *Foch: Supreme Allied Commander in the Great War* (Dulles, VA: Brassey's, 2003), 101.
141	"The Turks claim …" quoted in Michelle Tusan, *Smyrna's Ashes: Humanitarianism, Genocide, and the Birth of the Middle East* (Berkeley: University of California Press, 2012), 151.
142	"Both Reds and Whites …" quoted in Joshua Sanborn, *Imperial Apocalypse: The Great War and the Destruction of the Russian Empire* (New York: Oxford University Press, 2014), 252.

142   Information on the disputed death toll is drawn from Orlando Figes, "The Red Army and Mass Mobilization during the Russian Civil War, 1918–1920," *Past and Present* 129 (1990): 172.

142   Figures about anti-Jewish riots and attacks drawn from Carole Fink, *Defending the Rights of Others: The Great Powers, the Jews, and International Minority Protection, 1878–1938* (Cambridge: Cambridge University Press, 2004), 102–112.

142   Figure of 30 million drawn from Sharp, 166.

143   "compulsory exchange of ..." quoted in Bruce Clark, *Twice a Stranger: The Mass Expulsions that Forged Modern Greece and Turkey* (Cambridge, MA: Harvard University Press, 2006), 12–14.

145   "The weapon had bequeathed ..." quoted in Alan Kramer, *Dynamic of Destruction: Culture and Mass Killing in the First World War* (Oxford: Oxford University Press, 2007), 300–301.

145   Emilio Gentile, "Paramilitary Violence in Italy: The Rationale of Fascism and the Origins of Totalitarianism," in *War in Peace: Paramilitary Violence in Europe after the Great War*, 89.

146   "doctrine of conflict" quoted in Modris Eksteins, *Rites of Spring: The Great War and the Birth of the Modern Age* (Boston, MA: Houghton Mifflin, 1989), 314.

146   "Where formerly a wide ..." quoted in Aviel Roshwald, *Ethnic Nationalism & the Fall of Empires: Central Europe, Russia & the Middle East, 1914–1923* (New York: Routledge, 2001), 196.

Select Bibliography

Clark, Bruce. *Twice a Stranger: The Mass Expulsions that Forged Modern Greece and Turkey.* Cambridge, MA: Harvard University Press, 2006.

Dockrill, Michael L., and J. Douglas Goold. *Peace without Promise: Britain and the Peace Conferences, 1919–23.* Hamden, CT: Archon Books, 1981.

Eksteins, Modris. *Rites of Spring: The Great War and the Birth of the Modern Age.* Boston, MA: Houghton Mifflin, 1989.

Figes, Orlando. "The Red Army and Mass Mobilization During the Russian Civil War, 1918–1920." *Past and Present* 129 (1990): 168–211.

Fink, Carole. *Defending the Rights of Others: The Great Powers, the Jews, and International Minority Protection, 1878–1938.* Cambridge: Cambridge University Press, 2004.

Galántai, József. *Trianon and the Protection of Minorities.* New York: Columbia University Press, 1992.

Gentile, Emilio. "Paramilitary Violence in Italy: The Rationale of Fascism and the Origins of Totalitarianism." In *War in Peace: Paramilitary Violence in Europe after the Great War*, Robert Gerwarth and John Horne, eds., 85–103. Oxford: Oxford University Press, 2012.

Gerwarth, Robert, and John Horne, "Paramilitarism in Europe after the Great War: An Introduction." In *War in Peace: Paramilitary Violence in Europe after the Great War*, Gerwarth and Horne, eds., 1–18. Oxford: Oxford University Press, 2012.

Kramer, Alan. *Dynamic of Destruction: Culture and Mass Killing in the First World War.* Oxford: Oxford University Press, 2007.

MacMillan, Margaret. *Paris 1919: Six Months that Changed the World.* New York: Random House, 2001.

Manela, Erez. *The Wilsonian Moment: Self-Determination and the International Origins of Anticolonial Nationalism.* New York: Oxford University Press, 2007.

Marks, Sally. *The Illusion of Peace: International Relations in Europe, 1918–1933.* New York: St. Martin's Press, 1976.

Neiberg, Michael S. *Foch: Supreme Allied Commander in the Great War.* Dulles, VA: Brassey's, 2003.

Roshwald, Aviel. *Ethnic Nationalism & the Fall of Empires: Central Europe, Russia & the Middle East, 1914–1923.* New York: Routledge, 2001.

Sanborn, Joshua. *Imperial Apocalypse: The Great War and the Destruction of the Russian Empire.* New York: Oxford University Press, 2014.

Sharp, Alan. *The Versailles Settlement: Peacemaking after the First World War, 1919–1923*, 2nd Edition. Houndmills: Palgrave Macmillan, 2008.

Sternhell, Zeev. *The Birth of Fascist Ideologies.* Translated by David Maisel. Princeton, NJ: Princeton University Press, 1995.

Tooze, Adam. *The Deluge: The Great War, America and the Remaking of the Global Order, 1916–1931.* New York: Viking, 2014.

Tusan, Michelle. *Smyrna's Ashes: Humanitarianism, Genocide, and the Birth of the Middle East.* Berkeley: University of California Press, 2012.

Appendix 7.1: Timeline for 1919–1923

1919	*IMPORTANT EVENTS*
January 18	Paris Peace Conference begins
February 14	League of Nations Covenant
March 4	Comintern (Communist International) founded in Moscow
March 24	Béla Kun coup d'etat in Hungary leads to creation of a Soviet Republic
May 15	Greeks occupy Smyrna (Izmir)
June 28	Treaty of Versailles signed (Allies–Germany)
August 1	Kun's republic ends
September 10	Treaty of St.-Germain-en-Laye signed (Allies–Austria)
September 12	Gabriele D'Annunzio occupies Fiume
November 27	Treaty of Neuilly signed (Allies–Hungary)
1920	
March 16	Allies occupy Constantinople (Istanbul)
March 19	US Senate rejects the Treaty of Versailles
June 4	Treaty of Trianon signed (Allies–Hungary)
August 10	Treaty of Sèvres signed (Allies–Turkey)
1921	
March 18	Treaty of Riga signed (Poland–Russia)
October 18	United States ratifies separate treaties with Germany, Austria, and Hungary
December 6	Anglo-Irish Treaty signed
1922	
April 16	Treaty of Rapallo signed (Germany–Russia)
September	Burning of Smyrna
October 28	March on Rome which leads to Benito Mussolini assuming power in Italy
November 12	Washington Naval Conference opens
1923	
January 11	Occupation of the Ruhr begins
July 14	Treaty of Lausanne signed

8

Postwar. How Was the War Remembered and Commemorated?

Figure 8.1   War cemeteries and monuments from the First World War document the millions of war dead in this conflict. In the postwar period, political leaders sometimes used the dead for their own advancement or for an ideological purpose, as with Benito Mussolini's massive memorial to the war dead at Redipuglia. *Source*: Photo by author, 2012.

World War I: A Short History, First Edition. Tammy M. Proctor.
© 2018 John Wiley & Sons Ltd. Published 2018 by John Wiley & Sons Ltd.

In 1919, citizens of Kansas City in the United States raised $2.5 million in just under two weeks for a war memorial in their hometown to those who had fought and died in World War I. This accomplishment represented donations from almost a quarter of the population of the metropolitan area at the time and made it possible for the city to raise a huge monument named the Liberty Memorial. The site was dedicated in 1921 and the building itself was completed in 1926. Today that structure is the National World War I Museum and Memorial, and it represents the outpouring of money toward the commemoration of the war, not just in the United States but worldwide.

Elsewhere in the United States in that same year, in the tiny town of Pickerelltown, Ohio, a small column was erected. Today, drivers entering the town arrive at an obelisk in their path in the form of this stone memorial to the fallen of World War I, which sits in the center of the only intersection in this little town. It recognizes two Pickerelltown residents who died in the war—one on each side of the obelisk. Both of these men, Henry F. Bushawn and Forest E. Dubbs, died in France and are buried in American cemeteries in Europe. However, the monument is careful to distinguish between the two soldiers. While Dubbs was "killed in battle in France," Bushawn "died in France." We do not know from the stone if Bushawn was a soldier who died of influenza, or an ambulance driver, or a doctor, or an official in the Red Cross, but we do know that unlike Dubbs, he was not killed in battle. It is only by consulting their published service records, that one finds out that Bushawn, like Dubbs, was in the infantry. Bushawn, however, lingered a while after his injury and "died of wounds" in the Meuse-Argonne, while Dubbs was killed instantly during the German offensive at Montdidier-Noyon.

The Pickerelltown and Kansas City memorials help us understand one of the central features of postwar commemoration, namely that there were multiple approaches, numerous sentiments, and varied reactions to remembering the war and making sense of the conflict. While the Kansas City monument demonstrates an outpouring of civic pride and community grieving, the Pickerelltown stone shows the centrality of the combat soldier to the historical memory of the conflict. Both monuments demonstrate a crucial problem: how to show respect for the dead and their sacrifices while still maintaining the patriotic and nationalist justifications for war, many of which seem hollow in the face of so many dead and wounded men.

Added to this concern was the logistical question of how to deal with the sheer scope of the conflict and its casualties. Many families would never see their loved ones' graves because they were located half a world away. Added to this problem were the vast nameless dead or those missing. Erecting a grave for a known soldier at the site of a battle is a straightforward, if not an easy, task. Marking the life of an "unknown soldier" or creating a memorial for someone missing in action is a far harder task. Solutions to these problems ranged from massive memorial halls and monuments raised through public subscription or government subsidies to private shrines, memorial volumes of poetry, and other individual tributes.

Some postwar societies found it almost impossible to mourn the dead in any public fashion. In the former Russian Empire, the Revolution and Civil War superseded much of the public mourning for the war and made it hard for families to find collective means of petitioning the state for their losses, both emotional and physical. Likewise in Ireland, civic memorials sometimes sparked violence or opposition in the atmosphere of civil war that reigned in the immediate postwar years. Other nations such as Belgium had experienced invasion or occupation, so their postwar memory was mixed up with cries of collaboration and claims of resistance. Still other states such as Germany had to appeal to former enemies to retain war cemeteries in France and Belgium for their war dead. For all nations, marking the service of those who fought or labored became a politically charged act.

This chapter examines the notion that World War I left few families who were involved in the war unchanged, either because of the impact of injury or death or because of the less tangible effect of absence and violence. Memory of the war took a variety of forms from private memorialization to public commemoration to artistic or literary expressions. Each was an important component in building an historical memory of the war and in helping postwar populations cope with the aftermath of violence.

Commemoration in Stone

The process of making sense of the war and rebuilding the shattered landscapes and relationships the conflict had forged was neither easy nor quick. Political leaders spent time and money to enable the raising of local and national monuments, and workers logged countless hours digging up, identifying, labeling, and reburying dead. As Kurt Piehler has noted, "the war dead were still being pressed into service by their governments…since they were silent, the war dead could offer their complete allegiance to the nation." The commemoration of soldiers' service sometimes sparked political battles over national, ethnic, religious, racial, and familial identities, but few opposed the notion of marking the sacrifice of heroic male combatants.

Virtually all of these public monuments and cemeteries celebrated and mourned the combatant war dead—most of whom were male. Commemoration of non-combatant laborers and technicians, even of those who were formally drafted into the army, was more problematic. There are memorials that recognize those who worked visibly for the war, but typically these monuments make a distinction between those who labored and those who fought. For example, the Service of Supply, the US army's drafted military workforce, which was paid and uniformed by the army, is listed in a separate panel at the Meuse-Argonne War Cemetery in France, the United States' largest World War I cemetery. While missing combat soldiers from that conflict are listed on one panel under the phrase: "American Soldiers who *fought* in the region and whose earthly resting place is known only to God," the Service of Supply missing are inscribed on a separate panel, which notes "American soldiers who *died* in the Services of Supply during the World War and have no known graves" [emphasis mine]. Again, as in Pickerelltown, a distinction is drawn between those who fought and those who died in uniform, despite the reality that both groups gave their lives. For civilian contractors, there are even fewer memorials recognizing their service and sacrifice.

Civilians were left with few choices for highlighting their own contributions. Instead, civilian monuments often featured symbolic martyrs to the war. A good example of such memorials can be found in Great Britain, where citizens erected a prominent statue of Edith Cavell on Charing Cross Road near Trafalgar Square in 1920. Inscribed on the four sides of the monument are four qualities—Humanity, Fortitude, Devotion, and Sacrifice—but the most prominent inscription is that on the front of the monument at Cavell's feet—"Brussels. Dawn. October 12, 1915." Cavell, a nurse who helped Allied soldiers escape occupied Belgium, was executed by the Germans in 1915. Her death became a major theme of Allied propaganda during the war, and her postwar funeral had been a major public spectacle. Cavell, a martyr and symbol of German aggression, served as a perfect example of the kind of civilian heroism that was celebrated in the 1920s. Cavell and other executed civilians often symbolized sacrifice, but the monuments emphasized their victimhood rather than their heroism. Cavell's sculpture is pristine white, an idealized vision of the patriotic civilian war martyr.

In northern France and Belgium, similar monuments to the slain civilians of the war create a powerful language of martyrdom and collective grief. The war memorial in Leuven, Belgium, depicts scenes of atrocity and terror. Civilian experience is featured, but once again, the civilians are portrayed as victims of the German war machine, rather than as active war participants. Throughout the town, structures rebuilt after being destroyed by the German torching of the city during its invasion are marked prominently with a plaque containing a sword, flames, and the year 1914. The figures in these "martyrs' monuments" are victims of war, and their suffering is shown alongside the destruction of property and landscape. Postwar monuments portray civilians as objects of war, not subjects in the conflict; they are brave in their patience and suffering, but not heroes in the same sense that soldiers are. Yet, everyone involved in the war, whether fighting on the front lines or packing parcels for prisoners of war, felt urgency in their work and a patriotic pride in serving.

During World War I, both male and female civilians sought to prove their patriotism through activities they defined as active service. Civilians at home fronts and in occupied zones felt an emotional connection with the war and a sense of obligation to serve in some way, and they actively sought recognition for that service in the postwar world, which included working in war industries or volunteering for the multitude of war charities that arose. Often such civilians created ways to identify and recognize their war activities—armbands, uniforms, patches, registration certificates, and other external badges of their patriotism. News media during the war celebrated many varieties of war work, both civilian and military, but the promise of postwar recognition and commemoration was a much more difficult proposition. Barring a few unique cases, states emphasized the combat dead, placing them at the center of postwar commemoration rituals.

Postwar commissions in each nation oversaw the public memory of war. In general, these memorials to World War I fit into four broad categories. First, permanent war cemeteries for the burial of the dead became priorities. Second, monuments at the sites of battle to the known and missing of 1914–1918 also were important. Third, national or regional monuments to the sacrifices of war at home became central sites for commemoration (and later for protest). Finally, public monuments also emerged that marked ethnic, religious, or national subgroups within a state; these certainly served political purposes in the postwar. Each of these demonstrates an aspect of public mourning in the postwar period.

Beginning in August 1914, armies built cemeteries to bury the dead after battles, sometimes within hours of the soldiers' deaths. These cemeteries varied in form and because of the conditions under which the dead were buried, it was not always possible to fully identify the bodies. When practical, temporary markers of wood or stone marked the graves, and armies strove to keep detailed records of those who had died. As the war progressed, the numbers of unmarked graves or of those whose bodies were never found grew to enormous proportions, especially in the regions of the most intense, sustained fighting. Half of all corpses in France could not be identified. Even today, perhaps 80 000 Germans soldiers are still "missing" on the Western Front, lying in unmarked graves. Thus, when the war ended the former combatant countries faced an enormous task of identifying, reinterring, and memorializing the dead—known, unknown, missing. The regions that witnessed most of the fighting today host cemeteries for all the dead. A good example of the challenges this presented comes from a view of the former Western Front in Belgium and France, where armies of multiple nations clashed.

Known and Marked

Today in the region of the Somme, cemeteries dot the landscape. Each nation had to carefully plan its cemeteries to make them expressions of the sacrifices and service of the dead but also to make them sites for pilgrimage and com-memoration. Small and large cemeteries, some in irregular formation and some clearly planned after the war, contain the dead of Germany as well as the fallen from Belgium, France, and Britain, their colonies, and their allies such as the United States. France's war cemeteries contain crosses for its Christian dead, stars for its Jewish dead, and curved stones for its Muslim dead, demonstrating the sacrifices of a whole empire of people.

For Germany, the creation of foreign cemeteries represented a postwar political victory, albeit a hollow one. After a prolonged diplomatic dispute, the French and Belgians agreed to allow their former enemy to maintain German war cemeteries along the Western Front. Today most German dead lie in France, with smaller cemeteries scattered through multiple countries such as Poland and the Soviet Union. In Belgium, German dead are buried in four cemeteries in Flanders, where they had been relocated after the war from more than 100 temporary cemeteries.

For Great Britain, war cemeteries hold the dead of a massive empire—soldiers from India, Ireland, South Africa, Australia, Canada, New Zealand, and Great Britain lie side by side under white stones. Like the other combatants, Britain's cemeteries contain a mix of identified bodies and "unknown" soldiers. Some graves contain the remains of multiple soldiers and are marked only in general terms: "Five Canadian Soldiers of the Great War."

Britain provides an excellent example of the sheer size of the organiza-tional task of marking the dead and creating spaces for mourning and cele-bration of service. The British created a war graves commission as early as 1915, but beginning in 1921, their cemeteries were designed and managed by the Commonwealth War Graves Commission (CWGC), which eventually oversaw more than 2000 individual cemetery sites associated with World War I. The CWGC decided to create a unified stone marker for each of its dead, with common size, materials, and identifying information such as regi-ment, job titles, imperial status, and rank. It did, however, allow up to three lines of individualized inscription and each family was invited to choose a short sentence to include on the stone. Some chose to leave the stone blank or to use a template offered by the commission, but others were personal, often poetic quotations. One example from a British grave in France provides a good example: "Oh for the touch of a vanished hand and the sound of a voice that is still." Inscriptions were only rejected if they exceeded the allowable 66 characters or if the content was seen as unsuitable. Rejected inscriptions typically denounced the enemy or contained pacifist statements.

These were the kinds of decisions and negotiations that took place in each country that created cemeteries for the dead.

Another difficulty arose in considering the repatriation of bodies. The British decided not to repatriate, meaning that for some families who lived in imperial outposts on the other side of the world, a visit to a loved one's grave would be an impossibility. British officials knew that this was a hardship for grieving families, therefore they supported the creation of local monuments in virtually every municipality in the British Empire. The Canadian family of a dead soldier buried in France, for example, could go to the local memorial in the center of town to grieve, to mourn, and to decorate their son's grave in absentia. Often these monuments contained all the names of the war dead, so families could lay wreaths under their son's name.

Missing in Action

Postwar authorities faced an even more difficult task in dealing with the hundreds of thousands of soldiers listed as missing in action or unknown. A few of those soldiers appeared in the postwar period, mistakenly listed as missing and appearing when they were released from hospitals or liberated from prisoner of war camps, but most often these soldiers never returned. Without proof of death, however, families were left in limbo both in terms of their relationship to the state and their own grieving. Difficult questions arose especially in relationship to survivors' benefits from the government. Were wives of missing soldiers eligible for widows' pensions? States knew that families would want visible proof that their family members' sacrifices were remembered, so postwar nations built many monuments to the missing at or near battle fronts. A good example of such memorials was the cemetery and memorial to the dead of the Isonzo campaigns erected by the Italian government at St. Elias hill near Gorizia. Roughly 100 000 dead were interred here, most of them unknown (missing). Later under Mussolini, the site was reconsecrated when a massive monument to the missing of the war was erected in 1938 at Redipuglia (across the street from St. Elias). This recommemoration of the dead was not unusual in the interwar years as leaders sought to use World War I and its memory for their own political ends.

Today these massive monuments to the war dead are major sites for commemoration activities. The British government hosted a centennial ceremony at Thiepval (the Somme) Memorial on July 1, 2016, and the French government sponsored a similar memorial service at its ossuary at Verdun on September 22, 2016. The Menin Gate, a commemorative arch dedicated to unknown dead of the British Empire, hosts a nightly "Last Post" ceremony as it has done since the 1920s. Germany's major battle memorial at Tannenberg was destroyed during and after World War II, so little remains at the site for continued memorialization. What is important about these memorials on all fronts is that they had personal and national meaning in the 1920s and 1930s for those who had lost loved ones or those who had fought. However, over time the memorials changed meaning from places of personal grief to sites that marked World War I as an historical event.

Unknown and Eternal

Most of the former combatant countries also created "official" sites of mourning, typically in capital cities, for public ceremonies. These became the objects of parades, rituals, and ceremonies in the interwar period, particularly on important war anniversaries, the Armistice of 1918 foremost among these. One of the features of these World War I monuments was the maintenance of an eternal flame. The most famous of these is at the Tomb of the Unknown Soldier in Paris (under the Arc de Triumphe), where an eternal flame was installed in 1923. Other nations with memorials that include an eternal flame are Belgium, Poland, Portugal, Romania, and Czechoslovakia. Liberty Memorial, the Kansas City monument from the beginning of this chapter, has an eternal flame at the top of its tower.

Another way to create a unifying memorial for the whole nation was to choose unknown soldiers to bury in tombs in capital cities. Paris's Tomb of the Unknown Soldier has already been mentioned—the soldier there was buried in 1920 at the same time that an unknown British soldier was interred in Westminster Abbey in London. Other nations that created such tributes in 1921 include the United States (in Arlington Cemetery), Italy, and Portugal. Australia added an unknown soldiers' tomb to its war memorial in 1993, and the Canadians incorporated a similar tomb to the missing at its new war memorial in 2000.

Memorials as Dissent

As nations planned their memorials to sacrifice and patriotism, some ex-combatants and families of the dead found no place for themselves in these celebrations of national unity. Minority groups of all kinds sought to create their own monuments to war and to use these to forward their postwar claims for recognition, citizenship, or independence. Three good examples of such dissenting memorials include the Czech Legion monument and the Ulster Tower in France, as well as the Yser Tower in Belgium. Each of these demonstrates a different sort of postwar counter-memory.

The Yser Tower (built 1930), for instance, became the site for a burgeoning Flemish nationalist movement in Belgium that challenged the authority of the central Belgian government and of French-speakers in the country. The monument to the Flemish dead was in stark contrast to Belgian national memorials in Brussels and elsewhere, and it served as a flashpoint for rallies, marches, and sometimes violent action in the interwar period. The Czech Legion cemetery and monument near Arras serves a different purpose. It celebrates the birth of a Czechoslovak nation after World War I and commemorates the freedom fighters who threw off their Habsburg imperial uniforms to join the Allied side in World War I. It sits almost directly across the street from a similar monument to the Polish Legion, also freedom fighters for an independent postwar Poland. Finally, the Ulster Tower (built 1921) at the Somme, provides a selective look at the sacrifices of Protestant soldiers from Northern Ireland. It memorializes regiments that were predominantly pro-British and that represented the Loyalist side in the war for independence that followed World War I in Ireland. When Ireland separated from the United Kingdom during the interwar period, the Ulster Tower gained even more authority as the monument to the loyal Brits of northern Ireland. Each of these monuments underscores the political uses of memory in the postwar world.

Personal Grief and Memory

In addition to commemoration of the martyred dead, postwar commemoration focused on the concept of familial grief. Not only did public squares and city streets take on the memory of the heroes and martyrs of the war, but individuals also had to process their pain and loss. For widows, this could be particularly difficult because many of them were also struggling to make ends meet in the postwar environment. They battled grief at the same time that they had to support themselves and other family members. Small payments to widows and orphans from the state often did not cover expenses. For example, German widows awarded pensions found them almost meaningless for months at a time during the hyperinflation of the currency. One such widow wrote in a postwar account: "I was forced to send my youngest out begging in the neighborhood so that the others could take some bread to work." Another German woman's reduced circumstances speak for themselves—her husband made 400 marks per month, but her postwar pension only amounted to 69 marks for herself and two toddlers. Such hardship made it difficult for survivors.

During the war itself, having sons or brothers in active combat meant not only fearing for the lives and well-being of loved ones, but it meant a host of daily activities to support the men in their absence. Families wrote letters, mailed parcels, and performed the men's work, especially in rural households, and they spent time trying to learn about the war. Martha Hanna's moving portrayal of the war's impact on a marriage in France, *Your Death Would Be Mine*, shows clearly how invested Marie Pireaud was in Paul's wartime life, even through four years of separation. Marie assured Paul many times of her love, writing at one point "they could separate us for twenty years and we would love each other as much as on the very first day…" Marie was not alone in her feeling of connection with her loved one at the front and her sense of duty at home. Men and women at home fronts and in occupied zones saw themselves as part of the war, not as bystanders, but as stakeholders. With the end of the war, that activity ceased, and suddenly the challenge of reforming family units hit. Families faced the realization of permanent loss of loved ones, but they also needed to care for psychologically and physically wounded veterans. Children had to get to know parents they had rarely or never seen. The end of the war brought social upheaval for many households, much of which is absent from the historical record and which is difficult to memorialize.

One good example of the memorialization of grief is Käthe Kollwitz's sculpture, "The Parents," at the Vladslo German War Cemetery in Belgium. The statue memorializes her dead son's service in the war, not her own, but it does so by depicting the grief of those left behind, the survivors. The focus of this extremely moving monument to Peter Kollwitz is, as Jay Winter has persuasively argued, "a family which includes us all..." The mourning parents in the sculpture—father upright and stalwart, mother doubled over in her pain—stand as moving testaments to the war's effects on family life and the sacrifice of parents.

Another way loved ones feature in postwar memorials is as caretakers. Many monuments dedicated to fallen soldiers feature a woman as a foil to the dead man, usually a mother figure, a sweetheart, or a female angel. This explicit connection between the nation's dead combat soldiers and the mothers who sacrificed them helped raise the level of meaning, solidifying the nation's need to have a gendered call to arms. War's masculine battle front with its heroic dead is cradled in the arms of the female home front, staunchly sacrificing its loved ones. Perhaps the most iconic of these monuments is the massive structure at Vimy Ridge, which is dominated by the figure of a hooded, mourning woman. In other memorials, widows stand defiantly over a soldier's body or look wistfully at his grave, topped with his metal helmet and gun. In all these cases the explicit message of service "for the Nation" centers around the dead combat soldier; the other characters in the tableau highlight this primary sacrifice.

An extension of the stone female griever was in the organization of postwar pilgrimages to the battlefields and cemeteries of Europe. Even before the war ended, gawkers visited the sites of devastated villages and collected war "trophies" from former battlefields, but this industry expanded immensely after the end of the war. Guidebooks to the battlefields emerged almost immediately and a robust war tourism industry developed on the Western Front especially. France's Michelin began its series of battlefield guides in 1919, and Britain's Thomas Cook agency organized tours beginning that same year. The French and British governments both offered subsidized trips for relatives of the deceased to visit their graves in the 1920s. The line between wartime pilgrimage to visit the graves of loved ones and the voyeuristic urge to see the devastation as a tourist remained blurry throughout the interwar period. Towns near memorials and cemeteries maintained a flourishing business in war souvenirs such as soldiers' personal items and munitions. Those visiting the graves of loved ones could take home a piece of the war as a memento especially if all they could visit was an unmarked grave.

One such organized pilgrimage effort emerged in the United States during the interwar period: the Gold Star Mothers. Mothers of dead soldiers buried in France were chosen to go on pilgrimage to their sons' graves and to other important sites from the war. The example of Estella Kendall of Mason City, IA, demonstrates the Gold Star Mother system in operation. Kendall's 24-year-old son, Harry, was killed in action in France on July 15, 1918, and buried in the US Cemetery at the Meuse-Argonne. Kendall received a "letter of invitation" from the US Government in 1933 for "a pilgrimage to the Cemetery in Europe where the remains of her Son are now interred." In her short trip to France, Kendall saw the remains of trenches, shell holes, barbed-wire, and tanks, and she went to her son's grave to lay a wreath. On the US Memorial Day holiday, a large commemoration service took place at the cemetery with the Gold Star Mothers as the central figures, before an audience of thousands of French people. The trip finished with a visit to the site of the "Lost Battalion," a popular pilgrimage site for Americans. As Mrs. Kendall described it, a group of 600 US soldiers continued to fight for six days in the Argonne forest despite being surrounded by the enemy. When they were relieved, only about 200 remained. This visit helped provide meaning to the war, helping Kendall understand the heroic narrative of American participation and giving her a framework for understanding her own son's death.

Despite these possibilities for visiting the sites of the war or for being embodied in public memorialization, most grief and postwar caretaking remained private. Only in recent years have more historians begun examining the role the war played in postwar marriages, households, and families. The private nature of loss and sacrifice are hard to quantify and describe. One thing that helped people process the wartime losses was religion or spirituality. During the war itself, chaplains of all faiths accompanied armies, and soldiers brought with them folk traditions and beliefs. For example, folk beliefs, amulets, and good luck charms helped soldiers deal with the vagaries of war, and stories of the magical also helped inspire or explain the unexplainable. Historian Karen Petrone, for instance, recounts a postwar collection of tales that captures Russian soldiers' use of concepts of the magic of the forest to cope with war. In the book, written by a nurse about her experiences at the front, one tale features two soldiers discussing a "wood goblin" in the form of a small moving flame in the woods. Similarly, British soldiers wove a magical tale around the Angels of Mons, which interceded to save them in August 1914. The use of religious belief, spirituality, and even spiritualism (contact with the dead through spirit mediums) all featured in postwar societies.

Undoubtedly religious faith and other forms of spirituality helped people cope, but it is also evident that the war led some to lose faith in established religious certainties. In some cases, state policies, such as in the Soviet Union, made it difficult to continue public worship in established churches, synagogues, and mosques, but it is also true that individuals turned away from organized religion in the interwar period. For some soldiers, religious leaders had supported war and the imperial ambitions of political leaders, making them culpable in the bloodshed. Others simply experienced a crisis of faith in the midst of sacrifice and loss.

Cultural Memory of War

Perhaps those most able to capture the emotional and psychological impact of war were artists, a group that included musicians, painters, sculptors, writers, poets, and performers. In the years during and after World War I, war infused the imaginations of the postwar world.

Some of the most famous musicians producing works for concert halls were soldiers or had experienced war as a career-altering event. George Butterworth, a British composer, lost his life in the war, giving his music new relevance for audiences in the immediate postwar period. Austrian composer Arnold Schönberg was drafted at the age of 42, and the war may have accelerated the development of his postwar style, which was atonal and "modern." Another musical example is Maurice Ravel, already a known composer in 1914 in France. He served as a driver in World War I and penned a tribute to his fallen friends, "Le Tombeau de Couperin," during the war. In each of these cases, war disrupted careers and led to shifts in musical themes or styles that helped shape a postwar aesthetic that in many ways commemorated the fallen.

Visual artists also grappled with war and its consequences in their paintings, drawings, and sculptures. The most obvious artistic expression of the war was in the small and large memorials commissioned after the war. Edwin Lutyens, for instance, designed the massive Thiepval Memorial at the Somme, the Cenotaph in London, and the war memorial gardens in Ireland. Other sculptors designed hundreds of small municipal memorials throughout Europe or created busts to celebrate the war's heroes. War artists had accompanied armies during the war, so there was a documentary record of war's violence on display in the 1920s from official war artists such as Paul Nash (Britain). Other artists such as Maurice Neumont (France) worked for the governments creating propaganda (especially posters).

Some of the most haunting artwork comes from the soldiers themselves in the years following the war, as former soldiers worked through complicated emotions of anger, grief, longing, and fear in their art. The Dada movement is an excellent example of a generation of visual artists who embraced political and social critique in their works, some of which took unusual forms like collages and paper sculpture. Closely associated with Dada in Germany were artists of the German expressionist movement whose violent and angry portraits of war profiteers, military leaders, and soldiers themselves were raw and in-your-face. Examples of artists in this style include Georg Grosz and Otto Dix.

Other stories of war emerged slowly, and a real boom of war literature and film did not appear until about 10 years after the conflict ended. Most famous among this era of writers, poets, and filmmakers were Erich Maria Remarque's *All Quiet on the Western Front* (Germany 1929), Vera Brittain's *Testament of Youth* (Britain 1933), Ernest Hemingway's *A Farewell to Arms* (United States 1929), Mikhail Sholohkov's *Quiet Flows the Don* (Soviet 1928–1932), and Frederic Manning's *The Middle Parts of Fortune* (Australia 1929). These works joined earlier accounts by Ernst Junger in Germany and Henri Barbusse in France. Although each of the works centered around particular stories of war and nation, most of them provided a critique of the impact of war on the lives of individuals, demonstrating the upheaval of war on a generation. Even those writers and artists who did not explicitly address war in their work seem to have been marked by its impact. A good example is J. R. R. Tolkien, who served in World War I, and whose Lord of the Rings books contain countless references to life underground, to war, to comradeship, and to sacrifice.

Finally, it is important to remember that World War I was a war recorded in photographs and films. Postwar photography exhibits and expositions of war materials helped populations process the war experience in the years that followed. Films, such as Abel Gance's 1919 *J'Accuse* or the Hollywood version of *All Quiet on the Western Front* (1930) allowed audiences the opportunity to vicariously fight the war. For veterans, such films could raise uncomfortable or positive memories.

Conclusion

Part of the collective forgetting that marks all commemoration of sacrifice and service emerged from real concerns that a "return to normalcy" must be the order of the day. Citizens had to provide stability and support as the massive war machines demobilized, but they were also required to rebuild and inhabit the new nations rising from the ashes of war. Soldiers had a role in this reconstruction, but much of the work fell to the non-combatant populations. Civilians were urged to look to the future, not to the past. In Brussels, Belgium, for instance, the civilian memorial is inscribed with one short phrase: "To Our Martyrs." Most other countries have no memorial to their civilians in war. Perhaps the problem with commemorating civilian service in World War I is the fact that memory is a process rather than a static event. The war ended (in most places) at a specific hour and day, but the forces unleashed by the war did not, on the personal or societal level. Civilians never had a moment where they tucked away uniforms or signed a paper releasing them from service, and for some the end of the war marked a whole new period of heroism as they dealt with familial and societal impact of all that World War I unleashed.

In the end, the war left populations wondering what the sacrifices were for and how to make lasting memories of those they lost. While the story of "our glorious [combat] dead" helped justify the losses, it did not really answer the questions that lingered with families and friends of the dead. As Geoff Dyer reflects in his memoir, *The Missing of the Somme*: "What happened in the Great War remained incommensurable…This is what was heard in the two minutes' silence of Armistice Day and is heard still in the perpetual silence of the cemeteries." As Dyer points out, World War I happened on an unimaginable scale. Even the statistics fail to really make sense to postwar generations.

This chapter lays bare the roots of the trope of war that focuses on the futility of the sacrifices, the senselessness of the slaughter, and the divide between ordinary soldiers and their leaders. For those who remembered dead sons and husbands and who had been promised a "war to end war," World War II was a betrayal of trust. It appeared to be evidence that their sons and brothers and husbands had fought in vain. It also negated the sacrifices of women, men, and children who had gone without basic necessities, suffered from the devastation of airstrikes, or fled from their homes in front of advancing armies. Memory of war is not stable. It changes as those who lived through it die, and it transforms in relationship to the events that follow it. Even the obvious naming of the conflict itself, the Great War, required change with the advent of World War II. The Great War's memory as World War I is a very different thing when it is viewed through the prism of later conflicts and political developments than it was in 1920. In short, World War I has become part of a larger tale of the twentieth century that goes beyond the events themselves to encompass the aftermath in all of its bloodiness and pain.

Citations

Page   Source
152   Information on the building of the Kansas City memorial is drawn from Matt Campbell, "As Centennial Approaches, National World War I Museum at Liberty Memorial Will Take Center Stage," *The Kansas City Star*, January 10, 2014.

152   Bushawn and Dubbs service records available in *Official Roster of Ohio Soldiers, Sailors and Marines in the World War, 1917–1918*, Vols. 3 & 5 (Columbus, OH: F. J. Heer, 1926).

153   "The war dead were still …" quoted in G. Kurt Piehler, "The War Dead and the Gold Star: American Commemoration of the First World War," In *Commemorations: The Politics of National Identity*, John R. Gillis, ed. (Princeton, NJ: Princeton University Press, 1994), 168.

155   Information on unidentified and missing bodies drawn from Stéphane Audoin-Rouzeau and Annette Becker, *14–18: Understanding the Great War*, Translated by Catherine Temerson (New York: Hill and Wang, 2002), 217.

159   "I was forced ..." quoted in Karin Hausen, "The German Nation's Obligations
        to the Heroes' Widows of World War I," in *Behind the Lines: Gender and the Two
        World Wars*, Margaret Randolph Higonnet et al., eds. (New Haven, CT: Yale
        University Press, 1987), 128.

159   Pension figures drawn from Hausen, 137.

159   "they could separate us ..." quoted in Martha Hanna, *Your Death Would Be
        Mine: Paul and Marie Pireaud in the Great War* (Cambridge, MA: Harvard
        University Press, 2006), 121.

160   "a family which includes us all ..." quoted in Jay Winter, *Sites of Memory, Sites
        of Mourning: The Great War in European Cultural History* (Cambridge: Cambridge
        University Press, 1995), 113.

161   Kendall pilgrimage information drawn from the National World War I
        Museum, Harry N. Kendall Collection Acc. #2000.30; Gold Star Mothers
        Collection, Kansas City, MO.

161   Story and "wood goblin" recounted in Karen Petrone, *The Great War in Russian
        Memory* (Bloomington: Indiana University Press, 2011), 52–53.

164   "What happened in the Great War ..." quoted in Geoff Dyer, *The Missing of
        the Somme* (London: Phoenix, 1994), 123.

Select Bibliography

Audoin-Rouzeau, Stéphane, and Annette Becker. *14–18: Understanding the Great War*.
    Translated by Catherine Temerson. New York: Hill and Wang, 2002.

Dyer, Geoff. *The Missing of the Somme*. London: Phoenix, 1994.

Garth, John. *Tolkien and the Great War: The Threshold of Middle-Earth*. Boston, MA:
    Houghton Mifflin, 2003.

Hanna, Martha. *Your Death Would Be Mine: Paul and Marie Pireaud in the Great War*.
    Cambridge, MA: Harvard University Press, 2006.

Hausen, Karin. "The German Nation's Obligations to the Heroes' Widows of World
    War I." In *Behind the Lines: Gender and the Two World Wars*, Margaret Randolph
    Higonnet et al., eds., 126–140. New Haven, CT: Yale University Press, 1987.

Laqueur, Thomas. *The Work of the Dead: A Cultural History of Mortal Remains*. Princeton,
    NJ: Princeton University Press, 2015.

Official Roster of Ohio Soldiers, Sailors and Marines in the World War, 1917–1918. Columbus,
    OH: F. J. Heer, 1926.

Petrone, Karen. *The Great War in Russian Memory*. Bloomington: Indiana University Press,
    2011.

Piehler, G. Kurt. "The War Dead and the Gold Star: American Commemoration of the
    First World War." In *Commemorations: The Politics of National Identity*, John R. Gillis,
    ed. Princeton, NJ: Princeton University Press, 1994.

Winter, Jay. *Sites of Memory, Sites of Mourning: The Great War in European Cultural History*.
    Cambridge: Cambridge University Press, 1995.

Zenna Smith, Helen. *Not So Quiet...Stepdaughters of War*. New York: Feminist Press, 1989.

Appendix 8.1: Timeline for 1917–1938 Showing War Memorial Related Events

1917	Imperial (later Commonwealth) War Graves Commission created (Britain)
1919	German War Graves Commission created
	Wooden Cenotaph in London
	Abel Gance's film, *J'Accuse*
1920	Stone Cenotaph in London
	Tomb of the Unknown Soldier (Paris)
	Tomb of the Unknown Soldier (London)
	Permanent Ministry of Pensions created to organize war graves (France)
1921	Ulster Tower (Somme)
	Liberty Memorial (Kansas City)
	Tomb of the Unknown Soldier (Arlington, VA)
1923	Eternal Flame (Paris)
1927	Dedication of the Tannenberg Memorial (destroyed 1945)
1929	*All Quiet on the Western Front* (novel)
	A Farewell to Arms (novel)
1930	*All Quiet on the Western Front* (Hollywood movie)
1932	Käthe Kollwitz's sculpture dedicated at the Vladslo cemetery
	Thiepval Memorial (Somme) dedicated
1938	Mussolini dedicates a new memorial to the Italian war dead at Redipuglia

9

Postscript: World War I in Context

Figure 9.1 World War I straddled the divide between past wars and ways of fighting and the new technological modern combat of the twentieth century. This German officer and his horses are reminiscent of cavalry images of the past, yet these figures are altered forever by the gas masks that each is wearing. *Source*: © Imperial War Museums (Q 52280).

World War I: A Short History, First Edition. Tammy M. Proctor.
© 2018 John Wiley & Sons Ltd. Published 2018 by John Wiley & Sons Ltd.

One of the perpetual questions asked today about World War I is a basic one, namely when did it end? Schoolchildren will tell you that it ended on the eleventh hour of the eleventh day of the eleventh month in 1918, an easy and neat way to remember the Western Front Armistice. Certainly one might argue that the armistices marked endpoints or even that the various peace treaties finally concluded the war. These dates do provide clear closure for the history books, but they fail to capture the long-term effects of the war politically, socially, culturally, and economically. For all those involved in this five-year modern war, the end was often not at all clear cut. This short postscript lays out some of the complexities of understanding World War I in its larger historical context.

The politics of the wartime world infused interwar political rhetoric and structures, no more so than in the case of the dictatorships of the USSR, Germany, and Italy. Josef Stalin, Adolf Hitler, and Benito Mussolini used the structures of militarized states and economies to build their interwar empires, but they also used the logic of total war to make a case for public sacrifice. In other parts of the world, the war cast a long political shadow over the newly created states and mandates. Wartime alliances helped determine postwar leaders of these regions, and broken promises from the war led to long-term animosities. In terms of individual political impact, world leaders who led nations as late as the 1950s had been shaped by the war, often as participants. Harry Truman was a World War I soldier; Winston Churchill led the Admiralty and served as an officer at the front. Adolf Hitler and Benito Mussolini used people's memories of the war to forge nationalism, often speaking of their own war service or the sacrifice of men for the national good. Governments also faced new responsibilities as a result of war, with the creation of permanent intelligence bureaus, pension agencies, and other social service organizations designed to mitigate the long-term human impact of war.

Political fallout from the war popped up again and again in the interwar world. In the United States, more than 40 000 former World War I soldiers participated in the "Bonus March" on Washington from May to July 1932 to demand benefits from the US Government in the form of a war service bond they were due to receive in 1945. Perhaps no images better capture the continued impact of the war than the photographs of US troops led by General Douglas MacArthur evacuating the encampments by force with cavalry, bayonets, and, in the end, fire. MacArthur, who had acted beyond his orders from President Herbert Hoover, proclaimed at a press conference that he "had liberated the besieged people of Washington" from a force similar to the Germans who occupied northern France during the war. In other nations, veterans demanded relief and recognition of their service as well.

Virtually every nation had veterans' associations designed to provide social interaction for those who had served and to act as advocates on issues of pensions, invalidism, and other postwar problems. The largest of these veterans' associations was in France, where more than 40% of veterans joined.

For those who had been displaced by the war, the need for aid remained a vital one. Refugees, released prisoners of war, and people who had lost their homes all required assistance as they tried to rebuild their lives. Given the scope and nature of the problem, international humanitarian aid agencies that had been formed as temporary war relief societies turned into permanent organizations that still exist in some form today. Good examples are societies such as Save the Children, founded in Britain in 1919, or the American Friends Service Committee (Quakers), which was created in 1917. Each of these worked to feed children, build new housing, help prisoners of war find work, and develop programs for continued war aid well into the interwar period. Some of these agencies still had operations in place in Europe by the 1930s, so they began working with victims of the Spanish Civil War and with Jews and other refugees.

War's impact on society also lasted well into the twentieth century. The population policies led to radically restructured living situations for millions of people, who now found themselves residing in new countries and with newly defined national identities. The Muslim population that had been forcibly relocated from Greece to Turkey coped with a foreign language, a fledgling government, and a whole new life. In the states that were born from the war, such as Czechoslovakia, ethnic tensions long dormant began to re-emerge as minorities within the country sought recognition and participation. In all the former countries that had fought in the war, the social fabric had to be mended. Permanently disabled and psychologically scarred veterans needed care, war orphans and widows sought financial support and assistance, and communities reformed without some of their most vital citizens. To use an American example, in 2010, the United States was still providing assistance and compensation to roughly 10 000 surviving family members from World War I.

Just as such social effects are hard to really quantify, the cultural impact of the war also remains impressionistic. Certainly war transformed art, music, literature, and social mores—often this shift in mentality is attributed to a "loss of innocence." A better way to think of the cultural shock of the postwar world might be to consider the fact that many people lost their certainty about the notion of progress. The war demonstrated that all things modern and advanced are not necessarily helpful to humanity, and many cherished ideas lost their influence as a result of the conflict. This loss of certainty led to anxiety about the future, and opened up the possibility of new political movements, and new cultural forms of expression. The Jazz Age, with its perceived hedonism and topsy-turvy social rules typifies the postwar period.

Perhaps the most invisible yet important cultural transformation to come out of World War I was the persistence of violence, militarization, and mechanisms of wartime control. Suddenly the unimaginable had become possible not just on the battlefields but in the cities, the concentration camps, and the skies. World War I proved to be a testing ground for many of the tactics employed by militaries and civil governments in subsequent conflicts, most notably the Spanish Civil War and World War II. Structures designed to deal with wartime disruption became permanent; a good example is the institution of daylight saving time. The rise of communism in the Soviet Union also created the preconditions for the battles of the future.

Finally, it is important to remember the economic impact of World War I. Governments expanded and changed their systems of revenue and expenditure to meet the demands of a larger bureaucracy, but they also struggled to stabilize a postwar world reeling from wartime debt and the need for rebuilding. Claims for pensions and disability coverage strained local and national budgets (as well as family resources), and new organizations emerged to evaluate and process such claims. A good example from the United States is the Veterans Bureau, founded in 1921 to consolidate services for US servicemen and women. The Bureau became the Veterans' Administration in 1930.

Beyond the short-term economic impact, the war also led to long-term debt and physical costs for the states involved. The Belgian bomb removal squad, Dovo (formed 1919), still removed nearly 200 tons of munitions each year up to 2014, and as recently as 2014, people were killed by World War I unexploded ordinance. The cost of maintaining such bomb disposal squads and unusable "red zones" that are too dangerous for farming or industry continue to be drains on the public budget. Finally, an amazing fact that drives home the long term economic effect of the war is that Germany finally paid off its World War I reparations bill in October 2010, which it had been paying off and on since 1919 and through various renegotiations of the debt.

For me the best representation of the war's legacy is in the destroyed villages of the war, many of which could never be rebuilt. These villages speak to all the aspects of the war's memory and impact—political, social, cultural, economic, physical. In the Verdun area of France, the village of Fleury disappeared under 90 000 tons of high explosives in 1916. In 2014, the ground is so "hot" still that no agriculture, construction, or digging is allowed, and there are areas where humans are not allowed to walk. Yet, Fleury has a mayor, who symbolically represents the village. Fleury has a commemorative chapel to mark its past. The village also features a series of signs that represent the places where shops stood, where children went to school, and where families lived. Today one can walk through the imaginary streets with their imaginary buildings, surrounded by the remains of shell craters and by trees planted in the 1920s, and one can visualize the world that was lost.

Citations

Page	Source
168	Information on the Bonus March drawn from Jennifer D. Keene, *The United States and the First World War* (Harlow: Pearson, 2000), 79–80.
169	Figure regarding French veteran association membership drawn from Julia Eichenberg, "Veterans' Associations," in *1914–1918-online. International Encyclopedia of the First World War*.
169	Figure of 10 000 surviving family cited in Matthew LaPlante, "100 Year War: The Growing Expense of America's Battles," *Salt Lake Tribune* (December 30, 2010).
170	Background on the Veterans Administration available at History of the Department of Veterans Affairs, http://www.va.gov/about_va/vahistory.asp
170	Information on Dovo and bomb removal drawn from "Behind the scenes with Belgium's bomb disposal unit," BBC News (March 21, 2014). http://www.bbc.com/news/world-europe-26663643?ocid
170	Information on 2014 Belgian deaths from unexploded World War I ordnance is cited in Luke Garratt, "First World War Bomb Kills Two Construction Site Workers 100 Years After it Was Fired at Belgian Battlefield," *Daily Mail* (March 19, 2014).
170	Information on Germany's war reparations available in Margaret MacMillan, "The War to End All Wars is Finally Over," *International Herald Tribune* (December 27, 2010).
170–1	Background on Fleury described in Vincent Kessler, "The Ghost Villages of Verdun." *Reuters* (March 20, 2014). http://widerimage.reuters.com/story/the-ghost-villages-of-verdun

Select Bibliography

"Behind the scenes with Belgium's bomb disposal unit," BBC News, March 21, 2014. http://www.bbc.com/news/world-europe-26663643?ocid. Accessed December 30, 2015.

Eichenberg, Julia: "Veterans' Associations," in: *1914–1918-online. International Encyclopedia of the First World War*, ed. by Ute Daniel, Peter Gatrell, Oliver Janz, Heather Jones, Jennifer Keene, Alan Kramer, and Bill Nasson, issued by Freie Universität Berlin, Berlin, 2014. doi: 10.15463/ie1418.10270

Garratt, Luke. "First World War Bomb Kills Two Construction Site Workers 100 Years After it Was Fired at Belgian Battlefield," *Daily Mail*, March 19, 2014.

History of the Department of Veterans Affairs. http://www.va.gov/about_va/vahistory.asp. Accessed December 30, 2015.

Keene, Jennifer D. *The United States and the First World War*. Harlow: Pearson, 2000.

Kessler, Vincent. "The Ghost Villages of Verdun." *Reuters*, March 20, 2014. http://widerimage.reuters.com/story/the-ghost-villages-of-verdun. Accessed December 19, 2015.

LaPlante, Matthew. "100 Year War: The Growing Expense of America's Battles." *Salt Lake Tribune*, December 30, 2010.

MacMillan, Margaret. "The War to End All Wars is Finally Over." *International Herald Tribune*, December 27, 2010.

Index

World War I: A Short History, First Edition. Tammy M. Proctor.
© 2018 John Wiley & Sons Ltd. Published 2018 by John Wiley & Sons Ltd.

Printed and bound by CPI Group (UK) Ltd, Croydon, CR0 4YY

13/04/2025

14656463-0001